W9-BBM-278

PETTICOAT PIONEER

PETTICOAT PIONEER

THE STORY OF CHRISTIAN COLLEGE

OLDEST COLLEGE FOR WOMEN
WEST OF THE MISSISSIPPI

Allean Lemmon Hale

Revised Edition

Library of Congress Catalog Card Number: 68-57508

North Central Publishing Company, Saint Paul, Minnesota

To

MARY PAXTON KEELEY

First woman graduate of a school of journalism
and my first writing teacher

Contents

Illustrations

Foreword

CHRISTIAN COLLEGE, founded January 18, 1851, was the first college for women chartered by a state legislature west of the Mississippi. It is now the oldest women's college in the west. Organized by an early president and trustees of the University of Missouri, it was conceived as a sister school to that institution, which did not accept women until 1868.

Christian's story is unique because it opened immediately on a collegiate level, rather than evolving from an academy or seminary like most women's colleges in the East and South. Before Vassar, Smith or Wellesley existed, Christian offered a four-year Baccalaureate degree in a day when female education usually meant wax-work and embroidery. Now a two-year college, it has furnished 117 years of continuous higher education for women.

Its story is also typical: of the frontier, of American women and their social progress, of American democracy which said all of its members must have equal opportunity. The struggles recorded here might be those of almost any of the small, independent colleges which dot the map, and have shaped the thought, of the United States.

Because of its age, its archives are also a unique and valuable documentation of changes for women. These Christian College historical records are housed in the Western Historical Manuscripts Collection at the University of Missouri library and were the source material for this book. The book was first written for the College centennial in 1951. This revised edition adds a chapter, bringing up to date the history of this Petticoat Pioneer.

ALLEAN HALE

I

PLANTED IN THE WEST 1844-1851

We hope that a critical yet generous community will encourage this original enterprise . . . of the first FEMALE COLLEGE *in the West.*
—JOHN AUGUSTUS WILLIAMS

IT WAS FOURTH OF JULY, 1843, and firecracker hot. Since early morning all roads leading to Columbia, Boone County, Missouri, had been crowded with horses and wagons. The blazing sunshine caked the ruts on Broadway and glinted on the instruments of the Columbia brass band, tuning up at the Courthouse. There the procession was already forming. Before eleven o'clock it began to move majestically down the hill and across town towards the six gleaming columns of the new university building.

Among those first in line was a tall, courtly man who carried one arm slightly askew. He was thinking of the prayer he would offer on this solemn occasion. To Elder Thomas Allen, to most of the rural crowd who had sacrificed pennies and dollars, this morning was an almost incredible fulfillment. They were about to dedicate the first state university west of the Mississippi.

The name, "T. M. Allen," had appeared on the rolls of every important educational movement since his migration to Columbia in 1836. Soon after his arrival he had been made a trustee of Columbia College, the secondary school for boys which the town fathers had founded in 1833, only twelve years after the town itself. That same year, they had set up for their daughters a girls' high school, the Columbia Female Academy, on whose board he would eventually serve.

Almost immediately upon settling in Boone County, Allen was in the midst of the agitation to locate a state university there. Other central Missouri counties were competing for the site and from 1835 to 1839 the contest was heated. Just when it seemed as if neighboring Howard County would win, Boone Countian James S. Rollins and others overnight raised the subscription price which topped the bid.

"The agony is over," wrote Allen to his friend John Gano in Kentucky. "The University is located in Columbia. . . . Who will make a good President? . . . I want one distinguished member of our folks, a professor—."[1] He thought of his son, William, who would be one of the first students. Then he thought of his daughters, Ann Rebecca and Mary. No university, as conceived in 1839, would be open to females. In his mind's eye the gilded dome of the first state university in the West faded a little. He put down his pen.

In the decade before 1850 Missouri was the West. Not the wild West, for by 1845 Texas had been annexed, nor quite, any longer, the far West. From Independence across the plains led the Oregon trail and every Missouri border town had its signpost pointing "to Santa Fé." Another exodus was about to begin, of pilgrims with bright new picks in their hands and the glittering sands of the Sacramento in their eyes. The Indians were gone but across the Missouri river in Kansas Territory their wigwams rose. Civilization had taken root and was growing up like the green shoots which work through earth turned by the plow. But the plowshare itself, that sharp point of westward migration which had commenced in Virginia and cut a furrow through the center of Kentucky, still rested in Missouri.

Columbia, county-seat of what was even then called "Old Boone," lay in the center of the state. Its pleasant rolling landscape must have reminded those first Kentucky migrants of the blue-grass back home, for family after family had come with their slaves and their blooded horses and Grandpa's cherry cupboard hoisted into the back of the wagon.

It was not so much a settlement as a transplanting. With some concessions to environment—the ice dropped out of the julep—this spot in the new West became a bit of the old South. It had the southern characteristics: the concern with religion, the hot blood in politics, the respect for tradition and culture, the delight in good living. People strung up their hickory-smoked hams. They built a race-track. The men organized a county fair and the ladies a temperance society. And because these southern stockraisers, who farmed in order to set a good table, had sometimes studied medicine or law as well, they hired schoolmasters and opened subscription schools for their children. As their roots grew deeper into Boone County it had seemed less desirable to send their sons back to Transylvania or the University of Virginia. That is why they had aspired to a university of their own. When in 1843 the classic columns actually rose above the mudholes of their village of seven hundred or so, most of the citizens felt they had achieved the ultimate. "Columbia, Athens of Missouri" had a satisfying ring.

Thomas Allen should have been among the most satisfied. He had helped to lead the winning campaign. He was on the committee to choose the site for the school, was elected president of its curators, arranged for its cornerstone to be laid. Now the University was a fact but the old uneasiness nagged him as he looked at his daughters, growing tall. He picked up his pen to write a postscript to his letter of five years before.

"Do you know of any good Brother well qualified to take charge of a female school," he wrote John Gano; "if so, I wish he would come to Columbia. . . . A competent person of the right *grit* would soon overcome all opposition."[2] In that query, perhaps, was born the idea of Christian College for women.

It took "grit" in the America of the 1840's to suggest a higher education for women. The possibility was only being explored at the time that Missouri and Columbia came into being. That year, 1821, Emma Willard, opening a girls' school at Troy, New York, demonstrated through her pupils that the female brain could comprehend such subjects as algebra. Following her had come those other pioneer teachers with their experiments: Catharine Beecher with her girls' school at Hartford, Connecticut; Mary Lyon of Massachusetts with her Mount Holyoke Seminary. This was so far beyond all previous American efforts that its founding in 1837 was the impetus for girls' seminaries to spring up all over the country. There were even a few by 1850 which called themselves colleges. But there were none in the west that lay beyond Missouri.[3]

So T. M. Allen's query was precocious, even in 1849 when the answer came.

Thomas Miller Allen in 1849 was one of the best examples of Missouri's merging of south and west. Fifty-two years old, of commanding voice and presence, he was what his contemporaries described as "an ornament to the community." Influential in University affairs, he was a trustee of six other schools in and out of Missouri and was in later life a member of the Board of Visitors to West Point. He was a founder of Columbia's first fire insurance company, a member of the county Fair board, active on the state railroad commission.

Born a Virginia gentleman, descendant of first families, he had graduated in law from Kentucky's Transylvania University. He owned slaves, rode "one of the best mounts in the county," and hobnobbed with the aristocratic Whig-Presbyterian clique which dominated Columbia. Two of its leaders, Major James Rollins and Colonel William Switzler, were his close friends, and he was kin to the Garths and the Russells. He was not as wealthy as Austin Bradford, his neighbor on Two Mile Prairie, or Eli Bass down the road who held most of the county's slaves. Nevertheless, he had been able to subscribe $600 to the young university. He sent back to Kentucky yearly for bulls which had pedigrees as long as his own, and maintained a pleasant hospitality at his country home. Most important to him, he was wealthy enough to pursue his real interest, which was preaching.

It was preaching that brought Allen to Missouri. Where others saw trees to be felled and virgin prairie to be plowed, he saw souls waiting to be fired by a new gospel. He was one of those who had early grown restless with the rigid practices of the Presbyterian church dominant in the Kentucky-Virginia region. Quibbling over creeds seemed artificial in the backwoods. Why should men in buckskin let their salvation hinge on dogma pronounced by a bishop in gold cloth? Religion was threatened in America as men either left the church entirely or formed into new, warring sects.

Out of this apathy and division in the early 1800's came a new Reformation, as democratic as America itself. It urged a return to the simple Christianity of Jesus. It said a Christian needed no creed but the words of the New Testament, which each man could read for himself. It preached that all branches of Christians should forget their differences and *unite.*

"Christian" or "Disciples of Christ" were the names chosen by this group of reformers whose leaders, Barton W. Stone and Alexander Campbell, met in Georgetown, Kentucky, in 1832. Thomas Allen, who had come under the impact of both men, had previously given up law to spend his life in their radical cause.

For it was a thrilling concept which sent men into the wilderness armed with a pen and a Bible. It was a race to the frontier, a battle for souls, and it had all the excitement of conquest. Allen's letters over a period of thirty-five years reflect this dramatically, whether he wrote in his early days that he had "taken 16 scalps," or as the Civil War approached: "I kept the artillery of Heaven going night and day."

When Allen came to Boone County there were three Christian churches of perhaps a dozen members each. Other counties had not as many. By 1850 there were 30,000 members of the Christian church in Missouri, owing largely to the zeal of this one man. He went everywhere—by steamboat, by stage-coach, on horseback. He preached tirelessly—in schoolhouses, in log cabins, in town halls. He baptized in cold pasture streams. Once he hit quicksand but pronounced the benediction before climbing out. He took no money. He used no notes. A backwoods audience did not "hold" with a preacher who read his sermons. He had as large an acquaintance as any man in Missouri[4] and half-a-dozen towns named a street for him.

His travels caused him to lose a wife and lose his health but he kept going. Perhaps he, like John Wesley, was "a brand plucked from the burning." As a youth, he had been struck by a falling tree in a storm and had escaped with a damaged arm while his companion and their horses were killed.

At night, though he was "much broken down," he wrote detailed reports of his progress to Alexander Campbell in Virginia for publication in his *Millennial Harbinger.* One letter described a Christian church girls' school he had visited:

> It was a lovely sight, to see upwards of 100 young ladies emerge from that splendid edifice, and march, with all the regularity . . . of well disciplined troops . . . to the meeting house. Oh that our country was filled with such institutions!

This was one of the sentiments dearest to Campbell, President of Bethany College, and to the Christian church. As an ultra-democratic body it had from the beginning felt an obligation to educate females and orphans as well as males. Most schools, in this school-founding decade of the forties, were sponsored by church groups and the Christian church was well to the front in activity.

So it was Allen, the Christian, as well as Allen, the friend of education, who wrote in 1844 to John Gano for the name of a "good Brother well qualified to take charge of a female school" in Columbia.

If Allen from the first held the flint of the idea, there were others who helped to ignite it. There was Alexander Campbell himself. On a tour of the west arranged by Allen he visited Columbia in 1845 and spoke for two hours on education to a crowd of hundreds. He had just sent a paper on the subject to be read to the College of Teachers in Cincinnati before such educators as the Beechers and the Stowes. Doubtless Allen discussed with him the need in Columbia for a college for women. They may have named names of those they knew who might promote such a project.

But the real steel to Allen's flint was D. Pat Henderson. David Patterson Henderson was not quite forty the summer of '48 when he came to Missouri to hold a "protracted meeting." A native Kentuckian, he like Allen had heard Barton Stone and had been diverted from a law career to the young church movement. He was aggressive, and his energy channeled into journalism and evangelism. At thirty-one he was associate editor of Stone's *Christian Messenger* and was known as one of the most magnetic speakers of the brotherhood. He "acquitted himself handsomely" in the lengthy public debates which were popular in that day. Though it was an era of oratory he, like Allen, was a plain speaker. A newspaper account describes him as "attracting the élite of Louisville"—than whom there were perhaps no more élite.

Allen met Henderson and joined him on tour. In the long dusty days of travel the two had time for plans. They complemented each other. They saw the same field, but through a different end of the glass. Allen's passion was for the particular: each handful of believers who got together under a tree and had to be nurtured to the point of filling a meeting-house. Henderson had the speculator's focus on far horizons. He thought in terms of traveling all over the Mississippi Valley, of raising thousands of dollars, of swaying multitudes.

Indeed, he had a mesmerizing effect on people. In an America fascinated by transcendentalism, he was something of a mystic. He had explored the occult and even tried hypnosis. He drew friends as a magnet—powerful friends, everywhere. There was the New Orleans newspaper editor who helped him raise money. There was the Louisville lady who lent him her thirty-room mansion. There was the Irish convert who sent him a gold nugget from California and promised to build him a church if he would come out. There was that lanky Illinois lawyer who had practiced law in his court and was to remember him politically after becoming President of the United States.[5]

Allen recognized Henderson's influence. Allen knew they shared the same ambition. For though Henderson had no children but an adopted infant niece, he had recently aided in founding a female school at Eureka, Illinois.

Henderson was such a success with his meeting in Columbia that the congregation urged him to remain as its minister. He must have conferred with Allen and Allen may have thought, Here is the man! Now is the time! For as a current trustee, he knew that the Columbia Female Academy was having trouble keeping open.[6] Henderson accepted the pastorate on one condition: that the local Christian church leaders would help him establish a collegiate institute for women. Then he returned to Illinois for five months to settle his affairs.

Meanwhile, those church leaders had their hands full with education. It so happened that at least five of them were then curators of the state university. And the University was having a stormy time.

Politics was affecting it as, twelve years before the Civil War, it affected every phase of American life. In Missouri the fight between the Whigs and the Democrats over the extension of slavery had reached a climax and in Columbia, county-seat of the "banner Whig county" of the state, it was feverish. One result was that the longtime Democratic opposition of the board of curators got the upper hand. Christian church members Caleb Stone and Turner R. H. Smith were the leaders of this opposition. They immediately began to fight to oust the Whig president of the University John H. Lathrop. Since most of the local Whigs were Presbyterians and the Democrats tended to be Baptists, Methodists, or Christians, religion suddenly was an issue and the nickname "Campbellite" a fighting word.

This was the situation to which Henderson returned in February, 1849. In May, Lathrop resigned. Caleb Stone became president of the curators with a decisive voice in choosing Lathrop's successor. In September the Rev. James Shannon, president of Bacon College in Kentucky, was elected president of the University.

It was not strange that a Democratic board should elect this strong pro-slavery Democrat. It was not strange to elect a minister. (Both of the candidates had been ministers, and one of the charges against Lathrop had been that he did not concern himself enough with the moral and religious training of the students.) But was it a coincidence that the new president of Missouri University should come from Harrodsburg, stronghold of the Disciples, and that he should be a minister of the *Christian* church?[7]

James Shannon was a tempestuous Irishman, said to have been one of the most brilliant graduates of the University of Belfast. He had come to America at twenty to head the Sunbury (Georgia) Academy, a Presbyterian school then called "the Yale of the South." In 1830 he became professor of Ancient Languages at the University of Georgia at Athens and while there helped to found Mercer College nearby, a Baptist coeducational college. In 1836 he became president of Louisiana State University, then called the State College and located at Jackson.

His career in religion had been, at first glance, erratic. (One of his enemies said that Shannon would have turned Mormon had he lived in a Mormon community!) Actually, his personal evolution of faith followed the pattern of the Christian church itself, for he was first a Presbyterian, became a Baptist minister, and was drawn to the Christian church movement about the time Barton Stone and Alexander Campbell were forming it.

It was his interest in the new concept which led him to give up his lucrative position in Louisiana to become president in 1840 of the infant Bacon College, a training school for Christian ministers. Nine years later when invited to Missouri he was fifty, a power in the church; dynamic, colorful, but seeming to thrive in an atmosphere of contention. He had worshippers, or enemies. And such powerful new enemies as Senator Thomas Hart Benton were muttering that he had ruined every institution with which he had been connected.

Was there a conspiracy to dominate Columbia with Christian church educators? Did Henderson through Stone exert influence in choosing Missouri's new president? Did the election of Shannon relate to the founding of a girls' college?

Shannon later said that founding a college for women had been the subject of correspondence between leaders of Missouri and Kentucky Disciples "from 1848 on."[8] He definitely considered the project when he visited Columbia in October, 1849, to decide on the presidency of the University. For he had eight children to educate and five of them were girls.[9]

Whether by coincidence or conspiracy, upon Shannon's acceptance things begin to happen.[10] No sooner had he returned to Harrodsburg than Dr. Samuel Hatch of that town appeared in Columbia. Hatch was a colleague of Shannon at Bacon College. He proposed, through the Columbia paper, that he and another colleague, Professor Henry H. White, would be willing to emigrate to Columbia "with a view of establishing, on certain conditions, a Female Collegiate Institute of the highest grade."

It is certain that Henderson stirred up general interest in Hatch's visit. He and Allen arranged a meeting in the sheriff's office for exchange of views with the visitor. Undoubtedly Allen enlisted all the friends of education, regardless of creed. On November 23, 1849, the Columbia *Missouri Statesman* carried the notice which marked the first step in the founding of Christian College:

PUBLIC MEETING.

Female Collegiate Institute!!

We are requested to give notice that a public meeting of the citizens of Columbia and Boone County will be held in the court-house in this place on

☛ TO-MORROW EVENING ☚

at candle-lighting to devise ways and means for the establishment in this place of a Female Collegiate Institute. ☛ The *ladies* are especially invited.

It is significant that it started as a community venture. The newspaper reported the remarkable interest and unanimity of feeling of "our citizens of all parties and denominations." The names on the planning committees were those which had answered previous rollcalls when the town fathers had gathered to take a forward step in education. The paper recorded continuous civic action. But in that day of division could any attempt at unity succeed?

Unfortunately, the action of those two weeks lies in shadow. We know that two plans were in turn submitted and voted down. They agreed on a thirty-acre tract with buildings and apparatus worth at least $10,000. They disagreed on the number, identity, and degree of power of the trustees. Money was subscribed and withdrawn. Finally, a committee of six ladies and six gentlemen was appointed to work out a compromise. It is tantalizing that we cannot hear "quite an interesting debate" which arose to wreck the compromise, or the "few remarks" then made by Professor Hudson, Acting President of the University.

All business was tabled "until another day." But the day was never set. The enthusiastic editorial account of the noble pile which was to have risen on Garth's Hill west of town gave way to the curt statement that "irreconcilable differences as to details had arisen."

What were these "irreconcilable differences?" If we knew the motives of the contestants, as well as their names, we might have the answer.[11] For example, Dr. William Jewell was chairman of the meeting. He was a warm admirer of Alexander Campbell—but he had just given $10,000 to endow a missionary Baptist college for men. Would he have endowed a like college for women? How did it happen that Baptists Warren Woodson, Moss Prewitt, and Jewell were—under the first plan—controlling trustees of a school whose administrators were Christians? Was it a way of checking on each other or a real attempt to unite their interests? Why had the Presbyterians been left out?

Perhaps religion had less to do with the controversy than politics. Was it significant that the alternate plan launched by Switzler and Rollins would add not only three Presbyterians but a majority of Whigs to the board of trustees?

More likely the conflict was the opening gun in a personal feud between the Rollins-Switzler clique and James Shannon. William Switzler, editor of the powerful *Missouri Statesman* and a friend of former President Lathrop, had begun to attack Shannon before the latter had warmed the presidential chair. Doubtless he was now attacking Shannon's friends, whose coming he viewed as an attempt to remove Bacon College to the University of Missouri. Certainly the stringent stipulations of Switzler's platform for a female collegiate institute suggest a great distrust of Hatch and White. His platform also added both himself and Rollins to the trustees.

No doubt the realistic Allen saw that such a combination would be doomed from the start. He moved the rejection of Switzler's plan and for once the three friends parted ways. Switzler, Rollins, and others withdrew with some spite to revive the Female Academy.

Dr. Hatch went back to Kentucky. William Hudson thoughtfully pocketed the subscription list. Old Dr. Jewell went up to Liberty to devote his attention to the school named for him. The day seemingly ended in failure, but out of it were to come not one but two women's colleges in Columbia. Perhaps a third school was generated in the pang of discontent which D. Pat Henderson experienced and which usually led him to new horizons.[12]

The last scene in the founding of Christian College took place on Christmas Day, 1850. A large company was assembled for dinner at Ellerslie, country home of T. M. Allen. Among them were Henderson in his tall silk hat and James Shannon in his white beaver; established physician T. R. H. Smith and young Dr. Walter Lenoir, just commencing his practice. The diners moved from the table to the rosewood chairs of the parlor. All eyes were on the man who had recently become president of the University of Missouri. He gathered up his coat-tails before sitting and dusted his chair, a fastidious gesture which somehow went with his small, neat hands and elegant gold watch chain. But he was no dandy. His eyes were those of a zealot—flaming, blazing blue. Those around him—some had known him in Kentucky—watched with differing emotions.

Hudson, the science teacher who had been university executive *pro tem,* saw him as a hero. In five months he had found Shannon to be learned, dedicated, decisive, of inspiring courage, of inflexible piety. Professor George Matthews viewed him in a halo, too, and had followed Shannon to this western university. Henderson was exuberant. Shannon would be the spark they needed to carry forward great plans. Greater plans, even, than those around them suspected. Young Dr. Lenoir and merchant Alexander Douglass did not know, at this moment, that they were linking causes with their future father-in-law.

Allen saw him with some misgivings. Secretly he was sorry Shannon had come to the University. A genius—yes; but a fire-brand. One who forced himself into situations from which he must battle his way out. He was not likely to further the cause of unity with his outspoken views on the frightful Negro question!

The young man for whom the dinner had been given watched with affectionate amusement. John Augustus Williams, the visitor from Kentucky, had been Shannon's pupil, lived in his home. He had known not only the dignified preacher-president but the absent-minded scholar, butt of college pranks. Williams' black eyes sparkled as he looked toward former schoolmate Robert Grant. However he was decorously polite, for Shannon had honored him greatly this day. Plans were all laid for him to assume charge of the long-awaited college for females. His speech before the town had been well-received. It looked as if his western prospecting trip was a success.

"Are we agreed, then?" asked James Shannon as the others voiced their Yeas. William Hudson drew the subscription list from his pocket and smoothed out its folds.

The plan finally agreed upon was for "a chartered institution under the control of a board of trustees composed solely of our brethren and friends." This seemed more secure than the original idea of a private school which might be sold or diverted to other uses. Williams much preferred that the subscribers raise the total investment than that he, as originally proposed, invest in permanent improvements two dollars for every one dollar subscribed. Shannon assured him $3,000, for this amount had been promised Professor Hatch. They parted in apparent agreement but, as it developed, with not enough detail as to where the remainder of the suggested $10,000 would come from. Henderson and Shannon sat down to work out the articles of the charter—much of which was written in the library of the president's mansion on the University of Missouri campus. Henderson is credited with the spirit and quality of the document; Shannon its by-laws. It reads, in wording almost identical with that of the University's charter:

> The trustees shall have power to grant such literary honors as are usually granted by Colleges or Universities in the United States, and in testimony thereof, to give suitable diplomas, under the seal of the Corporation . . . and every such diploma shall entitle its possessor to all the immunities which by any law or usage are allowed to possessors of similar diplomas, granted by any College or University in the United States.

As soon as it was completed they offered it to Allen for approval. It had also been discussed with Williams before he returned to Kentucky. When Allen suggested that Henderson go to the state capitol at Jefferson City to superintend the passage of the bill they both "earnestly solicited" that Allen go along to aid him.

The eloquence of the one and the influence of the other were successful. On January 18, 1851, the General Assembly of the state of Missouri passed "an act to incorporate a Female College," to be named by a majority of the trustees.[13] It was the first college for women to be chartered by a state legislature west of the Mississippi. "Christian Female College" was the name chosen a month later.

Twenty incorporators were named, half from the state at large and half from Boone County. Some of these "brethren and friends" may have been sitting in the Legislature that day, for at least five of the twenty were at some time legislators. Congressman John S. Phelps of Springfield, Greene County, was later to become governor of Missouri. Merchant James Cephas Fox, the first white settler of Monroe County, founded the town of Paris and the Christian church there. Elijah Patterson was a representative to the Legislature from Lewis County and a Christian church member. John Jameson, of a key family in Callaway, had been Speaker of the House in the Missouri Legislature and twice a congressman. He had recently given up a twenty-five year law practice to become a Christian church lay preacher. His daughter Bettie would be one of the first students of the new college.

The six from other parts of the state were equally influential. State Senator Wayman Crow was a St. Louis merchant-prince and philanthropist. He helped to charter the St. Louis Mercantile Library, the city Asylum for the Blind, and aided the young sculptress, Harriet Hosmer, in her career. A prominent Whig and a Unitarian of that western group which surrounded the Rev. William Greenleaf Eliot, Crow was soon to become a co-founder of Washington University in St. Louis. Crow's son was a student at the University of Missouri but his daughters had been sent back to New England schools. He was a close friend of Thomas Allen.

Lewis Bryan, whose ancestors had founded Bryan Station, Kentucky, with their kinsman Daniel Boone, was an early settler of aristocratic Palmyra, Marion County, Missouri. Prosperous churchman Bryan was to help educate one Christian College president and become the father-in-law of another. J. J. Allen of Huntsville, Randolph County seat, was a leader in his community and the "Sallie Allen" on the first enrollment was probably his daughter. Weston Favel Burch of Fayette, in Howard County, was a wealthy commission merchant with enterprises from San Francisco to Wall Street. He was a director of the Missouri State Bank, superintendent of the road company, a supporter of Howard High School in Fayette (now Central College) and had published in Fayette one of Missouri's earliest newspapers, the *Western Monitor*. Son of an Episcopalian minister, Burch had joined the Christian church.

Two who would give the new college much support, but

little money were Christian church preachers Moses Lard of Liberty, Clay County, and Samuel S. Church of St. Louis. Lard had daughters who would someday be educated at the college and become women of consequence in Missouri.[14] Church was a promising young protégé of Allen.

Doubtless these valuable men, carefully selected from nine leading counties of the state, were expected to exert their influence in filling the new Christian College. But it was the local ten who would, after all, have most to do with the moulding of the institution. Next after Shannon, Henderson, and Allen, were Turner R. Haden Smith and William Wilson Hudson. Hudson was a superior person, a Yale graduate, one of the original members of the University faculty and twice its acting president. A Whig, he was spiritually apart from some of the others in that he was a non-church member. However, he was devoted to their educational cause and was to assume the burden of following Smith as the school's early treasurer. Smith, an outstanding physician and son of a noted Kentucky preacher, not only wielded power as secretary of the University's board of curators but as a leading Democrat in the state. By 1852 he headed the only other state institution then in Missouri, the Asylum at Fulton.

Other Columbians were physician William McClure and ageing General Thomas D. Grant. Robert S. Barr, one of the wealthiest merchants west of the Mississippi and a founder of Columbia, did not live long after being named an incorporator but was a large subscriber to the girls' college. Flavil Vivian and Levi T. Smith soon died and their places were taken on the first board of trustees by the incoming President Williams and Judge Alexander Persinger.

If Allen, Henderson, Shannon, and Williams were the four leading characters in the founding of Christian College, these others formed truly "a distinguished supporting cast." Not many schools starting around 1850 could boast among twenty incorporators a dozen with collegiate education, three college presidents, five legislators, and five doctors or lawyers! Most of them had fostered the University or had been trustees of other educational ventures. All were public-spirited men who also built roads and libraries. Some had daughters, the majority had no such personal motive.[15] While most of them belonged to the Christian church, they stated explicitly in the charter:

> . . . into this institution, *no sectarian feature has been incorporated, and in it no sectarian influence whatever will be exerted.*

They were sure of their intention: to found a school on the *collegiate* level. And they had a sense of destiny as related to their day:

> Thus have we planted in our midst the first Female College in the West . . . that shall stand as a monument to the memory of its founders when they shall have been long called to their reward. . . .[16]

Their eyes, like Thomas Allen's, were filled with a vision of young women marching from schoolrooms all across the land.

II

THE DAY OF SMALL THINGS 1851-1856

For who hath despised the day of small things? for they shall yet rejoice . . . with those seven; they are the eyes of the LORD, *which run to and fro through the whole earth.*—ZECH. 4:10

THE MORNING WAS CHILLY, but the young man in the doorway was warm with excitement. Less than three months had passed since the Legislature of Missouri had chartered the state's first college for females. And now, on Monday, April 7, 1851, its president scanned the muddy hill for sight of his first student.

Across the square in the courthouse he had, the day before, delivered his inaugural address to an enthusiastic audience. Behind him the fire blazed in the seven-plate stove which warmed at least one corner of the Christian church meeting house. Beside the Bible on his desk were clippings which had already returned from journals throughout the state, announcing the school's opening. The Liberty *Tribune,* the Paris *Mercury,* the Jefferson City *Inquirer.* . . . Even the St.

Louis and New Orleans papers had copied, for these cities were self-styled gateways to the West, and this was a western venture.

> "Elated with expectancy, I went early," he recalled afterwards, "to matriculate the throng. . . . In an hour, all had assembled: seven girls!"

The historic seven, Anna Hitt, Emma Gordon, Ann Thomas Harris, Amanda Ellis, Mary E. Carter, Matilda Stone and Sallie Bedford, were equally excited. Doubtless they noticed, as they bowed respectfully, that their principal was handsome and his lady assistant attractively young. Augustus Williams leafed his Bible for a suitable text: "Despise not the day of small things," he told his college of seven, "for ye shall yet rejoice."[1]

That preliminary session lasted into July, to close with the state university. A local French professor, Henri Desrieux, completed the faculty of three, with Williams teaching the literary courses and Miss Jones the sciences. Susan E. Jones of Jacksonville, Illinois, a graduate of "one of the best colleges for women in the land,"[2] had previously taught at Walnut Grove Academy in that state. Her father was John T. Jones, Christian evangelist and friend of D. Pat Henderson and the three had been associated in the Walnut Grove enterprise.[3] She, like Williams, was staking her future on these small beginnings in the West, and the seven girls were well taught.

Meanwhile, others from out of town were writing to enroll and the trustees were faced with the problem of where to put them. While a building committee was still drawing specifications the Board had a chance to buy the unfinished mansion of Dr. James Bennett, a physician who had died in Hangtown, California, during the Gold Rush. The dwelling was brick, set in a forest of elm and maple trees on twenty-nine high acres just north of the town. The Board's transaction was with James Rollins, Bennett's executor and brother-in-law; that same Rollins whose donation of land had earned him the title, Father of the University.

He was not so eager to father the girl's school. Why its trustees should have dealt with him at all seems odd, for he and his partner Switzler had formed an opposition since the day their own plan for a female college had been rejected in the town meeting.

Perhaps their good friend, Thomas Allen, arranged the purchase as a way to win over two of the town's most influential citizens. Perhaps Rollins, the speculator, wanted to be sure of a finger in any educational pie which might yield a plum. He made favorable terms: a year's credit before payments started and 5 per cent interest for four years. The Board accepted his price of $5,500 and asked for a right-of-way to their new property—a forty-foot-wide strip connecting it with "the tenth cross street in town." Christian College Avenue—to be.

As the Board went about enlarging its property Williams inserted a paragraph in the circular he had just prepared:

> A commodious new building, with five large rooms, in a retired and beautiful part of the village, has been obtained for the accommodation of the College the ensuing session.

This quaint first *Circular of the Christian Female College*, published June 28, 1851, is valuable for its list of courses offered, texts used, and regulations of the new college. Clear and uncompromising, like the man who wrote them, they would sound a little grim to the prospective student of today.

> It is desirable that no young lady will seek admission into this school, who is not determined to devote her whole energy and attention to her moral and mental improvement. Those who cannot, for the time being, abstract their minds from the fascinations of society, or who aspire *merely* to a *superficial* or fashionable Education, are earnestly advised to seek elsewhere. . . .

Every pupil, "excepting those in black" is expected to wear the "cheap, plain uniform:"

> FOR WINTER—Plain worsted dresses, maroon or green. Green Hoods—trimmed and lined with scarlet. White aprons.
>
> FOR SUMMER—Pink calico or lawn dresses. White sun bonnets trimmed with scarlet ribbon. Aprons. . . .

The other regulations are listed under Roman numerals, like the Ten Commandments:

> II. All profuse use of ornament is strictly prohibited.
>
> III. No pupil shall appear upon the street, or visit any public place whatever, except by permission.
>
> IV. Pupils are not allowed to attend night meetings, without permission.
>
> V. No pupil shall receive directly or indirectly the attentions of gallants.
>
> VIII. No young lady shall contract any debts, or make any purchases without express permission from parent or teacher. . . .

It must be remembered that these details were not too stringent for that era. From Bible study to bonnets, Christian College in its development was so representative of the women's college movement itself that its early history is worth preserving.

What was, to its everlasting credit, different in its day was its determination to be more than a finishing school—"that mockery of the girl," so scorned by Williams. Neighboring schools might teach ornamental wax-working or hair-wreath embroidery. "This institution," reiterated the *Circular,*

> has been established with the view of affording YOUNG LADIES the opportunity of acquiring a thorough *Collegiate Education,* by introducing a more extensive course of study, and a more rigid discipline of mind than is usual in the ordinary school for girls.

Its curriculum would go "beyond the usual primary attainments of the Academy," and young ladies would be encouraged to pursue "a thorough and extensive course in the Mathematics, in Natural Science, in Belles-lettres, in Natural History, in Language, and in Philosophy."

Although most of the teaching would be by lecture and experiment, pupils were advised to secure the latest editions of the twenty or more textbooks listed for the four years.[4] Students who wished to teach were assured the advantages of a Normal school, and a primary, or preparatory department, was being organized.

The first regular session of Christian Female College opened the second Monday in September, 1851, with more scholars than space. Enrollment was already thirty-six, compared with the University's seventy-five, and the building was not yet ready. Arrangements were made to board out-of-town pupils "with the most respectable families" for two dollars a week, including washing. This proved dangerous, since the same families also boarded university boys. Several college girls were lost to matrimony that first year.

A student's father solved the situation. William Y. Hitt, at whose home President Williams and his family were boarding, offered the new two-room storehouse on the front of his property. His own home with its hill-top domination of the town was one of the most impressive in Columbia. There Alexander Campbell had visited and perhaps had discussed the idea of a female college with such leading Columbians as T. M. Allen and Hitt's brother-in-law, Dr. William Jewell.

Across the street was the lot which had been reserved in the original town tract (but never used) for Columbia's male college. A block west was the brick Female Academy. In this educational atmosphere Christian College held its first school year on the northwest corner of Hitt and Cherry streets. Both of William Hitt's houses are gone now,[5] and only his view remains—its sudden glimpse of road's end and open country reminding present Columbians of their rural origin.

As news got around girls kept coming. Future catalogs would carry stern injunctions to enroll on time, for insistence on a regular term coinciding with that of the University was another indication of Christian's collegiate intent. (Girls boarding schools of the day commonly received and discharged pupils at any time.) A certain casualness was inevitable in these pre-railroad days. The breakdown of a stage, low waters on the Missouri, even the competition of a county fair, were causes for delay. By mid-year more than seventy had matriculated. Of these, thirty-one were from other towns and five from other states: Illinois, Virginia, and Louisiana. Christian College was from the start more than a local institution.

At second semester Christian College had a staff of five: "Miss S. E. Jones, Principal of Natural History; Miss R. J. Galbraith, Principal of Natural Science and Mathematics; Jno. Aug. Williams, A.M., Prof. of Belles Lettres; Miss E. Van Allen, Instrumental Music, and Prof. W. Alexander, the Polite Arts."

Five was a respectable faculty for a starting school of the day. Missouri University's regular faculty numbered seven. Many girls' schools of the fifties were staffed by "the President and Lady" aided by one or two young relatives or students.

Christian's three women teachers were brought from other states. Indications are that Rebecca Jane Galbraith, of Jacksonville, Illinois, also had taught at Walnut Grove. Sue Jones, in her professional career, was to help establish at least two other schools in Missouri. Ella Van Allen of Kentucky, probably one of William's former students, was the "first-rate" music teacher he had sought from the beginning. All were advertised as experienced but little more is known about their credentials. William Alexander, who taught drawing and painting, taught the same subjects at the University. He was the first of several teachers Christian shared with the men's school in its "distaff side" relationship during those early years.

Williams himself taught literature, the Bible, education courses, Latin and Greek. His versatility was not superficial, for he later published several books and collaborated on a translation of the New Testament from Greek. He was an able musician and composer. In an era when congregations split over such issues as part-singing he dared to introduce the controversial bass, tenor, alto, and soprano into the Columbia choir. The overwhelming item on Christian's first budget was for "the engagement of four pianos" and it was doubtless the President's own interest which established the school's enduring reputation for excellence in music.

A sixth staff-member was Emma Gordon, a senior student who, upon graduation, would be assistant in the Academic Department to open the fall of 1852.

This academic department was another facet of the founding fathers' dream. The charter had authorized the trustees to establish various departments of the institution "whenever the interests of education should require it." Now Williams and Henderson came forth with the heady idea of interpreting this to include a number of "feeder" schools, female academies all over the state, preparatory for Christian College. The

Board agreed, suggesting only that Williams do most of the organizing during his summer vacation.

So this amazing young man, at the end of his first year spent in raising money, overseeing a building, finding a faculty, and teaching, managed to launch at least two additional schools. One was the academy at Christian College itself. The other was the Christian Academy directed by Dr. Winthrop H. Hopson at Palmyra.[6] No wonder a contemporary, meeting him, could write: "I was disappointed in the appearance of Mr. Williams. He is older than I expected and looks toilworn. His undivided energies appear to be exerted in the cause of female education."

A man could age rapidly in the bitter climate of Columbia, Missouri, in 1852. Scarcely had school opened than Williams became so ill that he had to be carried across the road on horseback to teach from a couch. That fall, while still a depressed invalid, he and his wife lost their two-year-old Mary Belle. He had to see his first-born buried in the grove at the back of the Christian College campus.

From where he taught on Hitt street, he could almost hear the hammers of the workmen as they added on to the building of the Columbia Female Academy. Although this school, according to its catalog and charter, did not aspire to more than high school level, in that day of faint educational boundaries it was a rival for patronage. Too, it was supported by the socially powerful Whig faction of the town.

The very name "Christian College" seemed a drawback. He had meant "Christian" in its broadest sense, to express the school's democratic, religious, and unsectarian character. But it was interpreted in a strictly denominational way.

Financial support of the college seemed threatened by one of its own founders, for Henderson was already restless. He had discovered on a trip up the Mississippi the perfect site for a great Christian university—a bluff overlooking Iowa, Illinois, Missouri.

Even to have the president of the state university as one's leading trustee was a dubious blessing, for it plunged the infant school into the midst of a virulent newspaper feud—and in an era when one editor thought nothing of calling another a "yellow-bellied, brass-headed ape." The Columbia *Missouri Statesman,* edited by William Switzler, was the political mouthpiece of James Rollins and the Whigs. It had commenced to fight Democrat James Shannon, literally before he reached Missouri. Shannon immediately fought back, through the columns of the rival *Sentinel,* edited by E. C. Davis.

Both papers "have taken off gloves and coats and enter into the strife," commented the Liberty *Tribune,* adding that it would not advise any parent to matriculate his son where he must enter "the hot bed of political and religious controversy."

The antagonism had been fed by the fact that Switzler, after Shannon's arrival, was excluded from meetings of the University curators, which he had always felt free to attend and report.

Christian College, Shannon's project, was caught in the middle of the feud, a slippery position for a new school needing good publicity.

In the spring, the worst had happened. Scandal, a duel, gunsmoke that blew over from the University to cloud the reputation of Christian College, when a university tutor shot his student in a quarrel over politics and religion. The shooting was in self-defense, and the tutor, Robert Grant, was acquitted. But it dragged in the name of his bride-to-be, Christian's Sue Jones; their friend, D. Pat Henderson, to whom Grant surrendered his still-smoking revolver, and James Shannon himself. Since three of Grant's kin were in Christian College at the time, its effect on the school may be imagined. It is probable that the dead boy's epithet, "damned Campbellite democrat," flew like an arrow to leave its mark in the college so vulnerably named "Christian."

But by June, 1852, these trials were behind. Ahead was the finished building and only the hurdle of examination week. In those days of limited entertainment not only commencement exercises but final examinations were public affairs, enthusiastically attended by the townspeople.

The comments of the daily press in June, 1852, would sound perfectly familiar today: "This is a gay week in Columbia. . . . Our Town is filled with strangers, and the cry is still they come."

From the current references to exams as "intellectual struggles," and "thrilling combats of intense interest to the spectators," it is clear that they were to the native Columbian what a bullfight is to the Mexican. Indeed, they had similar trappings, for the about-to-be slaughtered maidens, decorated with banners, would march down the street and into the exhibition hall to the blare of the town's cornet band.

The local housewife who acquired a good education by sitting through years of final examinations was first cousin to the woman in Dickens who knit beside the guillotine as the heads fell. The anxiety of parents, watching their offspring in competition with neighbors', survives in a letter of the Lenoir family:

> The house was crouded [*sic*] perhaps with as respectable and inteligent [*sic*] citizens as to be found anywhere. It was Court week and the Judge and gentlemen of the Bar was [*sic*] present, you can Judge better than I can describe my feelings on the occasion; When Ann Eliza was called on to read she took a pull at harts-horn and without agitation read her composition with proper emphasis and sufficiently loud to be distincly [*sic*] heard by the audience, and when done, I could hear whispers of applause all around me, and enquiries—What young lady was that? . . . I felt as though I was rich indeed. . . .[7]

To President Williams and his six candidates for the Senior class it was more than an ordeal. Seven years' teaching had made Williams despise public examinations as a farce and a fraud. In later days as an educator he was to discard them altogether. He had seen "literary" exercises where each girl carried a scrolled "essay"—which he knew to be a blank sheet of paper. Or a "botany demonstration" consisting of each pupil holding a flower!

At least there would be no parroted answers, no sing-song recitations by *his* students. They were well aware that judgment would sit with the audience, and that the perspiring townspeople had come not only to see the finished rooms but to answer the question: Is it practical to send females to college?

The young ladies came through with colors flying. They astonished with their logic, impressed with their mathematical proficiency. Tossed subjects at random from the audience, they composed poetic stanzas "considerably superior to most of the newspaper effusions of the day." They were taken into the depths of Locke by the President of the University himself, and "passed through unscathed." Given an editorial from the *Statesman* to criticize—"one," the editor confessed, "in our best vein,"—they proceeded to riddle it. They sparred brilliantly over the proposition: Resolved, That the tongue of man has caused more evil than that of Woman.[8]

A masculine witness reports:

> Notwithstanding the *angel-like* appearance of the fair debatants, they now and then gave evidence that they were *human* beings, and that they possessed a nature in common with our own sex; for like ourselves . . . they occasionally made light of the argument of each other, and the words "absurd," "preposterous," "sophistry," and such like, were sprinkled through the discussion.

Add the words of one who admittedly came to scoff but went away asking himself, How is all this accomplished:

> The young ladies are taught to *think*. They are *compelled* to think. They take nothing for granted, no matter by whom affirmed. They frequently differed from each other, and would argue zealously for their own opinions and against the opinions of the others. Sometimes, they would dissent from the books and differ from their teacher, and they never yielded the point until they were convinced by arguments.[9]

We detect a certain amusement in these reports of the argumentative young ladies who took themselves so seriously. Well might they be self-conscious, and in their triumph even a little self-righteous, feeling the weight of women's education on their shoulders.

The examinations were held in the new college building: the evening exhibitions and concerts in the Christian church. The afternoon of July 2, 1852, the College was formally dedicated, the choir singing an ode which the girls had composed.

That night the first anniversary was celebrated by an address on "Female Education" delivered in a crowd so dense as to be uncomfortable. Since the orator, Edwin Curtis Davis, was soon to become Superintendent of Schools for Missouri it is interesting to know that he compared Christian with the movement for higher female education in New England and with the Ohio Female College and the Wesleyan College of Georgia.[10] Distinguishing sharply between it and the ordinary Female High School, he declared:

> Thus have we planted in our midst the first FEMALE COLLEGE in Missouri. I do not mean to say the first female institution empowered to confer honors in Literature, by virtue of charters. By no means. I mean a COLLEGE, as defined and understood by SCHOLARS. . . .

The night was so hot he was forced to cut short his address. Many never got in the church to see the young ladies in white, against a background of green cedar artfully entwined to form the motto, TRUTH. But the week was an unqualified success. President Williams was lauded as a gifted teacher who used the Greek method of "drawing out the mind rather than putting into it." The public agreed with the stranger who had dropped in on his way through town and had written his sentiments to the paper: "Little did I expect to find such an institution, such teachers and such young ladies in the wilds of the far west!"

The trustees voted to publish in a literary annual the outstanding compositions of the week. (Here the descendants of Miss Martha Gordon may read her earnest plea to educate the country's future mothers, or Miss Carrie Jenkins' valedictory address: "A Blush, A Smile, and a Tear.")

Then they turned over the new building and grounds to the President, to run as he saw fit—with certain provisions. He must "under no circumstances allow to run thereon any stock other than his own." (This may have been interpolated by Caleb Stone, or another of those curators who had seen President Lathrop rent out pasture in an attempt to keep the University solvent.) So at last, the college took possession of the building which still stands as "practice hall" and the shady grounds which have been and are forever Christian.

The students were scarcely out of sight when President Williams set about distributing the one thousand copies of the new catalog.[11] (They went so fast he had to promise more, "as soon as they can be stitched and bound.") He had an author's pride in the fresh type, the format, the title-page, exactly like that of the University's, and the three-page list of student names. It was, truly, an ambitious volume; thirty-one pages in all, including Mr. Davis' address and the fifteen-page student supplement. Printed by Davis and Millan at the *Sentinel,* it was to win first place over publisher William F. Switzler's entry at the Boone County Fair. For James Shannon, who had thrown this, as well as the University's printing jobs, to his friend Davis, it was a victory. For Christian College, perhaps not, for it made Switzler more than ever determined to suppress all publicity of the school.

Fortunately, Christian had publicity experts of its own. Williams was an aggressive journalist. Henderson edited a magazine. Allen was the indefatigable western correspondent for the *Millennial Harbinger.* These three, with Shannon and Davis, supported the saying that whenever a group of Methodists got together they formed a choir and whenever a group of Disciples got together they started a paper. Certainly, whichever men wrote them, the early publications of Christian College are outstanding for their persuasive journalism. Their paragraphs on education would compare favorably with those famous treatises of Beecher and Lyons. It is doubtful if many women's colleges have a collection of catalogs dating as far back, as informative, and therefore as significant of social changes as does Christian.

This first catalog was full of information about the new domestic function of Christian College. Now that the plant was equipped, there would be accommodations for fifty boarding students. But it was to be more than a boarding school.

In the education of the Young Lady, it averred, Home and School should not be separated. While "it is a fundamental principle . . . of this college, that Young Ladies should receive as thorough intellectual training as is given to young men in our Universities," at the same time:

> Every daughter should be so trained in the *domestic school,* so taught in *useful* and *substantial* knowledge, so habituated in early life to the virtues of *self-reliance,*

> *self-denial,* and *economy* as to be able in the great drama of after life, to find in the energy of her character, and in the resources of her mind, that independence, that honor and that happiness, for which she is now, in most cases, absolutely dependent on social conditions.[12]

Like Emma Willard, Mary Lyon, and Catharine Beecher, Williams was concerned with the fact that, in his day, a woman without wealth had only three resources: to marry, work as a domestic, or to teach. The popular education of girls, so far, had been aimed at fitting them to attract wealthy husbands.

Years before, Mary Lyon had stressed the fact that even a wealthy wife needed to understand domestic matters or she would be dependent upon her servants. Her girls at Mount Holyoke were required to do a certain amount of manual labor. But it was Catharine Beecher whose lead Williams seemed to be following in introducing domestic sciences into the curriculum. She once wrote:

> The care of a house . . . the management of children, the instruction and government of servants, are as deserving of scientific treatment . . . as are the care of farms, the management of manure and crops, and the raising and caring of stock.
>
> Young men are provided with lectures on political economy, while domestic economy, as yet, has not been so honored. . . .[13]

Williams' catalog declared:

> Every *Adopted* Pupil will be required to devote a reasonable portion of her attention to Domestic Science —to the theory and practice of Good *House Keeping*. There will be, in addition to the *Collegiate Faculty,* a *Domestic Superintendent,* a *Matron,* and an *Assistant Matron,* who in connection with the *President,* will take absolute control over every such Pupil, as far as it regards health, manners, habits, finances, and morals.[14]

Quite an order, especially as it involved the "correction of incipient evil dispositions" and seeing that each girl sent home to her parents at the end of the month a detailed account of every penny she had spent!

Chief textbook for the course was "A Treatise on Domestic

Economy," by Catharine E. Beecher.[15] This 369 page volume covers every subject from "How to Build an Earth Closet," with diagrams, to "Good Temper in the Housekeeper."

Completing the new domestic staff of three was the Patron,[16] a resident physician who would supervise the health and physical education of the girls. This arrangement was probably responsible for another innovation—the teaching of Anatomy and Physiology by a physician. For many years this continued a custom, the founder of the University of Missouri medical school being one of the lecturers listed.

Was Christian's curriculum, however, "as extensive as any in the country?" Was it collegiate, even? Is it too pretentious to seek a link between Christian College in the West and those three great pioneers for female education in the East? These questions form endless tangents for research.

Briefly, it is indisputable that Williams knew the work of Emma Willard, for he has the heroine of his novel, *Rosa Emerson,* go to school to her at Troy.

He was acquainted with the Beecher family, although he was only a boy in Kentucky when Catharine started her experimental school in Cincinnati. (Founder D. Pat Henderson was also a close friend of the Beechers and took Henry Ward Beecher's pulpit when the famous preacher visited England.)

The possible influence of Mary Lyon is unexplored. Her pronouncements and those of Williams are strikingly similar. Like her, he advocated the use of the Bible as the fountainhead of wisdom and saw the purpose of education as increasing the individual's social usefulness. Like her, his paramount interest was in training teachers.

The early catalogs of Mount Holyoke and those of Christian College fourteen years later are available for comparison.[17] (Holyoke's curriculum, according to its founder, was based on that of her two predecessors at Hartford and Troy.)

These first catalogs of Holyoke and Christian show a marked similarity in subjects taught and texts used. Holyoke offered more Botany and Natural Philosophy; Christian more English, Mathematics, and Bible. With both, languages were optional, a fact which scholars might seize as proof that they did not reach the standards of the men's colleges of the era.

But it was not a confession that women could not learn Greek and Latin but a conviction that knowledge of these should follow more useful attainments which motivated Williams and these easterners. Christian was definitely in their spirit when it advertised:

> The branches of learning which we prescribe, are useful, either as practical or as disciplinary studies. We omit some, which, though *popular,* we regard as neither useful nor ornamental; and we have substituted others, *of which the Women of this country should not be ignorant.*

The level of these studies must be judged in the light of that day, not by today's standards. There was not until 1855 a girls' school in the east which aspired to the title, College.[18] In the fifties, probably only Oberlin College, in the entire United States, offered women the same courses and the same A.B. degree granted its men.

With Oberlin Christian did not compare, any more than the struggling University of Missouri compared with Harvard or Yale. With the eastern seminaries, with the Ohio Female College and the Georgia Wesleyan College admired by Henderson and Shannon, with such established women's "colleges" as existed in the south, she compared favorably.

Her earliest surviving diploma (1855), granted only upon completion of the four year course, reads:

> Whereas, By an Act of the General Assembly of the State of Missouri, Ladies may receive from this Board such *Literary Honors* as are usually granted by American Colleges and Universities . . . we do hereby confer upon . . . the Baccalaureate Degree of this Institution, and award to her this DIPLOMA, in testimony of her attainments, and of our high consideration of her as a Lady.

Little can be proven about the age of those early graduates, although they seem to have averaged eighteen or older.[19] A contemporary St. Louis newspaper reports that most of Christian's students were "about sixteen." Actually, ages seem to have varied from thirteen to thirty! Most schools then, including the University of Missouri, were graduating students two to three years younger than is done today.

It is significant, however, that five of Christian's first six graduates immediately became teachers or principals of other schools.

Perhaps it is more realistic to compare Christian's level of education with that of the University of Missouri before the Civil War. Except for such strictly masculine subjects at the University as surveying and road-building, and the aforementioned Latin and Greek, the courses of the two schools are almost identical for the four college years.[20] Since the same texts were used and sometimes taught by the same teachers, the quality of education received would seem to have been similar. Christian's Board *Minutes* show that in the beginning her trustees took an active part in her educational policies. With a philosophical scholar like Shannon or a scientist like Hudson to supervise, it is unlikely that Christian would have shoddy offerings in these fields.

Since early texts and courses did not vary much, perhaps the sort of teaching a girl received should remain as the real criterion of her education. Of this we have proof.

Emerging from John Augustus Williams' *Reminiscences*[21] written many years later is the picture of a true educator: brilliant, but full of common sense, dedicated, but humorous. Progressive, even radical, but never hot-headed. We see a teacher who threw out the customary many "branches" of learning in favor of fewer courses, better taught; who renounced the "pernicious rote system," in favor of a constant sifting for "the truth;" who, when a little country girl offered some effusion on "The Influence of the Crusades on the Civilization of Western Europe," advised her to write on something as familiar as "The Cow."

Here was a disciplinarian who felt that the simple injunction "do right" was worth a book of rules; a taskmaster who insisted that each waking moment be gainfully employed, who saw each student as a missionary, spreading this gospel of higher learning.

None of this seemed too formidable to girls of that day. They enrolled so enthusiastically that before the rooms were furnished Williams was having to worry about lack of space.

His catalog had been, like most such documents, a little

before the fact. When he stated that "the *Main Front Edifice* of Christian College will be ready," he was speaking of the only building on the campus. Doubtless he expected that, before the year was out, there would be the advertised addition of 50 x 40 on the foundation already laid to the back. The St. Louis *Times* of 1852 even described it:

> The building is one hundred and five feet in length, by fifty in width. Including the basement, the front portion is four stories high. The rear is three stories.

"When finished," it added, it would be "as convenient and as well arranged for the objects in view, as any building of its size in the Union."

But only the front was finished, the "elegant brick mansion" much as it looks today. The five rooms of the original Bennett house had been enlarged into sixteen, four on each floor including the ground, or basement. After one hundred years the elegance has worn off, but it still has dignity and charm. The fanlighted front door is pleasant, as is the curving stairway connecting the "two spacious halls." In the basement are the remains of the kitchen fireplace where the first meals were cooked, and partitions marking the dining room on the front, the store room, and servants' quarters.

The main floor had two large rooms on either side of the central hall, with a fireplace in each. The President's family lived in one of the back rooms and undoubtedly shared their front parlor with those seniors who had "drawing room privileges." The front room on the east served as President's study, school library, and classroom. There were four similar rooms upstairs and, reportedly, four in the attic. These must have been crowded indeed, with their sloping walls and tiny windows almost at the floor.[22] But girls of that day considered it no great hardship to sleep eight in a room with sometimes a trundle bed under the big bed.

The editor of the *Sentinel* comments that, to his way of thinking, President Williams could have taken in quite a few more lodgers!

It must have been, truly, a collegiate family, or they could not have done so well in so little space. What were they like, these first college girls, and what was their life? This was the

Victorian era, when only men were vile, and women were supposed to be weak and protected.

"A healthy woman," according to the editor of the June 7, 1855 *Missouri Dollar Journal,* "is a prodigy in the 19th century."

> Wherever you go, you see scores and hundreds of spleeny, sickly, feeble girls, who can hardly muster courage to make their beds, wash their faces or drive an intruding cow from the yard. Tell them about early rising, fresh air and healthy exercise, and they heave a sigh as long as the moral law and are ready to faint away. . . . No wonder that every year sweeps to the grave so many young women. . . . Do you know the cause? It is found in listless idleness . . . inactivity . . . late hours . . . thin shoes . . . muslin dresses . . . a horror of fresh morning air . . . and that detestable stuff stitched in pink and yellow covers, which is flooding our country. If they will do nothing else, young ladies will sit and read from morning till night sickly, sentimental, impure and licentious trash.

If this was the norm, it does not describe the young ladies of Christian College, who took calisthenics and had little time for yellow-backed novels. They were not the ultra-fashionable, perambulating about in six to eight petticoats; not if Williams had his way. Certainly they were not the extreme who dared appear in the new fad of Bloomers. They were ambitious girls whose parents could afford the $150 a a year tuition and saw reason to spend it on a better-than-average education.

A letter from one of these parents is perhaps typical. He has, he tells his Nancy, just sold $4,625.00 worth of mules "and also . . . George" to some neighbors in Pike county. His trading ability was obviously better than his spelling.

> . . . I want you to drive a head and not become discouraged . . . bee industrous and try to advance as fast as any of the girls and be kind to your school teachers Roommates and to all . . . speake harsh to none or evil of any so when I come over next summer that I may see and hear all speak well of you as they did last.
>
> I should like to see you standing a mong the Juniors next summer if you are I have a hansom preasant alloted off for you. . . .

> . . . tell Mr. Williams not to hold you back in your studies that it dont doe to hold a trotting horse back for fear you spoil his gate, so let you trot through and if you can trot and wont trot up with your class to make you. . . .[23]

President Williams was never one to hold back a trotting horse.

The girls rose by six, took a morning walk, and gathered for chapel. They practiced, attended classes till late afternoon, and wrote a daily composition on foolscap. They "worked enormously hard," for they were required to write a thesis showing they understood each subject before passing on to another.[24] Required subjects were:[25]

> *Freshman Class.*—Arithmetic (finished), Ancient History, Grammar (finished), Ancient Geography, Nat. Philosophy, Five Books of Moses, Composition, and Mental Arithmetic (finished).
>
> *Sophomore Class.*—Ray's Algebra, Vol. 1st, Nat. History of Animals, of Plants and of Minerals, Modern History, Rhetoric, Jewish Scriptures (finished), and Modern Geography.
>
> *Junior Class.*—Ray's Algebra, Vol. 2d, Geometry, Chemistry, Practical Botany, Physiology, Geology, Criticism, and The Four Gospels.
>
> *Senior Class.*—Trigonometry, Analytical Geometry, Mental Science, Logic, Ethics, Constitutional Law, Astronomy, English and Sacred Literature, and Acts of Apostles.

They used such textbooks as Wayland's *Political Economy,* Mrs. Lincoln's *Botany,* Whately's *Logic,* Alexander's or Paley's *Evidences of Christianity,* Parker's *Natural Philosophy,* Goodrich's histories. They studied Hume and Bacon, read Swift, Milton, Shakespeare, Irving, Young's "Night Thoughts," Pollock's "Course of Time." They aspired to write stanzas like those of Amelia or Miss S. Virginia Smith.

Pupils who were doing well in their regular work could pursue, at slight additional cost, the Optionary Studies: Ancient and Modern Languages, Drawing, Painting, Embroidery, Vocal Music, Piano, or Guitar. The choir was popular.

After the girls had finished their studies, practice, bookkeeping, and chores, there was the Bible lecture each evening

John Augustus Williams, 1851–1856

Graduating class of 1857

THREE FOUNDERS OF CHRISTIAN COLLEGE

James Shannon

CHRISTIAN COLLEGE, COLUMBIA, MO.

THE SIXTH SESSION OF CHRISTIAN FEMALE COLLEGE will open on the ***Third Monday in September next.***

A competent and *experienced Faculty* has been selected, with reference to their ability, fidelity and moral worth.

The *Domestic Department* is fully provided for, a Lady of age and experience having been engaged to spend all her time in its supervision.

COLLEGE FEES, PER SESSION OF TEN MONTHS, AS HERETOFORE.

Board and tuition, including washing, lights and doctor's bills, in the family, (in advance,)	**$150**
Tuition for day pupils in the regular College classes, ...	**36**
Tuition for day pupils in the Preparatory Department, ...	**24**
Tuition for music—Piano or Guitar, ..	**40**
Use of Pianos, ...	**8**

Ancient or Modern Languages, Drawing, Painting, Embroidering, &c., extra, at the usual prices.

For further information address *C. S. STONE, A. DOUGLASS* or *L. B. WILKES. Columbia, Mo.*

L. B. WILKES,
President C. C.

July 10, 1056.

COLUMBIA BAPTIST FEMALE COLLEGE.

THE CURATORS of this Institution hereby announce to the public that the first term of the College will open on the **1st Monday in September next,** under the management of Prest. WM. R. ROTHWELL, aided by teachers highly qualified to instruct in all the branches of Female education taught in the United States.

The College property is admirably located in the town of Columbia, Boone county, Mo., and cannot be surpassed in point of beauty and fitness for a female school. For the present the Columbia Female Academy has been secured as a school room, and parents residing at a distance can procure boarding for their daughters

Above: From State Historical Society of Missouri. Right: The College in 1873

omas M. Allen

D. Pat Henderson

Lanceford B. Wilkes, 1856–1858

Vinnie Ream, Bingham portrait

Joseph K. Rogers, 1858–1877

Left: President Bryant (left) and girls in 1881

Martha Washington Literary Society, 1889

nnet Girl

George S. Bryant, 1877–1883

89 Senior Class with William A. Oldham (1883–1893)

ANNUAL EXHIBITION
OF THE
AURORA SOCIETY,
Christian College,
Columbia, Mo.,
Tuesday, May 25, 1886.
CLASS OF 188

1864

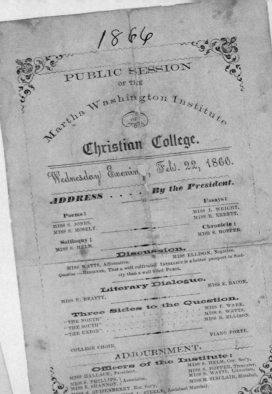

PUBLIC SESSION
OF THE
Martha Washington Institute
OF
Christian College.

Wednesday Evening, Feb. 22, 1860.

ADDRESS . . . . By the President.

Poems:
MISS S. JONES,
MISS S. MOSELY.

Essays:
MISS L. WRIGHT,
MISS R. ERRETT.

Soliloquy;
MISS S. HELM.

Chronicle:
MISS S. HOPPER.

Discussion.

MISS WATTS, Affirmative. MISS ELLISON, Negative.

Question:—RESOLVED, That a well cultivated INTELLECT is a better passport in Society than a well filled PURSE.

Literary Dialogue.

MISS E. BEATTY, MISS E. BACON.

Three Sides to the Question.

"THE NORTH" . . . . . . MISS F. WARE,
"THE SOUTH" . . . . . . MISS S. WATTS,
"THE UNION" . . . . . . MISS B. ELLISON.

PIANO FORTE.

COLLEGE CHOIR.

ADJOURNMENT.

Officers of the Institute:

MISS HALLACK, President.
MISS S. PHILLIPS, } Associates,
MISS E. SHANNON, }
MISS S. QUISENBERRY, Rec. Sec'y,
MISS S. HELM, Cor. Sec'y.
MISS S. HOPPER, Treasurer,
MISS S. WATTS, Librarian,
MISS M. SINCLAIR, Marshal,
MISS L. STEELE, Assistant Marshal.

Printed at the Statesman Office.

Commencement Exercises,
Christian Female College,
Columbia, Mo.,
June 1, 1887.

...SS OF 1881.

...	Miami, Mo.
...	Columbia, Mo.
...	...nton City, Mo.
...	...s Summit, Mo.
...	Lindey, Mo.
...nam,	Happy Valley, Mo.
...Downing,	Memphis, Mo.
...iams,	Boone Co., Mo.
...Kissinger,	Clarksville, Mo.
...Kitchen,	Hector, Kansas.
...Lenoir,	Columbia, Mo.
...igon,	St. Louis, Mo.
...ukens,	Columbia, Mo.
...ler,	Gervais, Oregon.
...dge,	Kansas City, Mo.

CHRISTIAN COLLEGE, COLUMBIA, MO.

PRIZE ESSAYS.

JUNIOR CLASS,

Tuesday, May 31, 1881,

2 P. M.

—PRIZES.—

First Prize . . . . . . Gold Medal, ($20.)
Second Prize . . . . . . Gold Medal, ($10.)

Matthews Litho. Phila.

...ORS.

... } Miss Dora Iiams.
... } Miss Katie Cook.
... Miss May Downing.
... Miss Julia C. Lenoir.

and church required on Sunday. They left the campus so seldom that this was probably a social occasion. They marched in their rows of green bonnets all the way from the college to town, carefully flanked by the President and members of the faculty.

If it snowed they might be isolated on campus as long as six weeks. Then a visit from such a notable as Alexander Campbell was a memorable affair. Only the young women teachers enjoyed the excitement of a Wednesday night prayer-meeting.

There are more secular glimpses: the botany class out combing the lawn for specimens, a gay circle of girls sitting on the grass, taking up the President's challenge to write him a song as he throws them a first line, gathering more soberly about him at night as he plays his recently published composition, "The Mary Belle Polka," named for his dead daughter.

It was on Saturdays—every sixth Saturday—that they had their callers and their infrequent, escorted trips to town. Here they were perhaps allowed to sample that delicious new confection, "soda," at one of Columbia's two fountains, or visit the exhibit of paintings which George Caleb Bingham had recently hung in the courthouse. On rare, delightful occasions they were guests of the university students at a literary society meeting. It is probable that on these evenings the boys obeyed their society's injunctions to Refrain From Spitting and Keep Feet off the Tables.

Perhaps these programs were the impetus for the girls to form a society of their own, the Mary Phelps Institute.[26] This met each Friday, when the girls would read original compositions, examine the new scientific specimens in their cabinet collection, and discuss how to enlarge their library, which was indeed the only one belonging to the school. Altogether, though there were periodic prankish invasions by the other sex, and perhaps need for the board fence which was constructed, the girls led a life insulated from the town: from the cholera scare, the political bickering, the gathering war clouds.

But they were normal girls. Although the President taught them a great deal, they apparently taught him some things, too, about human nature, or at least the nature of girls. There is a gradual tone of relaxing in the successive catalogs. The Bible becomes not *the* prominent, but *a* prominent text; its study condenses into Evidences of Christianity and the Life of Christ. Domestic chores are "encouraged" rather than "expected." An admonition that all clothing must be indelibly marked might indicate that President Williams succeeded no better than the average parent in reforming the habits of adolescents. Higher education was not making freaks of these lively daughters of the West.

"There must be something peculiar to the climate in Missouri favorable to the development of the person and congenial with beauty," speculates an out-state visitor to the campus.

> How different such young ladies are from the pale, sickly, hot-house plants of the old States. Already, some of the sensible young gentlemen of the old states are seeking for wives in Missouri. . . .

Altogether, it was a pleasant picture of life, that first year, like all first years in a new home, before the new wears off and the cracks appear in the plaster. Everywhere was health and vigor from "the bright eyes of the young ladies" to "the premium four-foot clover" found in the front yard! The school was booming. It looked as if nothing could stop Christian College.

It was this very refusal to be static that was to cause the trouble. The enrollment had increased from 75 the first year to 101 the second year, and 130 the third. The number of boarders had climbed from 36 to 50 to 70. By the third year girls were being turned away, and the advertisements of the college carried the warning: "Enrollment is strictly limited." The paper commented that twice as many could have been enrolled had there been accommodations, and declared: "There are two girls' schools in Columbia, neither of which can supply the demand." Then, in 1855 the Female Academy closed for good and some of its pupils came over to Christian.[27]

As new boarders came, the President put them where he could, among the enlarging faculty and the increasing number of pianos. He was forced to give up the primary school, all but his demonstration class of ten little girls (some of them orphans he was teaching gratuitously.)

He built two frame cottages flanking the main building, then added to the eastern one an "L" containing three rooms twenty feet square.[28] He converted the smokehouse into a classroom. In the spring of 1855 a newspaper reporter visited the campus, ostensibly to see the President's amazing new $150 revolving woodsaw, but actually to find out where he was putting all the girls.

And President Williams, gazing out over the still empty foundation, grew increasingly bitter. A limited enrollment was one of his standards, but he had never meant for it to be this limited. If subscriptions had been paid, if the promises of five years ago had been kept, he would easily have reached his ideal of 150 boarding students by now. Perhaps the trustees had got a good man too cheap.

For, underlying the booming growth statistics of the young school is the diverging downward record of an institution sinking deeper and deeper in debt. A chapter could be written on the early finances of Christian College, and it would probably serve as a history of most of the starting schools of its day.

Williams' original estimate of the minimum it would take to establish a female college was $10,000. (It is interesting that this was the very sum set aside five years later by the New York legislature to establish Elmira Female College, claiming to be the first in the East.) Of this, he expected the backers to raise $8,000. But the record of the *Minutes* show Shannon, more like a Scotsman than an Irishman, bargaining him into "coming out" for a donation of $3000. According to Shannon, Williams had understood that if no larger subscriptions could be raised, he was to match this sum with $6000 of his own money.

Actually, none of these sums materialized in cash. Christian College was started on a prayer and a piece of mortgage paper made out to J. S. Rollins.

The Board *Minutes* for the first six years reveal, in contrast to the optimism of the catalogs, a sorry struggle to exist.

Financing was ingenious. The President was to pay himself and his faculty out of the tuitions. Two agents, J. K. Rogers and H. H. Ready, were to travel and collect subscriptions, out of which they would be paid. Local building subscriptions were to be collected by the building committee, who were responsible for all bills. No wonder that into their initial report should creep that note of caution which was to become a counterpoint threatening the main theme: "Resolved . . . at no time to progress further than the amount of subscriptions will permit."

Before the grounds were even possessed the trustees had raised the tuition, suspended the brickwork on the extension and voted to require of President Williams four dollars return on every tuition. They were willing to relinquish this sum for two years, however, provided he would spend it in furnishing the new building.

This change of policy led to frequent misunderstandings over expenses. The Board would not acknowledge the President's bill for eleven stoves with pipes, a rail fence and latched gate on the west, or the plank fence between the yard and the grass lot. They did pay, however, for desks and for constructing "a privy of suitable dimensions."

There were constant crises. Henry Keene, the bricklayer, sued. Each time the interest on the mortgage fell due the trustees scurried about like principals in a melodrama. They passed vehement resolutions: "Something must be done." They worked out new schemes for urging or forcing subscribers to pay. They set a deadline for themselves to do the same. They worried about public opinion. "The college will never be considered as established until indebtedness is liquidated." Even the newspaper harangued their cause:

> Let our citizens then put their shoulders to the wheel and complete Christian College. *Double* her accommodations . . . and her halls will be crowded the first session they are thus enlarged. . . . Will our citizens stand idly by and see young ladies knocking at the doors. . . . ? For shame that [Boone] should be so blind to her own interests. . . .[29]

They vowed that the extension must be completed, and

in the same breath resolved to get no further in debt. They groaned around the conference table as the treasurer reported a balance on hand of sixty cents!

D. Pat Henderson made a stirring speech. Henderson alone, by the end of May, 1852, had raised $1,284.50 in the "foreign field." For this he sought no remuneration, being activated, he said, "by a single principle—the good of my race in cultivating the female mind and heart."

> I have been pleased and encouraged by the great unanimity which has characterized our proceedings in the discharge of our duties, as trustees of the *first* and *only Female College* in this state. . . .
>
> That we are surrounded by difficulties and embarrassments is too plainly seen . . . to be denied.
>
> From the accounts received, and the number of pupils obtained from abroad, I am cheered by the hope that we shall, by a united effort, succeed in demonstrating that we have not been pursuing "phantoms," erecting "airy castles" or building up "visionary schemes" which must end in "splendid failure;" but that with firmness of purpose, integrity of heart, as honorable and philanthropic men, we shall by the blessing of heaven, succeed in carrying into effect . . . the cherished purposes of our hearts.

He made the Board two propositions to clear the debt: one, that he would raise a sum equal to that raised by any other trustee, or, two, that he himself would raise half the money owed if any other trustee would do the same within the next year.

Though the Board thanked him and unanimously resolved that his name should go down on the books as "the early and steadfast friend of Christian College," his challenge was not taken up.

Perhaps others like T. M. Allen listened with scepticism. He was beginning to mistrust Henderson's stability. Perhaps the Board's inertia was too much for Henderson, the man who saw things in a big way. Within a month he had become a founder and trustee of Christian University[30] at Canton and was off to raise a $50,000 endowment for this first co-educational venture.

In the light of their day, the trustees and other subscribers were not greatly to be blamed. With typical American enthusiasm, they had hitched their wagons to not one star, but a constellation. River traffic was at its height and it seemed imperative to build a plank road between Columbia and its nearest port, Providence. Forward looking citizens were putting up money to get the railroad into Missouri. The so-called "State" University was still being supported by private subscriptions. There were only 1,000 people in Columbia, after all, and of these only a portion had pledged themselves to the ambitious task of founding a school of higher learning for females. Moreover, the same church members who were contributing to Christian College were responding to the canvass of the parent Bethany College in Virginia, the new Christian University at Canton, and the Kentucky Orphan School. Perhaps the wonder is that subscribers paid as readily as they did.

And across the border in Kansas suddenly there were skirmishes and gunsmoke which obscured the vision of the average Missourian to anything but the question: Will Kansas go pro-slavery?

In the unfolding conflict between Williams and the Board of Trustees, or more directly, Williams and Shannon, politics may have had a part. Williams was an abolitionist. Shannon was even then stumping the state with his famous speech proving by the Bible that slavery was ordained by God. Elder Allen's private prophecy that he would "bring down fire and brimstone on our heads" was coming true.

Williams and Shannon may have disagreed over such policies as the Normal School, a concept vital to Williams but which Shannon had fought at the University.

Although the drama as outlined in Board *Minutes* is shadowy we see Shannon growing more positive, petty, sometimes appearing interested in the quarrel rather than the College. Williams, *"that skilled diplomatist!—who is more than an equal for the whole Board,"*[31] remains bland but stubborn, answering accusations with cool rebuffs. Allen quietly vetoes the short-sighted resolutions, urging unity here as he had in politics and religion. More than a bit player is Caleb Stone, that power behind the University. (He was virtually keeping it in operation for Shannon during his absences.) We see Stone constantly checking, accusing, demanding an accounting, as he had five years before in his war on President Lathrop.

There is an overall tightening of the reins; whereas originally the President was to improve the grounds "as he sees fit," now he "*must* keep in good repair at his own expense all outbuildings, fences, etc." An issue of the catalog stating that all students are "allowed" to go to church each Sunday is called sharply in and the word "required" substituted. Even the circular woodsaw comes under suspicion, as it is hinted that the timber which was to be used for the College is being sold as firewood for private profit while Williams presents a bill for fuel.

Finally the President was asked to pay to date the four dollars on each pupil as rent on the building and grounds. He was accused of holding back money raised on subscriptions. A rumor sprang up in town that he had purchased a school in Kentucky.

Perhaps it was the July deadline of the Rollins note falling due which brought the situation to a head. At the closing of the fifth school year a committee of trustees visited the College and turned in a description of desperate overcrowding. Beds were everywhere. Young ladies were studying, sleeping, and practicing piano all in the same room. The President's family of four and the Patron's family of four[32] were each living in one room. The space in the basement used for dining was about "half the necessary size." Altogether, eighty-five boarders, eight teachers, eight family members, and eighteen servants were living on the premises in, apparently, the sixteen-room house and the two cottages totalling seven rooms. Since enrollment had then reached 147, there were some sixty others using the facilities.

The Board's solution seems further to insinuate that Williams had profited from the College. They approached him for a building loan of $7,500 in return for which they would mortgage the property to him. He refused:

> The entertainment of a proposition to do anything more for this institution in a pecuniary way, than what

> I have already done, must assume that a satisfactory adjustment has been made of all just claims growing out of my past expenditures for the improvement of the grounds and buildings, and also that the . . . assessment of $4 for each pupil . . . has been satisfactorily settled. . . .

It was a deadlock. In his former pupil the inflexible Shannon had met his match.

Allen was for a compromise that would induce Williams to stay, but Shannon saw only the issue of who was right and who was wrong. Insultingly, he demanded that Williams turn in an account of the number of pupils enrolled for the past two years and the tuition paid by each. Williams did so, and with it his resignation. Then, in a most sarcastic summing-up in Shannon's handwriting Williams is accused of having "for years" made a gross income of more than $12,000 on the College, while contributing little more to the physical plant than a couple of "cabins." (In preceding *Minutes* they had been referred to as "halls of instruction.")

Since the finances were confused a hundred years ago it is useless to try to clarify them now. The Board would seem justified in demanding that a certain amount of profit go back into the institution for improvements. However, Williams truly had the grievance he claimed: that they had always been too poor or too cautious to furnish adequate facilities for the number of students he was able to attract. Although he and his father apparently cleared enough to purchase the Greenville Institute, Harrodsburg, Kentucky, it is questionable how much money they made after deducting salaries, equipment, upkeep, and providing food, lodging, fuel, and laundry for the eighty-five boarding pupils.

Now with expansion blocked, the debt falling due, the finances of the drought-stricken country growing increasingly unstable,[33] it seemed a time to move.

Besides, Williams was homesick for Kentucky. He took one last look at the two small graves which now lay side by side at the back of the campus. He thought of the beautiful region around Greenville and its life-giving springs. . . .

Such was Williams' popularity that sixteen of his Senior class went with him to Kentucky. These Boone County names are on that first roll of Daughters' College at Harrodsburg which he named after his two little girls[34] and which still exists as Beaumont Inn.

The President and the Board parted with outward tokens of respect. They penned a resolution of regret, while he wished them success and invoked God's blessing on "our beloved institution." Then they voted unanimously that in the future any resigning president must give six months notice. Williams inserted a plaintive ad in the paper: "For sale—a one horse power woodsaw, adapted for a thrashing machine. . . ."

For his last Baccalaureate, looking down on his white-clad girls, the President delivered quite a beautiful sermon. He reaffirmed the importance to a Christian society of usefully educated women. His words were simple and his sentiments basic enough to credit a progressive educator of today.

He had no way of knowing whether they would take root. Doubtless he was discouraged; perhaps the times seemed out of joint. If the town fathers had acted in unity or the legislature voted funds as it had in New York state. . . . If a Matthew Vassar could have arisen, with his money and his desire for immortality, Christian College might, in all ways, have become first in the West. Perhaps Williams saw himself as a failure. Perhaps his aspirations had been too high for this still raw pioneer community.

He had no way of knowing even that he had set his stamp on Christian College. It would always retain something of the dictums he wrote so clearly into his catalogs; small, selective, serious in purpose. . . . "No education can be regarded as useful . . . unless it be adapted to the nature of the individual."

He only knew that in spite of humiliation, heart-break, harassments, in the turbulence of the times, he had tried to act with integrity. And as he turned back there would be those he had trained who might, after all, ranging the earth like "the eyes of the Lord," carry his work into the new horizons west of the prairie.

III

A YOUNG MAN IN BLUE JEANS 1856-1859

It has long been a cherished sentiment with us—no distinction of sex in the realms of thought.

—CHRISTIAN COLLEGE CATALOG, 1859

APPARENTLY NOT ONE remains of the five hundred circulars which were supposed to set forth the prospects of Christian College in the fall of 1856. The prospects were not good.

President Williams was departing, taking with him most of the furnishings, part of the student body and, according to Caleb Stone, two hundred of the three hundred books of the Mary Phelps library.

The Board of Trustees seemed to be breaking up. Chairman T. M. Allen had resigned along with Williams. James Shannon had made one too many of his violent political speeches and had talked his way out of the university presidency. He was rejoining Henderson, Samuel Hatch, and the Grants to promote at Canton the *co*-educational Christian

University which may have been their aim that fall of '49 in Columbia. Theirs was one of the first college charters to specify *equal* education of males and females.[1]

Christian's treasurer, William Hudson, had replaced Shannon as university executive and would have too many affairs of his own to concern himself longer with the girls' school. With less than five weeks to find a new president, rumor already had it that Christian College was prostrate. And, as if taking advantage of its embarrassment, across town a Baptist Female College was organizing for its first term.[2]

Immediately the Board looked toward Palmyra, the feeder school. Now, truly, the child could supply the parent. Associate principal Lanceford B. Wilkes was young but had more in his favor than expediency. Holder of an M.A. from the University, he already had served Christian College effectively both as agent and trustee.

It was Shannon who nominated him, just before shooting like a meteor from the Columbia scene. In doing so, he set his influence on the next twenty-five years of the college he had helped to found. Possibly he suggested that another of his outstanding graduates, Joseph Rogers, be hired as Wilkes' assistant. Anyway, Wilkes brought Rogers, his close companion of 1850-52 student days. Their lives had remained linked with each other and with Christian College, for each of them had traveled for it his first year out of school. Wilkes had married Rebecca, daughter of trustee Lewis Bryan. Rogers had married Jennie Robards, of its first graduating class. When Wilkes joined the staff of the Palmyra branch academy Rogers opened a Christian church female academy in St. Joseph.[3]

The day before Commencement the Board could advertise that "The sixth session of CHRISTIAN FEMALE COLLEGE will open the third Monday in September next. A competent and experienced faculty has been selected, with reference to their ability, fidelity and moral worth. . . ."

Expediency was a factor, too, for aside from Rogers and Professor Alexander the four new staff members are revealed to be last year's graduates. For $3,500 the President bought furniture for every room in the building, and made some improvements to the grounds. By September a reporter describes the College as "renovated." Enrollment had dropped by approximately forty, but still totaled ninety-nine as compared with the University's 108.

The brief record of Wilkes' administration lies within the covers of the 1857 catalog. It has grown from eight to twelve pages, reflecting the author's taste for purple passages. One such describes the lack of physical education in most colleges.

> Too numerous and lamentable are the instances on record, where the youthful aspirant for Literary Honors, in her rash zeal to secure the prize, has sacrificed health and happiness, and dashed the mingled cup of hope and promise from the lips of admiring friends and doting Parents.

There is a new stress on the physical. Whereas President Williams had "enjoined" the young ladies to take walks, now daily outdoor exercise is required at certain hours. Normal training is also emphasized:

> In view of the rapidly increasing demand for good teachers . . . to the other Departments of Christian College has been added a Teachers' Department. The peculiar object . . . the proper education of Young Ladies for Professional teaching. The Course of Study is so arranged, and recitations are so conducted, as to secure . . . *all* the advantages of a Normal School.

This effort paralleled current attempts of the University to establish a strong normal department.

Academic courses remain the same but, "because of the rising cost of living," tuition has increased to $160. Fees for optional studies are practically doubled and medical expenses are now extra. Regulations are, if anything, more strict in regard to meeting young men. Getting around these rules led to midnight visits and the first serenades. A university student of 1858 recalls Wayman Crow, Jr., singing "The Wrecker's Daughter," and Frank Venable strumming his guitar to "Peace Be Thy Slumbers."

Wilkes' catalog for the first time lists a CLASS OF SMALL BOYS, though some had attended the academy from its beginning. This was a concession to transportation problems of the day. Patrons found it convenient to send younger brothers along with their sisters to school; faculty members living on campus had sons. Thus, Dermot Brennan, Thomas and William Cave, Luther Crumbaugh, Edwin Haynes, Rollins Philips, Charles Shannon, Turner Cornelius, David and Owen Stone were the first males who could claim education at the women's college. The girls welcomed them as messengers from older brothers in the outside world.

But the greatest innovation is the Martha Washington Institute, "a Department of the College proper," which Juniors and Seniors are required to join. It was founded in 1857 by Professor Rogers and six of his advanced pupils. Modeled after the Union Literary Society in which Rogers and Wilkes had starred at the University, it was named Martha Washington because the men's societies had their yearly exhibition on George Washington's birthday. Hereafter, the 22nd of February would be the big day of the year for Christian girls. That morning they were guests at the University's program and that night the boys were invited to an "open meeting" at the College.

These programs were long drawn-out: roll-call, the president's "Address," numerous recitations and "literary gems," and the reading of the year's Journal. However, in the social half-hour following, many a match was made. Anticipation of these yearly high-spots enlivened the weekly meetings for, recorded along with attacks on Hume's philosophy or debates on the rights of women are controversies over whether club-members can afford a silk banner with their motto "Sit Lux," or may be allowed to wear pink, instead of dark red dresses to the program.

The trustees, in deeding over the remaining one hundred books of the defunct Mary Phelps society to the new organization, specified that a yearly record should be kept. Thus we have, from 1857 until 1897, three fascinating volumes of Minutes written by generations of earnest young parliamentarians.

The girls took their learned society seriously, offering honorary membership to persons they admired. (It is too bad they did not attach the letters of acceptance reported from

President James Buchanan and Sarah Josepha Hale, editor of *Godey's Lady's Book.*)

"But mostly we cut up," recalls one member whose fines for misdemeanors helped to fill the bookshelves. Aside from these Society collections, college students in early days often depended on the president's personal library, which they used for a small fee. To Wilkes goes the credit for proposing an independent library for Christian College, though its acquisition was voluntary for many years.

Wilkes was to play his biggest role in the development of Christian College not as president, but later when he liquidated its debts. But he did lend the school a certain aura with his reputation as a pulpit orator and logician. He became a famed mediator of arguments in churches throughout the state and, partly because of him, Columbia grew to be a clearing-house for the Disciples in the 1860's. Once he and Moses Lard got into such prolonged correspondence that he invited Lard down from northwest Missouri to visit until he could set him straight. Brother Lard brought his entire family and stayed at the College six weeks!

Preachers were perhaps easier to convince than young girls. A student recalls Wilkes, the professor, as "a Czar." One young lady who had given continuous trouble was finally called into his study.

"Cordelia," he said, "I've argued with you, I've commanded you, I've pleaded with you, I've prayed for you. Now I'm going to slap you in the jaw." And he did.

It was partially his incompatibility for teaching which caused Wilkes to resign at the end of a year and a half. That, and perhaps the old snag of the four dollars per pupil. The Board had dealt with him as inconsistently as with Williams, first letting him keep all profits to pay for his expenses, next asking him to pay the interest on the debt, finally demanding the four dollars return on each pupil. Wilkes refused. Caleb Stone scolded the others roundly for their vacillating policy. He prophesied that never again would the trustees of Christian College control its rent and tuition.

Stone was now undisputed leader of the trustees. Narrow and partisan as he had been in the University policies, it was he who steadied that institution during Shannon's tumultuous regime. Now he brought the same determined support to the college he considered its counterpart. Blunt, fearless, he was a shrewd bargainer for Christian where a sliver of land or a rate of interest was concerned. At Board meetings he made most of the resolutions, spread colorful protests upon the *Minutes* and doggedly maneuvered the group out of each financial pitfall.

University ties continued in the persons of trustees Bolivar Head and Sterling Price, Jr. Professors both, they were hot-heads, Shannonites, politically involved. Alexander Douglass, now treasurer, was Shannon's son-in-law. Of the other new trustees Walter T. Lenoir, John Machir, Jesse Boulton and Robert Lemon were to hold tenure and influence over thirty years. The bold signature, "David Gordon, Pres't," was to sign the fading *Minutes* until the Judge died in 1875. And the other old Boone County names, Joseph Estes, John Connelly (Conley), Archibald W. Turner, Robert M. Graham, Matthew Arnold and Theodric Jenkins, illustrate a significant fact—in the stop-gap crisis that was Wilkes' administration the Board of Trustees had become a local board.

This localizing was a sign of approaching war. It had happened at the University and was happening in schools throughout the land. Distinguished "foreigners" might lend prestige but it was the local group who had enough stake in the College to save it. They were related to it by business as well as by sentiment and religion. The College bought their wood, their pigs, their groceries or dry goods, called for their legal or medical services.

They were inextricably related to it by blood. Some had sisters who had been educated there. One or two had married Christian College brides. The majority had daughters in the school, or small sons. They had started a continuity. The "small boys" would grow up to marry Christian College girls, become trustees, and in time send their daughters. Christian College was acquiring roots.

The new Board approached the old problem. How to pay the debt and still build that northern extension? Resolving to do both, they floated bonds for $7,000 at 6 per cent. Then each trustee bought a bond! They were able to stave off Major Rollins for three more years with 10 per cent interest and a mortgage. At that, the minute they let the contract they saw they had underestimated building costs, so they turned to Wilkes for money from tuitions.

He refused to reconsider, but recommended Rogers for president, effective Commencement, 1858.

Meanwhile Rogers was elected to the Board of Trustees. One wonders if his nerve failed when he attended his first meeting and got on the inside of the finances. One item of business was a notice that former President Williams and his father were bringing suit for $1400. The other was that ten local trustees each held a deed of trust against the real and personal property of the Board, payable by January 1, 1861, *or property subjected to sale.*

It is interesting to compare the hectic facts with the words of Switzler, local historian, writing twenty-five years later. Joseph Kirtley Rogers "having taken charge of Christian College in 1858, the school had just arrived at a happy and prosperous period when Civil War broke out. . . ."[4] Old T. M. Allen wrote more accurately:

> Times are truly tight here—money scarce—confidence destroyed—many pecuniarily ruined—no sale for anything and all at a standstill but political demagogues & seeking politicians—Oh the darkness that covers the future.[5]

Fortunately, Rogers was no man to back down.

Eight years before, when the tall youth climbed off his mule at the gate of the University of Missouri, he had been teased about his homespun country dress.

"Rogers," jeered a sophomore, "where can we get some blue jeans broadcloth like yours?"

"There is none like it," he replied. "My mother made this." He was to face all his problems with such honesty, dignity and courage, but with little humor.

Perhaps Rogers, the President, would not have been the same had not Rogers, the boy, grown up breathing the heady air of Marion County. Fabulous Marion County, in northeastern Missouri, had been the setting for a typical American venture in Utopia. Two successful fictioneers drew on it; Dickens for the Eden of *Martin Chuzzlewit* and Mark Twain for the background of Colonel Mulberry Sellers in *The Gilded Age*.

The scheme, promoted by Eastern visionaries, had been to establish a $20,000 university in the moral wastes of the West. The university, but one of the attractions of a future metropolis to be known as Marion City, was laid out over 4,969 acres of land with different branches, like the spokes of a wheel, some fourteen miles apart. The curriculum ranged from preparatory school to medical and theological seminaries, from mineralogy to Greek.

This enterprise was to finance itself on what teachers and students could raise on the college farm. All were to spend their vacation harvesting hay and loading it on the steamboat for New Orleans.

"Marion College" was actually chartered in 1831; amazingly, the teachers and theologians arrived—men of real, if starry-eyed prominence. Students came, fifty-two of the eighty from outstate. "Massachusetts," "Pennsylvania," "New York," "Virginia," "Louisiana" were some of the frank marks that confounded the Ely, Missouri postmaster. Cosmopolitan discussions filled the dusty main street of Philadelphia. On Saturdays farmers gathered at Palmyra to chuckle over the $150 lots New Yorkers were buying in the nearby wilderness. Or they watched the grading of the railroad—the first in Missouri—that was to stretch to the Pacific coast.

At the hub of the dizzy wheel, a mile north of Philadelphia, stood the pioneer cabin of the Rogers family. Marion College was the school to which young Joe Rogers went in 1835 as a precocious lad of seven. This was the atmosphere he breathed, as he stared, with the other boys, at the gorgeous map of the Marion City that was to be, its Bank and Newspaper office and Theatre drawn in color. He was there later, when the bubble burst.

For the dreamers had reckoned without hell or high water, and they got both. When the easterners mixed abolition with their Hebrew, the slave-owners of Marion County rose up to drive them out. The Mississippi flooded the future metropolis and emigrants, arriving for months afterwards, found that their deeds entitled them to a malarial swamp.

Young Rogers perhaps learned from this two things which were to stand him in good stead when he became responsible for the fortunes of a college: a firm distrust of the visionary, and the practical value of being neutral.

He had always had his feet on hard ground. Carr, his biographer, describes his typical pioneer boyhood. He did all the chores of an eldest son, acquired the skills of an alert backwoods boy. But because hunting and fishing were as much necessity as sport he looked upon them with a utilitarian eye. (Later, when he needed potatoes to feed his collegiate family he saw no incongruity in planting them on either side of the school's front walk.) Where his schoolmates played for fun he played to excel, and enjoyed an activity in proportion as he could analyze and perfect it. He could not merely walk his sisters to school; he had to count the steps it took; just as years later he figured on the back of a ledger what each tuition would come to, divided by days and hours.

From log-puncheon to University, he sat at the head of his class. Later, the president of Missouri University was to pronounce him one of the three most brilliant pupils he had ever had, and Professor Matthews was to declare it an honor to teach Greek to men like J. K. Rogers. Like many precocious people he was impatient with dullness and had an uncomfortable tendency to sit in judgment. The position of mediator was often thrust upon him, for his decisions were fair and he had the gift of sending people away satisfied. There is an erudite letter he wrote, as a young man, when his brother-in-law inquired anxiously whether one could be a Christian and still go to *pick-nicks?*

Affable and engaging, Rogers had a gentility especially appreciated by women. As a youth at "play-parties" he would be more interested in the conversation of the matron next to him than in the games progressing on the floor. As a student he noted in his journal that whereas one young man was hard put to it to entertain one young lady, she could easily entertain three men. As a father, his letters to his daughters have a more tender tone than those to his sons. In view of his life career it is interesting to read this advice to Bowen Rogers, then a young man.

> It will be to your advantage to spend your leisure evenings . . . in the company of high-toned, intelligent young ladies; not in dancing or levity, but largely in animated, earnest conversation about persons and things, what you like and what you dislike, the merits and demerits of authors and pictures, this and that course of life, things honorable, pure and good. The young ladies ought to be fully your equals, in intelligence and general information, all the better if they are your superiors. . . . By all means, my son, cultivate a high regard for woman. . . . She is not perfect, she has her frailties, but she is, as a rule, a long ways better than man, purer in her thoughts, more disinterested and self-sacrificing in her life.[6]

No wonder he was to become a social lion with the ladies of Columbia!

By sixteen Joe had absorbed all the available education within miles and was teaching a subscription school near home. He had absorbed a great deal of preaching, too, and was striking out for himself in that direction. In that backwoods environ any speechmaking was community entertainment and, though there was a theater at Palmyra, twelve miles away, no respectable family would have considered attending it. (Performing make-believe was, in effect, to sin by acting out a lie.) When, as a modern educator, he included drama in the curriculum at Christian it was called "colloquy" and performed without a curtain.

The windy excitement of oratory, heard by torchlight, the razor keenness of debate, the urgency of souls rushing to be saved—no wonder every pious mother reserved for her eldest the place of the hero on the platform! The boy, Joe, drank in the sermons and to the man they always were to be recreation. He would get up from a sickbed to go to church, or finding himself on Sunday in a strange community, would hurry to hear what the preacher had to say. Once, in a Colorado mining community, he was reduced to attending a service entirely in Welsh. His is almost a lost attitude now and as incomprehensible as the fact that he would rise at four, in his university days, to study the Bible before class.

At twenty-two he wanted to teach. He wanted to preach. But he was on his way to Columbia to buy mules and become a farmer when the means to a career was put in his hands. It was Samuel S. Church, riding beside him, who persuaded him to enroll in the University instead. Another incorporator of Christian College, Lewis Bryan of Palmyra, lent him the tuition.

On borrowed funds, Rogers had done the four years' work in three. Though he was a strong six-footer the late studying and the hard work began to undermine his physique. There was such a "feast of good things" to be had at Columbia!

Many great preachers of the young Disciples movement passed through, and he heard them all: Lard, Church, Henderson, Shannon, Alexander Procter, Isaac Errett, Alexander Campbell himself. He went to church three times on Sundays, and when there was not a prominent Disciple available went to hear a Baptist or a Unitarian. At night he would carefully record their sermon "skeletons" in his diary. Other Sundays he would ride to Red Top or Dripping Springs and perhaps use some of these points in sermons of his own. Once, returning, he and another fledgling preacher met the venerable Elder Allen. The latter may have recalled the incident with a chuckle later, when they faced each other across a conference table as President and trustee of Christian College.

"Well, boys," he had asked, "Did you do any good yesterday?"

They answered they did not know.

"Did nobody *jine?*"

"No."

"Did nobody cry?"

"No."

"Did nobody get mad?"

"No."

"Well, boys, you must do better. I'm afraid you didn't do any good." And then the old man laughed.

Nevertheless, by graduation Rogers had found what he

meant to do. "I will teach when I preach, and preach when I teach," he declared.

Little is known of his first school in St. Joseph except that it opened December, 1854, on the corner of Third and Faraon. His partner was Edwin C. Davis, Shannon's cohort of Columbia days, now become state superintendent of schools. Rogers made just enough money that spring to marry his Christian College sweetheart, Jane Robards, daughter of the Mayor of Hannibal.

A record of his first teaching is an old clipping-book filled with student work. A school-girl's Going-Home Song—"For we'll leave these naughty *diggins* in the morning—" conjures up a St. Joe, gateway to the West: jumping off place for California and gold. The scrapbook went with Rogers a year later to Columbia. (When Wilkes summoned him to Christian College he had rejected his father-in-law's offer to build him a schoolhouse in Hannibal.) Before long, new clippings were being pasted in, signed by Rogers' most gifted pupil, Lavinia Ream.

There is not room here for the Cinderella story of little Vinnie Ream. Christian's first famous alumna, she was, while still a girl commissioned by Congress to sculp the statue of Lincoln which stands in the rotunda of the Nation's Capitol.

Vinnie and an older sister, Cynthia Ann,[7] had been left in the boarding school while their father was stationed at Ft. Leavenworth, Kansas Territory, as a surveyor for the Land Office. According to the 1847 date usually given for her birth in Wisconsin, Vinnie would have been ten when she entered Christian College in 1857. However, "L. E. Ream" is listed with the undergraduates for that year, not with the academy which included pupils up through twelve. The fact that she was recording secretary for the Martha Washington society shows she was at least a Junior. The Minutes she kept and her other writings suggest a girl of about fourteen.

None of her teachers in 1857-58 could have been so clairvoyant as to guess that within six years she would be sitting daily with the President of the United States in Washington, translating his anxious features into clay while he studied dispatches of a Civil War.

Did Professor Alexander recognize her talent? The one portrait she seems to have painted at school was a far cry from the doves and moss roses of most of his pupils. Perhaps he was equally impressed with her ability on the guitar. Rogers thought of her as a poet, carefully saving her farewell verses to room-mate Mary Persinger and an ode to "My Kansas Home." Also preserved at Christian are published songs and the painting of Martha Washington she later sent the Institute. A study of Vinnie hangs in St. Clair parlors and at the State Historical Society in Columbia her black eyes look down from a portrait by Bingham.

Professor Rogers' habit of offering his students' compositions to the paper illustrates his bent for diplomacy. Suddenly Colonel Switzler, who until now would scarcely spare a paragraph for a Christian College Commencement, was devoting a regular column to melancholy dirges signed "B. M. W." or "R. V. R., C. C." Such initials were easily deciphered by Columbia's proud parents. ("R. V. R."—Regina Victoria Royall—just happened to be a sister of Switzler's wife.)

Professor Rogers' urbanity had been felt in other ways: his tasteful Sunday sermons, his gracious wife. So the Board of Trustees had listened thankfully to his letter accepting the presidency of Christian College. Was he too urbane, too inexperienced at thirty to guide the ship which was rapidly heading for the rocks? They were quite willing to let him hold the wheel awhile.

Rogers began his administration like a practical man. There was no use spending money for a new account book. He took over the one Wilkes relinquished and wrote in it: "Note given for Negro hire, payable on or before 25th Dec. 1858—$390.55." This would give him five months to pay for the use of those dozen or more slaves who kept the wheels of the place turning. Hired from various owners, the Negroes drew the water, filled the pitchers for washing in the morning, made the fires, did the laundry, farmed, cooked, waited table. Those the students would remember were four who lived on the place: Aunt Caroline, the cook; Ned, the yardman; Harriet, the maid, and Uncle Charlie.

President Rogers agreed to buy the furnishings from Wilkes,

and asked for a complete invoice of everything—from the spittoon in the parlor to each cruet in the dining room. This price list is one of the most informative documents which survives concerning Christian College. Inventory of the original building before the wings were added, it gives us, not only a picture of the rooms and their uses, but a vivid glimpse of the life and times.[8]

Dishes, tumblers, and sheets, we learn, were much more expensive than tables, mattresses, and chairs. Doubtless a "Marseilles" spread or a linen tablecloth had to be transported by boat while a splint-bottom chair, made locally, could sell at a profit for fifty cents. The most expensive items, the four pianos, might well have been the originals Williams was so proud of.

Fourteen rooms for boarders each contained:

1 washstand	$1.50
2 bedsteads at $2.50	5.00
4 mattresses (2 moss and 2 shuck)	—
1 stove (and zinc)	6.00
4 or 5 splint-bottom chairs ea.	.50
1 pitcher	.50
1 bowl	.35
1 slop bucket	.75
1 chamber	.20

There was an embroidered "splasher" behind the washstand, a broom, a duster, and sometimes a trundle bed. The more expensive moss mattress was used on top of the shuck mattress. (Was it Spanish moss, we wonder, gathered from the live oaks of Louisiana and shipped up the river in bales?) The girls were expected to use their brooms and dustpans, the maids emptying the slop buckets.

The parlor—first room west of the entrance door—was distinguished by having rockers, a mirror, a carpet, the aforementioned spittoon, a piano with cover, and "winder" curtains. (Probably pronounced as spelled.)

The new dining room on the ground floor of the northern extension had red and "best" tablecloths, every article of china from fishbone dishes to egg cups, and sixty-nine chairs, including some high chairs. The inventory of the "library," or President's study on the east of the entrance, does not mention any books, but includes a school bell and a water cooler.

The miscellaneous list is the most interesting: a quilting frame, stoneware, nutmegs, a plow, seven blackboards, a globe, a map of the heavens, two cows, eleven sheep and fourteen hogs. All this, with other articles "too numerous to mention" Rogers purchased with a note for $2,679 to be paid by the opening of school, one year later.

Immediately, competent teachers must be hired. With his Marion College background, Rogers' standards were high. Wilkes was to remain as Professor of Philosophy and Constitutional Law. He himself would teach literature and botany; Professor Alexander, drawing, painting and guitar. For mathematics Rogers rehired another choice of John A. Williams, Professor William Pinckney Hurt, a Kentuckian of considerable experience as teacher and principal in high schools.

He brought in Frederick Pannell, an Englishman, graduate of St. John's College at Graveshead and formerly a chorister in the Cathedral there—"a fine musician and a composer of acknowledged ability." John D. Dawson was to teach history and elocution, and his wife, Mary Jane, to be principal matron. The Dawsons had for nine years superintended the Female Orphan School at Midway, Kentucky. The novice teachers were released.

When school opened in 1858 the trustees were so well satisfied with the way the new President was taking hold that they did not meet until almost Christmas. The first order of business was a shock, delivered by Bolivar Head:

> Whereas Christian College is now in debt for a larger amount of money than it can probably be sold for, and whereas it will have to be sold in a few years unless adequate means be provided to meet the accruing interest on its debts; therefore resolved—[9]

Caleb Stone jumped up to demand that the resolution be struck from the *Minutes*. It was dishonorable to the spirit of the founders. He alone had been present seven years before when the charter was read and to him the intent of permanency was sacred: (This) "property, . . . shall be held and applied in good faith to the purposes of education according to the provisions of this act, and in pursuance of the wishes of the donors, and for no other purpose. . . ." But he was in the minority and the more disillusioned trustees allowed it to remain, a blot upon the books.

Rogers managed to decline Head's resolution that the College president pay the Board ten dollars on every tuition of $160, a corresponding percentage on smaller tuitions, and 10 per cent interest on any tuitions unpaid at the end of the session.

He also declined to pay the Board a flat $600 a year rent. This would have been to their advantage, for when Rogers turned in his account, based on the original system of four dollars per regular tuition over fifty, it came to a mere $240. Caleb Stone had been astute in his prophecy.

Perhaps it was their common reaction to cynicism that brought Stone and Rogers together. It was fortunate, for it eliminated the friction that had previously sparked between the most aggressive trustee and the President. Each was to gain a growing respect for the other's shrewdness.

The city had proposed to cut a street on the western side of the College. Stone had wangled a fair price for the condemned piece of land and had re-sold what remained on the other side of the street for thirty dollars. Making the road would require taking down a section of the college fence, however. Topping Stone's self-satisfied report President Rogers turned in his own bill for moving the fence—three dollars and fifty cents.

A small incident, it illustrates Rogers' consistent financial policy with the board. That body was going to pay its way. No sum he spent on the College was too insignificant to itemize. He would record it carefully under the heading "What Christian College Owes Me," whether it was a new roof for the smoke house or a quart of paint. Enough small items, by the end of a year, made a surprising total. When he turned in his first annual account, the Board owed him sixty-one dollars more than he owed them! To some that $3.50 fence was beginning to look like a stone wall.

Moreover, though his rents were small he paid them

promptly, and it was the first time the Board had been able to count on settling with their President at the end of the year. They had to recognize a good business head, even on the unexpected shoulders of a college professor.

At the end of Rogers' first year the debt totaled $8,000. That long-planned northern addition was finished, however:

> The Extension is 60′ long, 40′ wide, and two stories high. It contains a Chapel 50′x40′ wide, a Dining Room 40′ long x 20′, besides a number of rooms adapted to recitation and boarding purposes.

Since after a year some imperfections existed—the roof sagged and there were no steps to the Chapel platform—the Board members went out to inspect it and the state of the College in general. It was to be one of their last concerted actions, for war clouds were gathering now and sparking the atmosphere was the jagged word, *Secede.* Their secretary reported:

> We found the edifice in a good state of preservation, except that some leaks exist. . . . The rooms used as dormitories and recitation rooms have an appearance of neatness & comfort. . . . The furniture & bedding are sufficient. In the absence of indications of those petty damages which so often occur in buildings used for boarding schools we infer that the discipline of the Institution is proper and effectual. The general condition of the Institution is satisfactory. The number of pupils is already equal to that of the last session & the prospects for an increase are flattering. Indeed when we consider that this school has been and is well sustained by public patronage during a period of unexampled embarrassment throughout the country in financial matters, we think there is good cause for congratulation on the part of the Board of Trustees. . . . Your committee are decidedly of the opinion it is mainly if not entirely owing to the successful efforts of the President to associate with himself Teachers of decided ability and faithfulness and the prompt and faithful discharge of every duty encumbent upon each officer in the Institution. . . .[10]

With these kind words the trustees went their separate ways, leaving the President of Christian College one year closer to the deadline of its mortgage.

IV

THE PEN AND THE SWORD
1859-1870

I would rather die than see Christian College go down.

—JOSEPH K. ROGERS, 1861

TO THE PRESIDENT OF CHRISTIAN COLLEGE the thought of the approaching foreclosure was as a red flag to a bull. Joseph Kirtley Rogers had never yet failed at anything he undertook. God willing, this would be no exception.

He had additional family reasons for wanting to succeed. There were two babies now, Fannie and Lenoir, besides the wife for whom he had vowed always to "have everything nice." The memory that her wealthy father had considered him no great catch, fired him yet. But more pressing was the thought of his own father, whose lack of business acumen had lost him their big brick house and 350 acres near Palmyra. Thinking of it, Rogers was more than ever determined to hold on to his own, and he swung away from the old man's openhanded ways just as in later years his own sons were to rebel from his practicality. He added his mother, father, and teenage brother to his list of dependents and installed them in the east cottage on the campus. There the old couple became Grandma and Grandpa to the college girls, who delighted to go in and help themselves from their barrel of apples.

First he examined the tuitions which Wilkes had raised. He noted that one-third to one-half of all the girls enrolled in academic courses were also studying music. And a president had never been required to give a rebate to the Board on music students. He raised this tuition from forty to fifty dollars—a difference which would not show up alarmingly in the catalog but would give him a great deal more to work with. He also added a slight fee for penmanship and for singing in the choir.

Whereas in early years catalog space had been devoted to concern lest some young lady of frivolous intent be enrolled, he now added a section labeled "Expenses." Terms were to be in advance, cash, not refundable, and subject to 10 per cent interest if not paid by the date of matriculation. This tightening was, of course, the difference between life and death in any institution in 1860.

Moreover, he collected the tuitions. Almost all the accounts which he so meticulously kept on each student were sooner or later marked "Squared." No item was too small to record, since, there again, a great many little things made a large total. Squire Austin Bradford might read that he owed, on his daughter Narcissa's bill, for one pair of shoestrings, use of library and ink, a slate pencil, and three postage stamps.

He sent terse little notes to the parents: notes which contrasted brusquely with the flowery compositions he set his classes to copying on Monday mornings. "Dear Sir: Will you please send the balance for Belle's tuition at once as I am needing the money greatly." If Belle's parent simply could not pay, he could send over one of his slaves to work at the College, or deliver fuel from his woodlot or hams from his smokehouse.

With his faculty Rogers assumed much the sort of pay-as-you-go policy he used in his financial dealings with the Board. A typical contract read:

> I have this day agreed with J. D. Dawson for the services of himself and Lady in Christian College for the session of 1859-60, at the salary of one thousand dollars, to be paid as follows: his family to be boarded at one hundred dollars each, his children to be taught at the uniform charges, and the rest to be paid in money. . . .
> J. K. Rogers.[1]

After deducting for the education of two young Dawsons, board for four, and certain other expenses for which the President had advanced funds—a freight express charge, vocal music, several dozen candles, a bushel of apples, and one fifteen cent copy book—very little cash exchanged hands.

A thousand dollars seems to have been the top salary for a teacher; less if his wife also taught. The idea of equal opportunities for women did not extend to paying them comparable wages, for the most they received was $250 a year. Considering the fact that young lady music teachers were the poorest paid and the most frequently replaced, it is interesting to read that their employer expected them to teach twenty pupils two times a week, to practice every day, and to conduct a regular college choir.

For at least one year the President recorded every cash expenditure, both personal and for the College. In his slanting, orderly handwriting, he accounts for each penny:[2]

2½	bushels meal at .60	$1.50
1	Latin grammar	.60
10	lbs. bacon at 6c per lb.	.60
½	doz. Cedar well buckets	4.50

Chickens, lard, peaches, lamp wicks, milch cows, featherbeds, such was the picturesque miscellany that confronted the father of a "college family." Only occasionally were there such items as "new boots," an outfit for one of the servants, or a daguerreotype to be used for publicity purposes. It all totaled up to a life that was sufficient, but very simple and rural. As one of the students later recalled: "There were no frills at Christian College."

Those few expenses which were beneath his notice fell to

his wife to record. Officially listed as Assistant Matron, Jennie Rogers was his helpmeet in many ways. In a cramped, feminine writing is her laundry list for the whole college for each week. There are staggering numbers of "chemises," "drawers," "linen shirt bosums," "good," and red tablecloths, together with the name of the servant responsible for their washing. No wonder that one of the first improvements Rogers recorded against the Board after the war was the building of a wash house, and that he added to the list of commandments the admonition: "No articles are received into the Laundry unless plainly and fully marked with the name of the owner."

It was Mrs. Rogers who trained the servants and saw that they performed their duties. It was she who founded the Friday morning inquisition in the chapel. Each girl must stand behind the desk on which was stacked her returned laundry. The matron then toured the room, examined the articles in each pile and commented on their state of preservation. To girls like Leila and Minnie Winans, reared in the deep South with servants to do the mending, it was an ordeal. "Our clothes were always in rags," Minnie recalled.

While the President and his wife applied themselves to the small economies which kept the College running, the trustees wrestled with higher finance. The books had become so discouraging that it was difficult to keep a treasurer in office. Unable to pursue any set policy they concentrated desperately on averting the impending date of sale. It was rumored the Catholics stood ready to buy the building.

The crisis was approaching with whirlwind speed, now, both for the country and for the College.

"Our State is all in a blaze," wrote observer Allen. "I could not make you believe the bitterness of *secessionists* towards all those who are *Union* men."[3]

And the girls themselves understood, as they walked through halls that might soon be vacant, or paused at the cistern to drink the delicious cold water that was like no other water in the world. Jenny Lard was to remember that taste years later when, as governor's lady, she arranged the sparkling crystal for official dinners. Her father, Moses Lard, and L. B. Wilkes were the "two noble souls" who in the very face of the gale "left their homes, went into our surrounding country and . . . plead with eloquent tongue the cause of woman's education." By June, 1860, they raised enough in new subscriptions to cover the mortgages. By the deadline of January, 1861, the trustees called in the many liens and transferred them in one to Dr. J. G. Jacobs, with another year to pay. They could not know they were starting a game of "hot potato" which was to continue throughout the war years; Jacobs would hold his burden until it burned his fingers; Dr. Lenoir would take it up from there, and in his turn hand it on to Jerry Dorsey.

They were content to be addressed as "saviours" by the eighteen-year-old salutatorian as she predicted that "years hence, when bowed and infirm, you take your final leave of this life . . . the great crisis of the College will be remembered, and you who bore it through the storm. . . ."

They rejoiced with her that "Oh! we are glad to say . . . the years as they roll out their courses, will each in its turn find a band such as this to wander amid these groves, and glad voices will continue to echo within these walls."[4]

Their applause had scarcely died away when civil war struck Missouri. Rogers noted the fact in his Journal, giving thought to his prose style:

> The Temple of Janus flings wide her brazen doors, and the red god of War rages through the once, not long since, proudest and happiest land on the globe. Since my last sitting blood has flowed, fraternal blood. . . . What a sight for men and angels![5]

A Christian College girl wrote in her diary:

> Our glorious Ship Union is aground. Her traitorous pilot Lincoln with the rest of her crew have betrayed her passengers and now we are beating against the terrible shoals of Revolution. . . . God protect us. . . .[6]

T. M. Allen dated a letter, "Boone County, May 22, 1861":

> The whole country is now in great excitement and we are daily in expectation of a terrible fight between the U. S. troops under General Harney and . . . State troops at Jefferson City . . . it was reported at Jefferson, that Harney's army was on his way there, to take the Governor and Cabinet—the alarm spread—volunteers were called

> for, and they have been rolling to Jefferson by hundreds.
>
> I live . . . 24 miles of Jefferson on the great thoroughfare leading north; and in the event of general war, should I survive, I wish to be near my family.[7]

There is one mention of war in the *Minutes* of the Board as on January 19, 1861, it assembled and "in view of the troubles now in the country" authorized the treasurer to collect all subscriptions if he had to sue.

It was to be the last meeting for some time where such men as Sterling Price, nephew of Missouri's Confederate general and Francis Russell, local Union commander, could sit together in harmony. As a parting legacy to the President, the Board released him from his yearly rent, holding him only to payment of taxes.

The University was tottering. Its young men were enlisting and it had no funds from the Legislature. Public schools were closing. Lizzie Brown, riding from Kansas City to Christian in a spring wagon, reported that the female college in Fayette had all the windows broken and the furnishings thrown in the street.

Teachers were leaving, travel was so dangerous that students were unable to come. More to be feared than the army were such wild guerrilla bands as Anderson's raiders in Howard County or the "Jayhawkers" who galloped down from Kansas and rode away, leaving wreckage behind. But the army was making itself felt, too.

"A *worm* . . . has recently made its appearance in our Country, and is making waste of our small grain;" wrote T. M. Allen, who no longer dared make his speeches on union and armed neutrality. "They are not on our farm yet, but are devouring the one adjoining. . . ."[8]

Family fortunes were toppling, as many a north Missouri merchant was forced to burrow his way to Confederate lines. Such steamboats as the BELLE MEMPHIS carried loads of "exiles" who lived on "parched corn and enthusiasm," sang "Dixie" and as they steamed past Cairo, emptied their shoes so that no Yankee dirt would infect the "promised land."[9] In Columbia, help was restless as the report spread that the flats below Boonville thirty miles away were black with migrating slaves.

Rogers saw that his only hope was to preserve a strict neutrality. He banned all newspapers from the campus (though he and Professor Hurt studied them privately.) He guarded himself from mentioning war, even in his diary. Nevertheless, he resolved to fight in his own way. He seized his pen and poured his passion into announcements in the *Statesman*.

> The hope of America is with the future; the present is lost, irretrievably lost; and, if to the wide-spread ruin of every material interest is to be added the wreck of our Institutions of learning . . . if the fountains of knowledge and virtue are to be dried up just when the flood-gates of vice and immorality are thrown wide—then indeed is the hope of our country a forlorn one. Parents—patriot, philanthropist, Christian—whatever else may be neglected, educate your children.[10]

If the College had been sheltered before, it now became a little insulated world of its own. Behind the plank fence life went on in deadly routine. The diary of Mary Louisa Caldwell, a Christian College girl of 1859-60, describes a typical blue Monday.

> Early to rise as usual that gong is never tardy. It is still dark yet I am dressed and ready to begin the many duties of the week. Oh how steep and arduous is the hill of knowledge. . . .

Every morning was the same. At five, a knock on the door, and four sleepy girls would pull the covers over their heads as Uncle Charlie came in to build the fire. When the small pot-bellied stove began to give off heat, along would come Harriet with water for washing. (Early risers in winter had to break the ice in their basins.) As soon as the simple wool dress was on and the long hair "done up"—the more prudent girls kept theirs clean by sleeping with it wrapped in silk—it was time for the morning walk. The serious purpose of "matutinal recreation" dissolved in the pleasure of being out, unsupervised, in the morning air. The long green skirts rustled through the leaves under the chinquapin trees, swept over the stile near the huge elm which marked the campus boundary, and on down the hill to the bridge across the ravine at the bottom. Beyond, the town of Columbia seemed still asleep—and there was a one-hour study period before breakfast!

In the dining room the girls sat at one long table, with the President at one end and Professor Hurt at the other. They had to wait while President Rogers cleared his throat and gave a long scriptural blessing.

Meals were mostly home grown. In the garden back of the College were potatoes, turnips, peas, mustard greens, beets, and that cabbage which Aunt Caroline converted into "the best slaw." The President had five acres of corn on an outlying farm and had planted a variety of apple trees around the College, carefully recording the location of each one: "E. side of chapel, near woodpile, between chapel and smoke house." It was an age of interest in scientific agriculture, and he made anxious little notations about each planting: "Finished out ends of row with blood beets—light moon;" or "May 20—Planted cabbage seed in bed—is it too late?"[11] Botany and horticulture classes were not only called to examine how a slip of Major Rollins' choice silesian honeysuckle had been planted in a potato, but were given hoes to ply or seeds to plant. Such applied horticulture had varying results. More than once Dr. Lenoir, the college physician, had to attend a student who had eaten too many raw turnips.

Every Sunday there was turkey, while Tuesday and Thursday were dessert days. These loomed so important to hungry adolescents that once, when a fire broke out just as apple dumpling was being served, Callie Duncan stayed behind to eat both hers and her neighbor's dumpling while the others ran to the fire.

After breakfast the entire college gathered in the chapel for roll call and morning prayers. Listed among chapel furnishings were three highchairs, and the tediousness of the occasion to younger members of the family is reflected by the fact that one prep school girl received demerits for "yelling out in chapel." Others relieved their boredom more subtly. Once President Rogers, who had been reading scripture to the accompaniment from the audience of a very squeaky pair of shoes, interpolated solemnly and with no change of voice: "If the young lady in the northeast corner of the room does not stop squeaking her shoes, I shall throw this book at her."

However, conscientious girls like Mary Lou had nothing to fear. She recorded:

> Oh yes. Met with quite an accident this morning; turned over a bottle of ink in my room, am afraid the President will be very much offended.

The next day:

> Have just told President Rogers of the spilled ink. He did not scold me as I expected and no doubt deserved. Heaven bless him. He is the best man, *almost,* that ever lived. He also gave me a pencil. I will try and repay his kindnesses by good conduct.

Classes stretched steadily from 8:15 till 12:15 and from 2:00 till 4:00. There was a tendency in the curriculum to concentrate all the sciences in one year and mathematics in another, which must have been discouraging to the Sophomore whose tastes did not run to Botany, Chemistry, Geology, Zoology, Physiology, and Astronomy.

Geology was largely an acquiring and examining of strange rocks which were locked in the Martha Washington society's new cabinet. These natural history collections were sought by schools all over the country. Wellesley in 1870 was just starting to build up a scientific collection in the same voluntary way which Rogers for years had taken when he begged:

> Who so poor as not to be able to contribute one volume to a Library, or one specimen to a Cabinet. . . . There are books without number that lie unread upon the shelves . . . specimens, Mineralogical and Geological, all over the country, in the possession of private individuals, of little or no value to them, but which would be highly prized by us. . . . Will not their possessors redeem them from the darkness . . . in which they rest, and turn them to a profitable account . . . the cause of Female Education?[12]

Botany was probably the only other science course not taught almost completely by textbook. It should have been popular, for its tours took pupils off campus along routes familiar to Columbia students of today: "out by the lane running E and W through the 'Price Addition' down to the Hingston—"

Rogers' interest in geology and agriculture indicates the continued influence of the University of Missouri upon the women's college. Professor Swallow, state geologist, was now prominent on the University staff and leading the movement to establish an Agricultural College. Engineering was the only field into which the female college did not attempt to follow the male. Classical languages, still not a general requirement for graduation from the University, were seldom elected at Christian. A growing prudery among parents of the day found Latin unfit for ladies and Katie Stone, caught by father Caleb with Pope's translation of *The Iliad,* was scolded for reading indecent literature.

In his catalogs Rogers laconically announces that "those who have the time and a taste for the study of Languages" may take a three year course in Latin and French. Evidently any wartime pruning of courses was in these ornamental branches. The catalogs make it clear that Christian's collegiate department remained organized into Freshman, Sophomore, Junior, and Senior years, each of which must be completed before passing to the next; and that "a regular Diploma would be granted to those Young Ladies only" who completed the entire college course.

The catalogs also shed some light on Rogers' teaching. Like Williams he scorned the memorized recitation and stressed that individual education which was to remain a hallmark of Christian:

> It is our aim, as far as practicable, to make the course of study and the mode of treatment a specialty for each individual case. Accordingly our first work in the reception of a pupil, is to ascertain her age, health, previous culture and mental aptitudes, and to select her studies, in nature and number, with special reference to these.[13]

In and out of class there was a stiff daily grounding in religion, which was taught with a fundamentalism naive to us. Dates of the Flood and of Eve eating the apple were fixed quite definitely—so many years "A. M.," *anno mundi,* from the beginning of the world.

On Sundays all secular interests were forbidden. Lou Caldwell records a bleak one:

> Went to church this morning. . . . Prof. Wilks continued his discourse on Orthodoxy. came home. studied my Bible lesson. Mr. Rogers paid us a very un-expected call. After dinner recited our Bible lesson. Had quite a discussion on . . . the Acts of the Apostles. Gained a great many new thoughts. After the lesson went in and spent an hour with Mrs. Dawson. spent the remainder of the evening in my room reading Gibbons History of the Decline and Fall of the Roman Empire. Felt in worse health tonight than have since I came here. Went to bed and took a good cry. . . .

No wonder that after several months she should head her diary entry: "Sunday—One more Sabbath nearer the grave."

After class life was gayer. There was leisure to explore the campus woods, gather walnuts, or look surreptitiously under a certain plank in the boardwalk to see whether some young man had left a note. This front walk had been paid for partly by the girls themselves, who got their money's worth by using it as a postoffice.

Late afternoons while President Rogers went for the mail, some would slip in the forbidden pleasure of dancing. (The President agreed with the *Atlantic Monthly:* "Waltzing is . . . Profane.") On Friday afternoons and evenings were the society meetings. Every night but Saturday the girls were herded into the chapel to study for an hour or two by the warmth of the two stoves. Then, recalls Mrs. Henry Clay Daniel (Lizzie Brown '65):

> Mr. Rogers would call the roll for each room and the "Bell sheep" would take her lighted candle from the table and lead the way, all the girls following in perfect order, one by one to her room. The coal oil lamps hanging in the chapel were then turned off and we were supposed to be in bed by nine o'clock.[14]

Saturdays were general cleanup days, when rooms were readied, hair was washed, letters written home. President Rogers had continued domestic training at Christian by grading girls on their housekeeping with the same system used for academic courses. Six was the perfect mark, going down to zero. Each girl was housekeeper for a week, her duty to "Have chg. of lights," "Be an example in room, Harmonize it and make it pleasant," and when that failed—this was the President's notation—"to report to me."

Once in about six weeks young men were admitted to the parlor. There they might promenade the Seniors under the watchful eye of some faculty member—and drop a coin in the "mite" box to help defray the cost of any refreshments. It was mostly at public entertainments they met, occasions held by President Rogers to raise funds, but social events, nonetheless. There were "strawberry festivals" on the lawn on warm June evenings, with the ladies of the alumnae or the church as donors. ("Admission $1, children half price.") Sometimes the $200 profit was the difference between the College running a week longer or not.

There were concerts and tableaux in the chapel, with plump parents and gangly university boys wedged behind the small seats. "I recall one of our entertainments, a pantomime, *Genevra* . . ." says Mrs. Daniel:

> We had no dressing rooms. I was to play the part of housekeeper and had to slip out and change my dress to a house dress. As I came back with my broom and dustpan I had to run along the side of the wall where the University boys were sitting. One of them said something saucy to me and I tapped him with my pan, to the merriment of the other boys. At the end of the play I had to handle a chest which I set on the floor. It fell to pieces and out dropped a real skeleton which those rascals had put in as a joke on me. Did I run out yelling?

She also gives another vivid picture of the times:

> —Will I ever forget the night bugs and flies that came into our unscreened windows on summer nights. I can still feel myself squirming at the piano on concert nights as I sat between two fat girls playing a trio, the little oat bugs crawling up and down my back beneath my thin swiss dress.

Church, of course, remained something more than a duty, with the girls buzzing over whether it was "red" or "green" dress Sunday, or whether that handsome young Richard

Shannon would be in the choir today. They lined up and walked discreetly in twos down to the Christian Church on Walnut, with President Rogers heading the procession and some "starch-faced old maid" flanking it. They halted at alleys and intersections while their guardians made sure there were no boys too near. The boys appreciated the sight, nevertheless, and eventually some campus poet wrote a ditty on "the bonnets." (Some say it was Eugene Field.)

Enormous green bonnets, with ribbons of blue,
Were seated in church, just six in a pew.
Did ever you teachers bethink in your mind,
How cruel the effort such beauty to blind?

Lights under a bushel, it was a disgrace,
To cover with cotton such a beautiful face.
Were college girls skittish, like scampering colts,
That blinders were needed for hindering bolts?

If out on the street C. C. girls wished to go,
In charge of a teacher they must walk in a row;
And where'er in Columbia those girls might be seen,
They were spotted at once by the bonnets of green.[15]

These first uniform bonnets were nothing more than the ugly "split bonnets" of pioneer days, later used for service in the country. They opened flat for ironing and had rows of stitching in the brim into which cardboard strips or splints were inserted for stiffness. They came so far over the face that the wearers were practically featureless. But ingenious girls got around this problem by cutting small eyelets between the splints. Eyes could be wandering over the audience while faces seemed to be turned dutifully toward the pulpit.

Eugene Field, the campus cut-up of 1871 who may have toasted the bonnets, was also credited with establishing serenades at Christian. The *University Missourian* of which he was literary editor, describes one such and years later when he returned to Columbia he went out and sang at Christian for "old times' sake."

For serenades, as for young gentlemen's calls, the girls had to write formal thank-you notes. (The gentlemen also preceded their calls with notes requesting permission.) They pasted the cards in their albums:

> For the delightful serenade the Gentlemen will please accept the thanks of Misses Emma Garnett, Ella Garnett and Lou Caldwell.
>
> Mr. Anthony Haynes requests the pleasure of calling upon Miss Sue Bruton on Saturday, the fourteenth of November.

There were a few—very few—other social events in the formal tradition. During the holidays bonds were relaxed for those whom war or distance prevented from going home. A letter from a university student dated December 25, 1860, indicates that Christmas at school had its compensations.

> Dear Sir: I have just returned from a formal visit to the young ladies of Christian College. . . . The girls, excepting the senior class, are permitted to receive visitors *only* during the holidays, and the parlors being opened for that purpose this evening, I gladly availed myself of the privilege of going over to make their acquaintance and enjoy a few hours of confabulation with them. . . . I shall not attempt to portray the beauty and colloquial powers of these fair inmates of Christian College, but suffice it to say, *I do not regret my visit.*[16]

Holidays were also favorite times for "town people" to entertain the college girls. These feasts at the homes of the Conleys, Carters, Hubbells, Brights, or Elkins, with university boys present and sometimes a fiddle going in the next room, were long-remembered occasions.

Perhaps the girls were allowed to witness such an important civic event as the arrival of Columbia's first train in 1867. (They could see the depot from their hill.) The Centralia Comet—great-great-grandpa of The Cannonball—was to figure largely in their futures as it carried not only them, but the mail.

Any other off-campus experiences were escapades, as the April Fool's day the Seniors played hookey.

> We were up before lights, stealing around like mice, for fear the servants would hear. I went home with Tish Jordan and Eliza Snoddy, whose uncle and aunt lived just beyond General Guitar's home, then new. The others went to James Conley's (Miss Melissa Jarvis lived with

> them.) All the girls planned on returning in the evening to meet at Col. Frank Russell's. He was the Federal officer in charge of the troops. . . . He led us, two and two, in fear and trembling, to the college. He rang the bell and had a few private words with President Rogers. Our greeting was dignified and cold. He led us into the library and we were sent hastily to bed without supper. . . .[17]

Perhaps they would not have got off so easily had not Colonel Russell had three lively daughters of his own in Christian. It was after his popular wife that the Junior "Cannie Russell Society" was named.

If President Rogers could not control the high spirits of his daughters neither could he cloister them entirely from the atmosphere of war. Merrill's Horse, a Federal detachment, was stationed in Columbia now and lifetime residents were being stopped on the streets and required to swear loyalty to the Union.

The University had closed. A fatal error, the president admitted later when confronted by the wreckage of a library and halls where troops had barracked. Rogers had gone sadly to the last meeting of the Union Literary Society but sentiment did not prevent his buying some of its desks at a bargain rate.

News leaked onto the campus. Mr. Jerry Dorsey, treasurer of the Board of Trustees, had "talked too much" and been banished. Elder Moses Lard, traveling from St. Joseph to Weston, had been attacked by drunken "Dutch" troops. Major Rollins had missed death by being absent when Bushwhackers foraged his home.

The Russell sisters brought reports of magnificent parades on Broadway, of Union meetings where Colonel Switzler spoke, of the beautiful flag presented to their father. There were whispers of war marriages, of brothers putting on the blue or gray. The campus May Day fête was distracted by the gleam of Federal bayonets. There were lugubrious entries in schoolgirl albums. In Sue Bruton's:

> Sukey—I leave this evening perhaps never mor to see you if so I hope you may think of me as one of your friends when thinking of the past I shall think of you when ever I think of home and its many pleasurs and

dear friend Sukey if it is never my happy lot to see you hear on earth I hope to meete you in heaven. . . .

John W. Baker, March 30th, 1863.

There was the day a neighbor of Fannie and Louisa Libscomb appeared from Westport. By nightfall the new hair trunk which had been made for their journey to college was packed and the tearful girls were gone. Mr. Libscomb had been ruined by Order Number Eleven. House and barns burned, he had fled to Texas.

Some inevitable bitterness escaped into the schoolroom. In 1861 Pauline Kellar wrote into her essay on "Changes":

> But may I not speak of changes more recent? Not long ago peace reigned supreme over our happy land. Then our sister states were close bound together in peace and harmony, and the "star spangled banner" with her thirty three brilliant stars waved over the North and the South. But, what a change has occurred, what wild confusion and discord, have swept over our once happy Country. The northern fanatics, have under a pretext of preserving the union, endeavored to oppress a free and independent people, and deprive them of the rights and freedom, secured to them by the blood of their fathers. . . .[18]

The harried President could not preserve neutrality in his own family. Once Mrs. Rogers had secretly loaded a whole wagon with blankets and counterpanes for the Confederate army. When the wagon was captured, and her astonished husband called on the carpet, it required all his diplomacy to resolve the situation.

There was the night some university boys crept into academic hall there and sawed a hole through the ceiling in the room where "rebels" were imprisoned. The captives escaped on horses of Union soldiers which were saddled and waiting in back of Dr. Victor's store. It was no jest to Mr. Rogers to hear his young brother greeted by companions as "you old horse thief."

Most memorable was the Sunday Dr. and Mrs. Lynn Banks came to dinner. Dr. Banks was the husband of Rogers' sister Mary, an outspoken southern-rights man. He had driven to Columbia with a feeling of being followed. Half-way through church he was aware, suddenly, of blue uniforms at the back of the room. Driving from church to the College, he stationed a colored nursegirl at an upstairs window. Just as they sat down to eat, she cried: "M'assa Lynn, M'assa Lynn, the sojers are comin'!"

He raced out the back door, across the college lot, and gained the dense woods northeast, near the present Banks' estate. Then, panting, he threw off his coat. His white Sunday shirt made a target for the circling Federals. He was ordered to take the loyalty oath, join the Union Army, or be shot. Like many another, he took the oath and was imprisoned—the first Union prisoner in Columbia.

Not so dramatic, but more threatening to the President was the everyday anxiety over whether he could make ends meet. Pupils were leaving daily. By that first June of the war, 1861, demonstrations were so violent that school closed with only one day of Commencement. But it would open in the fall, Rogers assured the audience.

He advertised in the paper that the College servants were for hire. Then, the story goes, he called his ebbing faculty in. He could promise them nothing for the next year. But if they would stand by and keep the school going he would feed them, house them, and give them a percentage of whatever was left from tuitions.

Some of them had nothing but I.O.U's. to show for the past session. But the majority—Hurt, Pannell, and Miss Laura Blair, teacher of the preparatory school, agreed to stay. Thus, with his skeleton staff behind him, Rogers was able to declare through the *Statesman* "once for all, and with emphasis:"

> —so far as it depends upon us, the continuance of the School is a certainty. Nothing . . . shall drive us from our posts. . . . The third Monday of September will find the faculty in their places—the rest will depend upon you.[19]

The school opened, but there is no catalog, almost no record of that critical year. The President's account book opens at "1861—"; the dash followed by pages suddenly blank, as if it were hopeless to go on. Only the student accounts continued, minute, painstaking:

Tuition . . . .
Books . . . .
1 india eraser . . . .
1 ball soap . . . .
Extra sugar . . . .

From the faded ink of these lists we deduce something of the struggle to survive. We learn that at its lowest in 1862 the school had fifty-six students, perhaps half of them boarders. How many were of college age cannot be told from catalogs of the war years but there were only three graduates in 1862 and four in 1863. And a door fee was charged for Commencement! Classes of small boys stayed above fifteen as local parents sought the comparative stability of Christian College. As other schools closed across the nation, Rogers thought of his increasingly as a citadel.

> We humbly think it a matter of no small importance that Christian College shall be sustained through the present crisis, which like some dread hurricane threatens to sweep down indiscriminately everything . . . within its fearful pathway. . . . Notwithstanding the stringency of the times and the disturbed state of the public mind . . . there are interests too vital to the cause of humanity . . . to be . . . disregarded.[20]

As parents took their daughters out of school, Rogers admonished:

> Retrench every other outlay, dispense with your fine apparel, your costly equipage, your sumptuous tables . . . but educate your children.
>
> Lay not up for your child sordid pelf, while the chambers of the mind are all empty . . . pamper not the body . . . while . . . the deathless spirit within, is in poverty and rags. On the contrary, know that a well cultivated mind is the richest legacy a father can bequeath. . . .[21]

So he continued to fight the war with pen and ledger.

It was a strain, daily, to turn from the fine lines of the ledger to the ivory tower of the class room. He was in deadly earnest as he drummed into the girls the facts of his own education, trying to make them see the contrast between the one-room schoolhouse and the art classes and pianos they might soon be losing. Because he was so serious, they loved to tease him. They sent him an anonymous ditty:

> President Rogers attended an old log school,
> Where they never celebrated "April Fool."
> He says that the seats were not very good;
> And that every girl had to wear a hood.
>
> All of us wear bright bonnets of green,
> Which 'tis said are the prettiest ever seen.
> So let's admit the President's right,
> And all wear hoods to church to-night.
>
> Then let's build an old log house,
> Where all's as quiet as a mouse;
> And do away with pianos and paint,
> And every girl look just like a saint.

Sometimes he lost his temper completely. Then he would snap his fingers—a terrifying sound—and the giggling would dissolve into an abjection which left him ashamed. He confided to his diary that he was "harsh and refractory," disposed sometimes to "ascerbity and crossness towards all around me." He prayed for "a more genuine urbanity of manner," and made New Year's resolutions: "To do no scolding, in school or among servants, but after having borne with their derelictions as long as my judgment says is proper, then without railing, or noisy and passionate demonstrations, to adopt the necessary remedy. The Lord help me. . . ."

How well he succeeded is described by one of his teachers, Belle Finlayson (Burdett):

> I never think of President Rogers . . . without my mind reverting with vivid distinctness to the fine legal acumen he displayed with refractory pupils. . . . The imperturbable expression of countenance he could assume, and the . . . irony with which he could clothe his language when occasion required. . . . The power of keeping perfectly calm himself . . . and at the same time probing with a few well-chosen words whose import was as keen as polished steel. . . . With that cool, impassive face . . . that steady, penetrating gaze which seemed to go down into the very heart's secrets, two or three magic words, and behold . . . the secret laid bare. . . .[22]

This control extended not only to himself and his pupils but to every detail of the College. "Eternal Vigilance" had replaced "Excelsior" as his motto. Everyone, from servant to professor, felt his eagle eye and began to find that whatever he did was acceptable, as long as it was done in the President's way. The President's way was usually the efficient way, one had to admit. Were there books out of place in room number eleven? The erring student must understand that petty carelessness can lead to large slothfulness. Had Julia neglected to polish the table silver? Standards must be kept more firmly in the midst of disintegration. Had Ned allowed one of the horses to become sick? The President had a sure remedy, copied last week into the back of his account book.

Morale was good at Christian College. The reputation for firm discipline spread; and those parents who still made the effort it required to bring daughters there did so because, as one expressed it, "it was looked on as one of the best schools in the country."[23]

Privately Rogers needed all his resolutions. The Board was too scattered to transact business. The church he so loved was torn with internal schisms and its pride in a new brick building forgotten in bitterness, deacon against deacon. Would to God, he prayed, that he might be the humble instrument of holding the church together. . . . Preaching for it was one of the things he did not think of in terms of money.

His natural melancholy emerged in the funeral sermons he conducted with growing frequency. One outline is typical: (1) Life is short and uncertain; (2) Its joys unsatisfying and unenduring; (3) Death is certain; (4) Judgment is certain; (5) Business of life is to prepare for death.

Like many another whose career forced him to be preoccupied with worldly "trash" he cried out against materialism.

"The spirit of the age is too intensely business," he wrote in the catalogs of the war years. "In the estimation of many, nothing is valuable that cannot be computed by the rules of Arithmetic."

> The daughter is sent off to school, spends the session, and returns home; the father pays the teacher . . . in the same commercial spirit that he would sell a house

or buy a farm; except that in the latter case many more questions would be asked. . . .[24]

He adds, significantly, that to him deportment is more important than proficiency—the former being an index to the heart, the latter to the intellect. John Augustus Williams might not have agreed, but perhaps Rogers better reflected the aspirations of his clients. And Williams, in his Kentucky college, was discarding as artificial the Commencement examinations Rogers strongly promoted:

> You know not, parents, the influence, for weal or woe, that your presence or absence on that occasion may exert on the susceptible nature of your child. The thought "Father and Mother will be present to see what I have been doing during the Session," possesses a more than magic power.

So the weeklong Commencements went on through the war years, although in June of 1862 Mary Alice Boulton, Emma Norwood, and Eugenia Shannon were the entire graduating class. The University was holding no Commencements, issuing no catalogs.

Then suddenly, the very walls of the College were threatened.

It was the usual August afternoon. Down town the bench-sitters spat into the dust or talked to Union soldiers yawning in front of the stores. The village accepted them now, and they, in turn, had relaxed to the point of not having sentries posted. Suddenly there was thunder, and at the sight of two hundred Confederate horsemen dashing down Broadway, the few Federals scattered. By the time word reached Colonel Merrill on the campus and the bugle sounded, the Rebs had stormed the jail, freed the prisoners, and all were galloping out past Christian College by the Paris Road. They paused at a pasture nearby to seize eighty army horses.

Merrill was furious. He accused Columbians of informing the rebels that no sentinels were on duty. He vowed to burn the town, the University, and the college buildings. After others had failed to dissuade him, Robert L. Todd tried.

"Well, Sir," he is supposed to have said. "You are to

blame for all this; you should have had guards on every road leading into Columbia. . . . Now, if you burn our town, our university and our colleges, our friends will kindle a fire under you, and I tremble for you at the result." Since Mr. Todd was a first cousin of Mary Todd Lincoln, that ended all talk of burning.

When Merrill then threatened to close the College, Todd reportedly took up the matter with President Lincoln. For years he kept Lincoln's letter saying he would not permit it to be done. (In 1911, at the Jubilee celebration of Christian College, Mrs. Rogers spoke of the "valuable assistance of Mr. Todd, during those troublous times.")[25]

Perhaps this marked a sort of turning point, convincing people that in reality, Christian College was here to stay. In 1863 enrollment started upward, and the loyal faculty received something over a hundred dollars apiece in cash. By the fall of 1865 when peace came, victory had also come to Christian College. It had its largest enrollment to date, 182 students and seventeen graduates. The faculty had increased to nine as compared with the five teachers and sixty-nine students at the University.

But there was a more significant change. When the reorganized board of trustees finally got back into the harness, it was apparent who held the reins. President Rogers presented his bill for improvements during the war years: additions to the west cottage, a brick wash-house—a total of about one thousand dollars. They gave him a lien on the property and accepted his offer to rent the College for $600 a year plus the four dollar rebate on each tuition in excess of fifty.

Not that financial struggles were over for the trustees. There were to be years of the familiar scrambling; crises averted by sudden saviours. Dr. Lenoir had held the bulk of the debt during the War, Caleb Stone had quietly contributed to Rogers' salary. But this embarrassing personal finance was still characteristic even of the state university, it must be remembered. The debt's assumption for the first time by a bank in 1870 was another proof that the College had attained community standing. The citizens of Columbia could not afford to see it fail.

President Rogers saw to it that the trustees did the scrambling. Though he had every confidence that he could run the College with a profit, he knew that no one man could relieve a debt, build an endowment, or initiate expansion. He continued to throw the problem squarely back to the trustees, and to present them, annually, with his bills for improvements which they were seldom able to pay. Rather they would add one more to his growing stack of I.O.U.'s.

They had purchased a new Minutes book. Its blue lined pages lacked the personality of the old yellowed ones whose scrawls were already fading, and its cloth cover was more businesslike than the old, crumbling leather. Optimistically, it was a thick book, with room for years of records.

One of the earliest insertions is the black-edged funeral notice of Thomas M. Allen, dated October 10, 1871. With civil strife over, Allen had immediately returned to the board of his beloved college. Now his death in a way emphasized the continuity of that institution, for its president preached his funeral sermon and one of its founders, D. Pat Henderson, returned to stand beside his grave. Two others, James Shannon and William Hudson, lay nearby, some in the crowd remembered as they listened to the tolling of the university bell.

Perhaps Henderson recalled that day, so long ago, when he had told the three of them that they were not "pursuing phantoms." Well, it was true, and they could rest in peace. Christian College, which they had founded on such high ground, was now on solid ground as well.

V

AN ACCOUNT IS SQUARED
1870-1883

Happy he whose business ledger . . . is square; happier he whose Acct. on Heaven's Ledger is square; & happiest he whose Acct. there shows a good balance of "treasure laid up" . . .
—J. K. ROGERS in his Journal, 1879

AT FORTY-ONE, in 1869, President Rogers had for the first time put on glasses. Through them he was to watch the drama of the next ten years rather as the *deus ex machina* of the old Greek plays: the god who sits in the wings and swoops down to intervene only when difficulties seem insurmountable. Or, better, he was the puppet-master, for he never ceased manipulating the many strings which kept the action going, leaving others to supply the passion, the fury, the progress of the plot. Letting the trustees collect subscriptions, try out new soliciting ventures, and shift the mortgages, he raised enough money with student benefits to pay each year's interest on the capital debt.

Never, through the years, in his orderly mind did he confuse the cubicles marked "sentiment" and "business." He was even able to watch while the hope for an endowment rose and was dashed, and when, to raise money for expansion, the trustees were forced to sell lots off the north end of the campus in 1870. But he was one of seven who bought a lot. When he saw that physical expansion was still blocked, he intervened again. He cancelled his notes against the Board, agreed to a lease with higher rent, and donated $1000 to the building fund. Thus they were enabled to contract for the long-needed wings to the main building. It was he who, when that building was finished in 1872, assumed the outstanding debt of $8000.

"We are happy to announce," says the catalog of 1871, "That the efforts [to enlarge the College] have been more successful than even the most sanguine anticipated." The $20,000 improvements consisted of two wings to the main building, three stories above basement, fifty-eight feet long each, by forty wide, and containing, "besides spacious halls in each story, thirty-four elegant and well ventilated rooms for boarders." An engraving of the College, included for the first time, is slightly misleading, for the third story was not added to the central building till some years later. We get a clearer picture from one irreverent inmate who remarked that "Christian College was a bird, with two wings, and the chapel as a tail."

A portico, whose lack James Shannon had bemoaned, now stretched across the south front. (A fine place for serenades on moonlit nights. When "Home, Sweet Home" left girls in hysterics they were sent upstairs to the sick bay adjoining the chapel where Ma Taylor revived them with asafetida.) A brick kitchen had been added to the dining-room in back, which "L" also housed the widowed Mrs. Banks, Matron, and her boys, Lynn and Hartley. Rogers had assumed the responsibility for their welfare now, as well as for the education of his wife's young brothers, Archie and Scott Robards.

President Rogers still taught Juniors and Seniors in his study and Professor Hurt taught in the chapel, used simultaneously as a study hall. ("Confusion most confounded," recalls Minnie Winans Horner.) Students still trooped to class in the cottages which sprang like mushrooms around the parent plant. One of these was the preparatory school, and at least one doubled as faculty housing, for one student remembers the music teacher telling her to hold high C while he ran to see if his duck was burning! There was a pond on the back of the campus, and though religion was not as zealous as in founding days, every spring would see a group of white clad girls baptized there or in Hinkson Creek.

The new wings housed the ninety or one hundred boarders, the Rogers and Hurt families, and others of the faculty. While choice end rooms had only two girls, most rooms held four. Even the dresser drawers were divided. The habit of frugality had become so entrenched at Christian College that a mother, being shown her daughter's room in 1880 was still able to exclaim: "Why, it looks like a prison!"

Save for a central square of carpet and perhaps an additional bureau, the hard straight chairs, the painted brown beds with blue-checked counterpanes, were much the same as those which Rogers had installed at the beginning of his regime. Doubtless some were the same, for Rogers' invoice of furnishings when he made Hurt his partner in 1870 is almost a duplicate of the list of furnishings bought from Wilkes in 1858.

By 1879 the building was lighted with gas, which was considered progressive since only recently had Columbia installed gas street lamps. Just after the new building was finished the catalog had announced that:

> a gymnasium, furnished with all needful appliances, will be provided . . . and each young lady will daily be passed through a select course of exercises calculated to secure proper physical development, to promote health, and to correct the evils frequently attendant on student life. Bath rooms also, furnished with cold and hot water, will be fitted up in the building.[1]

These improvements, however, did not materialize for some years. Although the state university was the proud possessor of one water-closet (the first in town) plumbing was still a novelty. In bad weather the college girls got most of their exercise, as did their mothers, by taking the required constitutional after each meal to the small buildings "out back." They were hidden from view by a hedge of osage orange.

There were streets on three sides of the College now. It was no longer an island, but a peninsula, for Christian College Avenue had been deeded to the town and was beginning to bloom with shaded houses and white fences. The town itself was still small (3,000 in 1870) and southern. Reconstruction had altered the lives of its landed families; "strangers" were moving in; road-building had brought the Irish. But the little Bass and Haydon boys who swam in Grindstone Creek still watched with curiosity any new Yankee playmate to see if a certain part of his anatomy really was banded in blue.

The girls who came to college now traveled by railroad, which new accessibility had increased the registration from small inland towns. Actually, the railroad was giving birth to the towns, for until almost 1870 girls were listed in the catalogs by counties. The sudden shift to dozens of place-names—Moberly, Sedalia, Macon, Callao—suggests whistle-stops on the railroad.

Population trends indicated in the first twenty-five years of Christian College catalogs are interesting as they dramatize the growth of the United States. In steamboat days students came from ports on the Missouri and Mississippi Rivers—Glasgow, Carrollton, Westport Landing (predecessor of Kansas City). An estate name, "Linwood," or "Rural Retreat" was sufficient address. Inland students usually came from county seat towns on stagecoach lines, such as Paris or Montgomery City. All of Christian's outstate students in the first ten years, except a few from neighboring Illinois, were from the South: Kentucky, Louisiana, Texas, Arkansas, Mississippi. Several from California reflected the Gold Rush.

After the war, Union victory brought an influx from northern states: Illinois, then Kansas and Indiana. Nearby Arkansas remained constant, and there were still students from Texas and Louisiana. A few from Colorado suggest President Rogers' travels there in search of health. Most Missouri girls continued to come from the older parts of the state, with a few appearing from the Ozark regions.

Outstate enrollment in the early 1880's was quite different. Texas led, with "Indian territory" next; then Kansas, Colorado, New Mexico, Oregon, California, Nebraska and Illinois. This would seem to reflect the settling of the far west and the fact that parents, in sending their daughters to school in Missouri, now were sending them "back East."

They found life changed very little at Christian College. They were still required to bring a uniform, but now this could be any simple dark dress and was worn only in public. They still had the bonnets, the girls, when allowed to vote on the question, having decided to retain them. But they had become fetching, expressing the wearer's personality. One alumna recalls a creation of puffed organdy and dainty "Val" lace, the brim faced with provocative pink silk quilting.

Rules—if the catalog is reliable—remained virtually unchanged, though perhaps more freely interpreted. Girls might resort to trickery to meet—and be kissed by—visiting male "cousins" at the Powers Hotel. Since in grocery stores downtown a farmer could help himself from the whiskey barrel, perhaps there was reason for the girls not to appear on the streets. An 1876 excursion to the Boone County Fair was hailed as the first time the student body was allowed to leave Christian College for other than church or school activities.

No one seemed to resent this perpetual maintenance of the *status quo*. Rather, it added to the reputation of the school, "one of the leading educational institutions of the West," according to the local paper.

A good part of the school's reputation was that of its President. He had attained great prestige as a financier, educator and disciplinarian. In church circles his name was synonymous with fairness and diplomacy. Called on to mediate disagreements anywhere in the state, he would consider the problem carefully, whether the colored preacher or a visiting bishop presented it. If a meeting threatened to be critical he was appointed chairman, healing the situation with tact. He could not bear to see anyone do less than his best. If a preacher offered a stumbling sermon and Rogers was subsequently asked to pray, he would weave into his prayer the sermon's points and make them seem somehow better than they were.

He had the respect, now, that wealth brings, for careful habits had accrued a good income. He had reconciled an old feud. Colonel Switzler, whose lack of support had once handicapped the College was now a trustee and Rollins, the socially prominent, had sent his daughters there. Indeed, a small note of snobbery had crept into the catalog with the statement "We must be certified of the good character and social standing of those applying for admission."

Rogers was a curator of the University on equal footing with its most distinguished educators. President Samuel Spahr Laws once spoke of him as "that alumnus best qualified . . . to take the Presidency of his *alma mater*."

He had scores of friends, for his rigidity was apparent only to those who asked him to compromise between what he saw clearly as right and wrong. He saw nothing preposterous in demanding that day students keep the same evening hours as boarders, cancelling a Christmas vacation because it was a waste of time, calling upon an alumna in another town to reprimand her for going to dances.

In daily life he was charming, cultivated, tactful and sociable. The record of marriages and funerals he kept during the seventies reads like a social register. The governor's daughter, the general's ward, former students from everywhere, every one wanted to be married by President Rogers. He buried many of the town's pioneer citizens and most of the College's earlier trustees. One is impressed by the distances he was summoned to perform a wedding ceremony and the high fees given him.

In a private notebook he titled "The Altar and the Tomb," he recorded each occasion:[2]

> MARRIED, on Tuesday, circa 2½ P.M., at residence of the bride's father, A. W. Roper, Glasgow, Mo., in the presence of a brilliant & cultivated company, Mr. Samuel Jackson Conley of Columbia, & Miss Candace Roper. How bright & beautiful a thing is love! . . . $20.
>
> *Dec., 1871* Married, at the res. of the bride's Uncle, Col. John Doniphan in Weston . . . Mr. John F. Murphy of Helena, Montana Ter., & Miss Lizzie T. Morton, an old pupil. A large & elegant company present, and a sumptuous and tastefully arranged supper . . . $100.

It was only human that his sentiments should be more expansive for a $75 wedding than for a two dollar one. After one such he wrote: "Where little is given, little will be required." Of a couple who paid him four bushels of corn he commented succinctly: "Both young and green."

There is an amusing story of Rogers' last Commencement, June, 1876. Heretofore, the girls had always been required to wear the simplest sort of white dresses—"like Quakers," one recalls. After twenty years of bucking rebellious graduates, President Rogers gave in. "Wear anything you like," he told them.

There was a mad scurry. There were frantic letters to parents. The girls rushed to get white satin gowns with trains, fancy tarlatans with the forbidden overskirts, elbow sleeves, corsages. . . . Each one wore a solitary, dangling curl. As they came down the aisle the murmur rose: "Is that Christian College?"[3]

There were apparently no major changes in the curriculum in Rogers' twenty-five years of influence, although incoming teachers must have brought changes in method. Nor did his attitude toward the status of women vary. His most radical career suggestion to a student was that she might become a telegraph operator! A survey of Rogers' graduates made by Carr shows that most of them were still becoming housewives or teachers; their other energies going to churchwork. But it had not been long since Columbia's woman lawyer, a Vassar graduate, had been spit upon by men as she walked out of the courthouse.

Possibly Rogers' chief intellectual contribution to Christian College was through the quality of teachers he chose. He was aware of this, and on retiring wrote the Board: "I cannot close . . . without calling to your attention the teachers who have been my colaborers. Whatever success has attended my administration is due largely to their ability and faithfulness."[4]

"Dear old Pinckney Hurt" stands first in tenure and perhaps in the memory of old girls. He served the College almost a quarter century, teaching under the first five presidents and becoming financial partner with both Rogers and Bryant. His pupils teased him until his red whiskers shook, or learned to divert him from a problem in mathematics to reminiscences of his Mexican War experiences.

Frederick Pannell brought to Christian an excellent musical training and fame as a composer. His twenty-year influence established the musical leadership which Williams had initiated. In other years of travel he taught at almost every city of size in the West. In Columbia, he was *the* musician, leading the band at the elaborate civic programs popular in those days. He was a familiar sight, carting his instruments around in a wagon, sounding the pitch with his tuning fork at the Christian church. It almost broke his heart when the first organ was installed there and turned over to a younger hand. Columbia remembers him with a "Pannell Street."

John Prosinger carried on the tradition of imported music teachers. While Pannell specialized in voice, he taught instrumental music for ten years. He will be remembered for his thick German accent and for one notable concert where he had all his students repeat the same composition on different instruments. "Vun Long Veary Day," was the way he announced the piece each time, and it was one long weary night to the audience before the program was over.

The outstanding scholar Rogers brought to his faculty was Joseph Ficklin. A mathematical prodigy from childhood, he was educated at the Masonic College at Lexington (the transplanted Marion College of Rogers' youth) and apparently had only his A.B. when he came to Christian in 1864. While there, certain of his contributions to scientific journals and solutions to problems were published. The University, reorganizing after the war and looking for a man to fill its important Chair of Mathematics and Engineering, saw "that little fellow over at Christian College." Ten years later Ficklin had his Ph.D. from the University of Wisconsin and was recognized in the United States and Europe for his scholarship. He served as a trustee of Christian for two decades.

Andrew Walker McAlester deserves brief mention because, though his connection with the College was slight, it shows the opportunities afforded girl students of that era. He was one of the distinguished physicians of the Mississippi valley, founder of the University of Missouri medical school, and he came over to Christian to lecture the young ladies on anatomy and physiology. Dr. Woodson Moss (also a University staff-member) followed him as medical lecturer at the College.

These three men illustrate a change which was taking place in the long "distaff side" relationship between Christian College and the University of Missouri. They were among a group, beginning in 1851 with William Alexander, who had taught the same subjects to both schools. Some such duplication of teachers would continue but oftener in the future Christian would be a stepping stone for novices to larger opportunities.

For while Christian was standing still, academically, the University was feeling growing pains. During the 1870's it would reach into new fields, begin to expand from the male college of pre-war days into a true university. For two decades the size of both student bodies had compared favorably (and in 1867 Christian's enrollment had exceeded that of the University's by 15 per cent).[5] Never again would this be true.

The fundamental relationship between the two schools had ceased in 1868 when the University cautiously admitted its first women students. Although they were not allowed to "mingle" with the men, they kept coming until by 1872 there were sixty enrolled. (This year a girl first received a B.S. degree.) When a dean of women was thought necessary in 1879, the University found its first lady principal on the staff of Christian College. To the University Mrs. O. A. Carr brought the continued influence of the girls' school for she had been a pupil, years before, of John Augustus Williams.

The most notable woman who taught at Christian in its first twenty-five years was Caroline Neville Pearre. Caroline Neville had taught for Williams in Kentucky and at Christian and, as Mrs. Pearre, was hired by Rogers in 1875. Previously she had become the most talked-of woman nationally in the Christian church, having dared what no other woman of her day would do. At the Cincinnati Convention of 1874 she walked into a hall full of men, took the platform, and pleaded the cause of foreign missions. Her success made her the founder of the CWBM, Christian Woman's Board of Missions. She brought the same daring to Christian College when in those sex-shy days she explained with charts and pointer the facts of human reproduction.

Virginia Neville, her sister, was with the College from 1866 until 1874. One of her pupils recalls: "She was a magnificent teacher; Wordsworth was almost her God . . . I can hear her now, her deep voice like a barrel-organ, reading to us from 'Yarrow Unvisited.' "[6]

Caroline Neville started a three-generation chain of inspiring literature teachers at Christian College when she married the father of student Henrietta Pearre. Henrietta, upon graduating, joined the faculty in 1875 and taught until 1883 after her marriage to Edmund, son of L. B. Wilkes. Of entirely different temperament from her step-mother, she was equally idolized. One of the favorite stories of "old girls" is of the time "Miss Nettie" became so exasperated with a sluggish class that she cried: "I'd as soon teach a room full of broomsticks as you girls!" The next morning, when she appeared, each chair held a broomstick.

She would have been pleased to know that another seventy years would find her daughter, Mrs. Cynthia Wilkes McHarg, at Christian initiating the old classics to eager new minds.

But the prince of teachers was George S. Bryant. When Elder Rogers in 1871 had married Professor George Bryant, principal of the Independence high school to Miss Maggie Ferguson of Columbia, he had noted them as "an interesting and promising couple." One year later Bryant was on the faculty of Christian. He was a Bethany College graduate and held a Master's degree. For the next five years he was to teach philosophy, mainly, but sometimes literature and history. He was the true type of scholar, as remote from the world as Rogers was practical. "He would have been more at home in the streets of ancient Greece than he was on Broadway," declares Rose Allison Banks.

Another recalls how clearly he taught and how he made everything live. There survives a small green programme marked Commencement, 1881. The cover design is pure Egyptian, pyramids, palm trees. . . . The connection between these and a Christian College Commencement would be obscure to most, but to old students of Bryant it would bring back enlightened evenings. For the Rosetta Stone was the exciting discovery of their schooldays, and often had they followed while Bryant led them along the sandy plains of Egypt. Under him the old after-dinner programs of self-improvement apparently relaxed. His listeners never forgot the trials of Paul on his missionary journeys or the snarls of the peasants as they stormed the Bastille.

"He was casting his pearls before swine," declares Mrs. Banks, at ninety, but the women who sat in her class on Sunday mornings would not agree. She is but one echo of others who describe him as "a great man. The greatest single influence in my life."

Where the girls respected or feared Rogers, they adored Bryant. As Rogers' health grew worse it became apparent that Bryant was to succeed him, and in 1877 he became President. But Bryant found it distasteful from the start to try to fill the footsteps of Rogers, the financier. Although he recognized the need for funds, it was not in his nature to solicit or to make public speeches of promotion. His conviction was that if a man make a better mousetrap the world will beat a path to his door. He concerned himself only with the mousetrap; he was so determined to send forth graduates who knew their subject matter that even after final examinations he drilled them in a review of the course.

Administration was irksome, and his six year presidency was shot with disappointments. No sooner had he taken over his first lease of the College than he was offered a position at the University which he coveted and for which he was cut to the cloth. Too conscientious to resign, he had a parallel frustrating experience a few years later, in 1883. This time he returned to Independence.

Other facts confirm the impression that Bryant was primarily the teacher and that his administration was actually an extension of Rogers'. He appointed no trustees. His strongest board members were those Rogers had installed around 1870: William C. Robnett, James Estill, James Ferguson, John Hubbell, Joseph S. Moss, N. T. Rutherford and Robert Clinkscales. Perhaps out of consideration for Rogers, his very catalog did not change until 1879—three years before the latter's death. Then it assumes a new personality, non-pietistic, simple, almost folksy—as when it states that "The moral influence of the home relation is worth a *ton* of rules."

His restatement of the purpose of the school is interesting:

> . . . to furnish young ladies all the advantages for thorough and complete education that are enjoyed by the best appointed Colleges, and in addition to this . . . a *Christian* education.

He repeats that the policy of the school is liberal, not sectarian. Discipline is still parental, no system of student "espionage" being allowed. Gold medals are offered, for the first time, for the two best essays written from the Junior Class.

Three innovations are worth noting, in view of the times. He stresses the safety advantages of *gas lighting* and declares that "All other things being equal, this should have its weight in determining the choice of a school." He describes the new TELESCOPE, in one paragraph, and dwells on THE LIBRARY. Its 620 volumes—"not books for juveniles—but books which will go a long way in developing and rounding up one's character" are listed in Bryant's last catalog (year ending 1882). Whereas Rogers had flatly forbidden "any works of doubtful morality," Bryant suggests that access to a good library will guide the young ladies' tastes away from trash. He includes as worthwhile the works of Mark Twain, which Rogers would likely have classified as dubious.

Administratively, Bryant did little to change the *status quo*. He was never a trustee of the College, nor present at board meetings. There Rogers retained the chief voice, and continued to guide fiscal affairs until his death in 1882 towards the end of Bryant's regime.

It was Rogers who, on retiring, had pointed out in strong terms the school's need:

> My heart's desire . . . for years, has been to see the College endowed in such a sum as would place it beyond the contingencies which necessarily attach to unendowed institutions. That this end may yet be attained in the not distant future, I have not wholly despaired of. One thing is certain, unless it is done, the days of the College

> are numbered, and its friends might as well prepare for its funeral.[7]

This was too bitter a prophecy for the trustees, who omitted it when they spread his resignation on the *Minutes.* It was Rogers who suggested the means of finally liquidating the debt when he proposed that they send L. B. Wilkes into the state as agent. Again Wilkes came to the rescue, and in 1878 Christian College was for the first time free from debt.

Then Rogers did a characteristic thing. He sent the Board a bill for thirty-five dollars for blinds which he had left installed in the window of the President's study!

How finally to estimate this man who, to many, for a quarter of a century *was* Christian College? We are tempted to balance factors, as he would have done; to arrange him neatly on two sides of a ledger. But his human contradictions will not be stuffed into cubbyholes.

He is a vanished type, difficult to comprehend: the benevolent despot, with the Victorian concept of Duty as "Stern Daughter of the Voice of God." Few today could understand a man whose sense of duty sent him to a Commencement program while, a few doors away, his son lay dying.

However, one could choose at random a significant tribute from a dozen really distinguished men who knew Rogers. The University's foremost scientist, Schweitzer, wrote:

> I knew him as a curator of the University and as a citizen of Columbia, clear-headed and warm-hearted, strong-willed and sympathetic, well informed and endowed with unusual executive talent, he made the College, I think, what it is, and certainly gave it direction . . . he could calmly place his burden upon the shoulders of his successors, well knowing that what he had done, had no need to be done over; they could build as upon a strong and sure foundation.[8]

Did Rogers, through his new glasses, take a near-sighted view of education? He seemed as unconcerned with the need for change as Augustus Williams had been convinced of it. In his administration the school had evolved from a progressive, almost radical venture into a conservative mold.

The testing days of female education were over. Women's

colleges had sprung up across the land. Never again would it be a problem of survival because there were too few, but because there were so many. Christian could no longer function as a counterpart of the state university. Did Rogers realize that to survive, Christian College must change?

He had noted the birth of the great women's colleges in the East—Vassar, Smith, Wellesley. He envied them their founding wealth and perhaps did not sufficiently mark their high entrance requirements. With the Easterners' lofty provincialism they were still congratulating themselves as pioneers. But Christian was in its thirty-second year.

He had brought it through the fire-bath of Civil War, the depression and reconstruction following. He had paid off its debt, tripled the value of its property and established a yearly enrollment of well over a hundred.

Perhaps by his quarter-century insistence on the same standards during such shifting times, Rogers did something for Christian College that no other could have done. He converted the founders' dream of a collegiate, Christian education for women into a fact. If it lost some of its scope in the conversion, that was the inevitable compromise between dream and reality.

Before closing his ledger for the last time he could write with honesty: "My account with Christian College—*Squared.*"

VI

AGAINST THE GASLIGHT 1883-1893

Young men and study are incompatible.
—WILLIAM A. OLDHAM, 1885

WITH BRYANT RESIGNING in April, 1883, and Rogers dead, the trustees of Christian College looked to the South for a president. A University of Kentucky graduate, a principal in the Lexington public schools, a Christian Church preacher there, William Abner Oldham was known as "an experienced educator and a ripe scholar." He also fitted Columbia's picture of the southern gentleman.

When Mrs. Oldham unpacked their trunks at Christian and young Lila, Silas, Abner, Mary, and Susan romped up the broad hall stairs on their tour of investigation, everyone felt quite at home.

But here the *status quo* ended. Underneath his jolly, rotund appearance the forty-year-old president showed aggressive qualities. With a newcomer's perspective he saw the needs: the venerable school, now surrounded by competitors. There were five other girls' colleges within thirty miles; younger schools, whose buildings were newer. There was little stigma, now, to the coeducation offered by public institutions.

First, Christian College must be enlarged, declared Oldham. The original plans for raising the main building and towers to the level of the wings must be carried out immediately. The elegantly deceptive engraving in the catalog must become a reality or clients would take their patronage elsewhere. The Board listened, and since times seemed prosperous, concurred. By 1885 the College was no longer "a bird," but a unified three-story structure with ornamental iron fretwork the length of its fireproof tin roof.

The new President was shrewd enough to learn what he could from the past. On his arrival the Board had appointed one of its members "to procure if possible a full file of the catalogs of Christian College from the beginning up to the present time" and turn over to President Oldham for preservation. A complete file could not be found. Perhaps, as it was, the President had read too many, for he was to continue to point out to the trustees certain unfulfilled promises of previous years. What about the bath rooms, "with hot and cold running water?" What about the gymnasium? What about the fact that young ladies were still forced to practice at pianos scattered all over the College, so that they had to make an appointment to secure a free one?

Again building on the past, he counted his alumnae. There were 322 living; thirty-five dead. He had taken care to be introduced to the community by the society of alumnae itself, with a nice speech by Mrs. Nannie Walker Lenoir[1] which challenged each member of her audience to send back one student to the College each year. It was the first occasion in the history of the College where mother and daughter had sat side by side as alumnae, and was made more significant by the presence of Mrs. Sallie Bedford Robinson, first valedictorian. Mrs. Lenoir mentioned that the idea of securing an endowment for Christian College was "not preposterous," a theme which Oldham took up vigorously.

He used the catalog as his medium and addressed himself chiefly to the Christian Church in Missouri.

> "Whose is Christian College?" he asked. "At the present writing Christian College is the only exclusively female school of the Christian Church in the state. . . . Beyond all dispute, it is the property of the brotherhood. . . . It has been built by the liberality and energy of divers men of God, and is now run in the interests of the Christian Church. . . . If, by patronage of alien schools, they are built up, and your own destroyed, upon whom shall censure fall? Who but ourselves shall reap the bitter fruit?[2]

Later presidents were to imitate his efforts to arouse a conscience about the school in the Christian church. But that loosely-knit body was seldom to help, just as it was never to interfere. Its one attempt to bring the College under its jurisdiction had failed,[3] leaving Christian with an intellectual freedom not always characteristic of church-affiliated schools. It continued true that local trustees and college donors were usually members of the Christian church.

Oldham's ten years of catalogs stand out among the others as a study in transition. They record the several ways in which he attempted to push his barque off its mossy rock into the main stream of progress.

After organizing the alumnae and appealing to the church, he attacked the college curriculum. The contradictory nature of his changes indicates that they may have been his answer to two threats. The first was the competition of public high schools. As these increased and yearly raised their standards, the old seminaries were being forced out of existence. Many a so-called "college" was on a not much higher level. Even the University was being queried by high schools of the state as to where their work left off and its began.

To define Christian's position Oldham added a Classical Course which required an additional year and carried an A.B. degree. It was the four year "literary and scientific" course of former years with Latin, trigonometry, astronomy, and two years of French or German required. Accordingly, after 1889 candidates for graduation were listed for the first time as A.B. or B.L. Perhaps he knew that it was a concession to progress few students were prepared to make, for he once remarked ruefully that "the curriculum is now too high for the average Missouri girl." In 1890 Mary Frazier Oldham was listed as the only A.B.

Another revision which sought to define scholarship levels was a grading system on the basis of 100 down, with 96 an honor candidate, over 75 a passing mark, and under 60 a failure. This followed the system used at the University and seems to have been more exacting than that used in similar southern girls' schools of the day.

The second threat, the co-education offered by the state university perhaps accounted for new courses which were, by contrast, designed to appeal to women. President Oldham wrote:

> I am not opposed to co-education. I doubt its wisdom in many cases. Young girls of immature character *are not safe* in mixed schools. Others, more mature, may, we think, advantageously attend well-endowed and well-officered institutions where co-education is permitted. The seclusion of the boarding-school, however, cuts off that great thief of time, promiscuous company-keeping, and enables the young lady to devote her attention exclusively to the work.[4]

This was propaganda later presidents were to employ. Indeed, Oldham, in all his methods might be called the first of the moderns, who felt that "psychology," publicity, and capitalizing on individual features were as necessary to keep a private school going as the old standards of scholarly worth.

Such finishing-school specialties as "Elocution" appeared, a forty day course conducted by two gentlemen experts from Kansas City. "History of Art," was introduced and "Sensible Etiquette" by Mrs. Ward was listed as a textbook.

The 1885 catalog announced the creation of a Conservatory of Music under "a German professor." In the eighties any musician of repute must sojourn in Germany, just as thirty years later the mecca would be an *atelier* in Paris, or the Conservatoire de Fontainebleau. The study of the German language became fashionable and Christian announced "a German table" in the dining room.

A complete three year course of study in music was listed,

above the preparatory level. It included harmony, counterpoint, composition analysis, and its requirements seem to correspond rather well with those of today. Intermediate pupils studied the exercises of Koehler, Heller, Loeschorn, Czerny, the sonatinas of Clementi and Mozart, for recitals played Mendelssohn's "Song without Words" or Schubert's "Moment Musical." Seniors must be able to play Chopin and Liszt, Bach's "Well-Tempered Clavicord," Beethoven's more difficult sonatas. All stringed instruments were taught, as well as pipe organ. There was a concert series announced, "with some of the best musicians of our country."

In 1885 Christian gave its first degree in Music. The number of pupils enrolled and the many graduates show that the important music school dreamed of by Williams and Rogers had materialized. "The department of music," declared the catalog, "is second to none in the State."

Other course changes were simply in name. "Psychology" replaced "mental philosophy," "physics"—"natural philosophy." In 1886 laboratory work was listed under chemistry but the available scientific apparatus was still meager:

> . . . a large number of Geological specimens, a valuable Microscope, with a fine selection of Physiological objects, and Anatomical models, illustrative of Anatomy and Physiology. The College has also the use of a pair of fine Stereopticons, by which the latest and best way of impressing the sciences . . . will be introduced. A number of slides illustrative of Astronomy have been purchased. . . .

In place of the intensive study of Rogers' and Bryant's day in the five books of Moses and the Gospels themselves, two semesters were spent on Milligan's "Scheme of Redemption," a book *about* the Bible. Finally this evolved into a single course, "Evidences of Christianity."

Physical education for a while took a colorful twist, the girls performing military drill on campus, in red coats. (Undoubtedly the influence of the University whose Lieutenant Crowder had organized a ladies' cadet band. The University ladies drilled with light guns and *without* corsets. However, they must retain their hats!)

The most significant innovation made by Oldham was his last, in 1890: a course in shorthand, typing and bookkeeping. Perhaps to defend this he quoted a recent Commencement speaker: "Some of the most womanly women I know have beat back the black battalions of poverty with . . . no spear more minacious than a stenographic pencil."

This would have been a shattering thought to John Augustus Williams, who used "the swift-flying needle," as emblematic of womanhood. Shocking, too, would have been such words as "emancipation," "rights of citizenship," and "galling dependency," random samples from baccalaureate addresses of the opening nineties.

Inside the old college, the trappings were much the same: the bowls, pitchers, embroidered "splashers," just as the uniforms were the same. But the girls inside the uniforms were changing.

In downtown Columbia livery stable operators were complaining that their business was dying because nowadays it was cheaper for a young man to take his girl out on a tandem bicycle than to rent a horse. Probably this had no more effect on the sheltered college girls than did the first football game in 1890 or the forbidden novels of Émile Zola. But though football and bikes were barred along with yellow-backed novels nothing could keep the restive ideas of the nineties from seeping between the boards of the fence.

Oldham himself averred publicly that the female college graduate need no longer choose between marriage and life as a dependent. He cited medicine, writing, the lecture platform, and the mission field as newly open to women. "I admire both the pluck and good taste of the lady who gave as her reason for not marrying, that she was not willing to give up a sixty dollar per month salary for a ten dollar husband!"[5]

Perhaps his recognition of the changes brewing accounts for the stern preachments in his catalogs. Judging from these, Oldham seems to have been more preoccupied than former presidents with the subject of boy meeting girl. The same rules are in effect: no trips beyond the college enclosure unchaperoned, all correspondence subject to inspection, no callers except on Monday nights. (Instead of the former

Saturday.) But the injunctions are much more emphatic. Assuring parents that "Every effort will be made to preserve the maidenly purity of those entrusted to our care," he adds:

> Our experience teaches that evil, and only evil, comes from students paying or receiving visits. . . . With reference to calls from young men we would be especially emphatic. Young ladies meet young men in going to and from College, and straightway these young men wish to call. Parents sometimes weakly yield.
>
> Please leave this matter entirely in our hands. . . . After graduation young ladies may, if they desire, give much of their time to the society of young men. While in school it is different. Young men and study are incompatible.[6]

Yet boy did manage to meet girl, although sometimes it took a catastrophe to bring them together. An exciting event to students of 1892 was the burning of the University.

On Saturday night, just before a meeting of the University Athenaeum Society a fire started in the society's room in the administrative building. One of the few objects saved was the Conant portrait of Joseph K. Rogers which one of the members pulled from the wall. The students and town rallied to save the other buildings. (Mr. Alex Bradford of Columbia still claims a weak back from carrying books down the three flights of Switzler Hall's steps.) The University was yet on a precarious enough footing that it was not only a question of one building being burned. Total destruction might give some rival community another chance to bid for the state university.

The Governor hurried over from the Capitol to lend his support to President Jesse. Christian College invited the university students to use its chapel and classrooms. They answered through the Columbia *Herald:*

> The female colleges are offered to us. They say they can embrace the entire University. And we say that, even in our demoralized and disabled condition, we can embrace them.

President Oldham well knew the pitfalls that awaited eligible young women, for he had three popular daughters of his own. They were in on most of the mischief of the day, whether it was the stealthy barricade of the door while each girl puffed a cigarette or the time a group accidentally entered a barber shop and saw men with their naked faces covered with lather! It was becoming more difficult than in former years to keep a young female cloistered, just as it was becoming more troublesome to keep her bonneted.

"Much difficulty is experienced," admits the catalog of 1889, "in securing uniformity of dress." And it urges plaintively: "no silk trimmings, no beads. Please . . . the plainer, the better." In the elegant eighties this was the subject of much complaint from the girls to Mrs. Fine, the Matron, who sewed for them. For years they had been getting around the bonnet rule by bringing from home any fluffy conception a doting mother could dream up. President Oldham had sought to curb this trend by having the bonnets made (for $2.70) after the girls arrived in Columbia. The last two catalogs of the eighties record a significant change of verb: "N.B. Bonnets should be made in Columbia to secure uniformity," and a year later: "N.B. Bonnets *must* be made in Columbia." The bonnet was on its way out.

It is puzzling to try to reconcile Oldham's rigid discipline, as he expounded it, with his remembered popularity. Perhaps his harsh dictums were simply those of the parent, hopeless of enforcing them. Student memories are uniformly fond: of him standing in the door listening as a young instructor sunk her class deeper and deeper into the morass of mental arithmetic. How he excused her, took the group to his own study, and in five minutes explained the matter in the most lucid way imaginable.

Old students remember how they would curtsey to him as they left the study hall in the evenings. . . . His croquet contests with trustees John Conley and Robert Clinkscales, continued into the twilight by lantern or in the rain with umbrellas. The same gentlemen at chess in the parlor, under the steel engravings. (That period parlor: the pink roses on the Brussels carpet, the plush album, Mrs. Soule's painting of "King Lear," and on the marble-topped table a Rogers' group called "Weighing the Baby.")

They recall how he forgave the hungry girls who ate all the ice-cream ordered for a wedding reception. How he brought his gold-headed cane down on the head of the boy who tried to sneak into the line as they walked to church! His trials with the hair-styles of the day which dictated bangs dripping with flaxseed at breakfast in order to be becomingly frizzed by supper.

One last injunction is stressed in the catalogs to the extent of being surrounded by pointing fingers:

> ☛ HEALTH ☚
>
> Rich boxes of cake and confections bring dyspepsia, and sickness of other kinds. During the past year many pupils have lost days from school by this means. Our table is abundantly supplied with wholesome food. These confections breed many altogether un-necessary ills. They take the mind of the pupil from her studies; they lead to untidy ways and filthy rooms . . . do not send them.

Yet the girls of Oldham's day report that when he caught them enjoying such a delight, he only laughed. He knew of their efforts to boil eggs over the gas jet or fry oysters on brown paper at the back of the stove. It is possible that the evils the good doctor warned against so vigorously were those which tempted him most.

He was a short, stout man, fond of good eating, although so absent-minded he would sometimes read through a meal and have to be reminded. His students recall him with large white napkin tucked across his expansive front—hiding the heavy gold watch chain which usually dominated that region. All the faculty, families down to babes in highchair included, ate at the college, as did numerous guests who came and stayed for weeks. Perhaps, as one trustee conjectured, the fact that they ate so well was one reason the College never made much profit. The fact that they received so much of their pay in board, the faculty might have said, would account for the few years most of them stayed.

Professors Pannell and Hurt were the old-timers still in service. Young W. H. Pommer was the German music professor who headed the new conservatory. After graduating from the Royal Conservatory at Leipzig, he studied at the Musical Conservatory of Vienna for an additional year. He brought his bride to his first position at Christian College.

His career, like his baby daughter, grew up on the campus. Soon, published compositions began to add to his fame and he was asked to head the music department of the University of Missouri. Otto Tiede, who took his place, had married Evelyn Bryant, a Christian alumna. He had not studied in Germany, but from a Dresden graduate. He was a blond, small man whose suits the girls borrowed for parties on Saturday nights.

Another who "married into" the college was Joseph B. Skinner, M.A., whom Oldham had brought from the University of Kentucky to teach Latin and Mathematics. He had married Julia Lenoir, daughter of the college physician (and grand-daughter of founder James Shannon). She had studied music at Christian from the time she was a child of seven, through her teens. Professor Skinner was called back to Kentucky as president of Hamilton College, and after he died there, she became head of the Cincinnati Conservatory of Music. She was one of Christian's first graduates to have a distinguished career.

Mrs. S. A. Iglehart was Christian's best-remembered primary teacher. She scorned the *Kindergarten* (recently introduced into St. Louis) and was just as determined that her daughter and grand-daughter not attend kindergarten as that they should be graduated from Christian.

Mrs. Soule, art teacher (the Miss Forbes of Rogers' faculty) was a young Kentuckian already receiving notice for her portraits in Columbia.[7] Mrs. Annie Dobyns Bourne is remembered for her pretty face and ostrich plumed hats. The Misses Sally and Lucy Morton taught music during most of Oldham's regime. The other faces came and went around the long dining table—the Rev. John Mountjoy, adored by the girls, "Brother" Shouse, another Christian Church preacher, Oldham's trustees: William A. Bright, Sinclair Kirtley, Slater Lenoir, F. D. Hubbell; sometimes Shannon Douglass from Kansas City or James Clinkscales from Carrollton. Only the figure at the head of the table remained the same, the paternal face with its generous whiskers.

For in many ways, where Williams was the educator, Rogers the administrator, and Bryant the teacher, Oldham was the parent—the last of the Papas for the little collegiate family. Who after him, in the first warm days of spring, would interview each girl personally to make sure she had not taken off her long underwear?

Certainly, most of his activity was designed to ensure the creature comforts that any father would seek for his brood. He never ceased to push his main line of attack—modernization. When, after the first five years his contract was renewed, he immediately brought up the subject of building. The enlarged dormitories had been a great step forward. Girls no longer had to keep their trunks before their doors in the hall. True, the out-houses were now lit by gas. Unfortunately, the "baths with hot and cold running water" and the steam heat were not as advertised.

But new classroom space was a necessity if the College were to survive. After thirty-five years students were still trudging from east to west cottage for classes or music. The academy pupils still sat on benches in the one-room school, for all the world like the country. The President had in mind a three-story brick academic hall, somewhat on the plan of the agricultural building of the University. There should be classrooms, primary school space, a chapel with a real stage, a library, and the long-promised gymnasium.

Apparently in July, 1887, for the first time in the history of Christian College, money was not too scarce, for the necessary $5000 was subscribed in a month. That summer the three-story brick chapel was erected just to the east, its second floor connected to the east wing of the dormitory by a covered chute. The ground floor held classrooms, parlor and office, and upstairs was the galleried auditorium planned to seat 600. Balancing the chapel tower on the west was the old east cottage, tacked to the new building for use as art rooms. The former chapel was partitioned into practice rooms. There was still no gymnasium, but the chapel had a bell, so Aunt Harriet would no longer signal to the world by beating on her Chinese gong that Christian College was having its breakfast. Poor Harriet was doomed along with the symbols of her life-time—the lamp chimneys to be polished, pitchers filled from the well. Soon she would be one of the legends of the College to which she willed her weary bones.[8]

The new building was accompanied by new propaganda in the catalog of 1889:

> The entire Literary Curriculum, from the primary years, has been remodeled and enlarged to meet the need that is being felt more and more throughout the West, for the higher education of young women. . . .
>
> Too much importance cannot be attached to the PREPARATION necessary to enter the College proper. . . . Most failures in College may be traced directly to feeble and defective elementary training. In view of these facts we have made our Primary and Preparatory courses exceptionally complete; and we feel assured that they offer advantages, in the way of preparation . . . not easily secured elsewhere.

Still there were no study desks or opera chairs in the new chapel; not to mention curtain and scenery for the stage, which addition had been planned "to prepare young ladies for *all* the duties of life." (Such old straight-backs as Caleb Stone would have gasped, but the presidents of Christian College had always shown a partiality for the dramatic arts.)

The usual benefit concerts and lectures having failed, Jerry Dorsey, who after twenty-five years was perhaps the most influential member of the Board, thought of an old rule of the trustees which had so galled the first President:

> Many years ago this Board restricted the power to create a debt and whereas an emergency has arisen for money to complete improvements already ensuing. Therefore, Resolved . . . that said resolution (be) suspended indefinitely . . . and Building committee (be) authorized to borrow sums necessary to complete chapel, purchase desks, and opera chairs, curtains and scenery for stage. . . .[9]

The committee on finance went to an interesting source for the money. "We have secured the sum of $2000 from Blind Boone . . . due in twelve months from date at 6% interest." Blind Boone was a Columbia negro concert pianist who had acquired wealth and fame in repeated tours on the continent. His mother had "belonged to" the Shannon family and he tried out his early notes on James Shannon's square grand piano which is preserved at the College. Thus, the uneducated son of a slave took his place among the gentry as one of the financial saviours of Christian College.

But again they had scraped the bottom of the barrel. Hard times were setting in. In January, 1890, the treasurer reported no cash on hand. It was necessary to raise the tuition. As an economy measure, students henceforth were required to bring their own counterpanes, sheets, and pillowcases.

Still President Oldham did not give up his battle for creature comforts. From 1890 on the *Minutes* of the Board are enlivened by constant references to steam heat, bath appliances, and water closet facilities. Finally the Board resolved: "Whereas the time has come for a forward movement in the heating of Christian College, in order that it may compete successfully with other institutions which are fully provided with modern improvements . . ." that it would float a bond for "an expenditure sufficient to provide a better and more comfortable water-closet system than that now in use, to be executed on the plan of an expert in such matters. . . ."[10]

All the stepping stones President Oldham laid to progress are gone from the Christian College campus. The wings, the red tin roof, the gas-lit privies, the chapel and the bell. Perhaps, then, it will not be irrelevant to immortalize him, as he requested, by a letter he wrote the trustees in his hour of triumph.

> I desire to express for myself, faculty and pupils most heartfelt thanks to the board for the splendid heating apparatus recently purchased. . . . It . . . has given us perpetual summer within the walls of the College. Not only is the apparatus a success . . . but also an ornament adding much to the beauty of the rooms. We also express thanks . . . for the new water closets, . . . which are a perpetual delight to all and add to the satisfaction and comfort of the pupils and faculty. I cannot think of anything else necessary to the well being of your renowned and venerable school, unless it be the addition of bath rooms . . . with bath rooms the cup of our earthly joy would be full.

He goes on to estimate that six bath tubs, at a cost of about fifty dollars, could be placed in the west wing cellar, since the hot and cold pipes were immediately above.

> A drain pipe leads out from the building into the west pasture and I do not think a bath once per week for each girl would injure the appearance of the west pasture in the least. (The only result would be an added verdure.)
>
> I cannot close without expressing to the Board my high appreciation of the . . . labors of your committee who had the work of heating the building by modern methods. . . . A record of their services should be preserved among the archives of the Institution.[11]

If the bathrooms he longed for were ever installed he must have done it himself, for his accounts in final settlement with the Board note "$90—for putting in bathrooms." There were fewer to enjoy them, however. In the last years enrollment had dropped. In January, 1892, Oldham wrote with characteristic bluntness: "Gentlemen: I am not for reelection. I thank this board . . . for its uniform courtesy, and for its support in trying emergencies. . . ."

Thus the gay nineties were ushered into Christian College, made somewhat gayer by the addition of steam heat and bathtubs. When Oldham sold his furniture, put on his black derby, and left, no one realized he was taking with him the last of an era. He was the last president who had known personally the old giants: Henry H. White, Moses Lard, John Augustus Williams, those who had pioneered the school. He was the last of the preacher-presidents . . . the last Papa for the College Family. Although the little group waving him good-bye did not realize it, they would never be a "family" again, just as they would never again wear the myrtle green bonnets.

So we leave them, figures that flicker against the gas-light, in the decade which formed a bridge between the old and the new.

VII

A PAIR OF WHITE GLOVES
1893-1920

A woman's chief glory, next to cultivating her heart and mind, lies in society and its functions.
—LUELLA WILCOX ST. CLAIR, 1894

IF THE TRUSTEES OF Christian College knew an era was passing, their actions did not show it. In typical pattern of the past they went back to their Athens: Lexington, Kentucky. J. W. Porter, president of Hamilton College, the women's branch of Transylvania, was approached. (The fact that he was referred to throughout the Minutes as *Mr. Poter* may indicate that the Board still had a southern cast.)

He refused, but they found another prospect there, a young man who as business manager had been chiefly responsible for operating Hamilton. Franklin Pierce St. Clair was sought out in Colorado, where he had removed for his health. When he and his attractive wife stepped off the train in Columbia the Board was captivated. For once, they invited a prospective president's wife to sit in on the interview.

Luella St. Clair was full of vivacity and sparkle. Professor St. Clair was courtly and intelligent. Such old timers as Jerry Dorsey and Dr. Lenoir remembered another mustached young man and took it as a good omen when the contract was signed. If they thought that the hollow footsteps of J. K. Rogers might at last be filled, they did not even imagine the imprint of a tiny feminine heel.

That was a busy summer of 1893. The first glance had been enough for the decisive young matron. Now followed studied sessions over paint swatches, wallpaper samples, carpet, while the new President looked into the account books and their five-year old daughter chased squirrels on the lawn. Evenings when they were not being entertained, the couple sat under the out-moded gas jet in the parlor and planned; mornings there were workmen to supervise, packing boxes to uncrate. It was a happy, hectic summer. It was a race to have everything ready by the time school opened in the fall. Sometimes Luella would look at her husband with anxiety, knowing the strain that was being put on his delicate heart.

Finally there was not one of the crude washstands, the splint-bottomed chairs, the square pianos, left. By September it was announced: "Christian College is completely refurnished throughout with new golden oak furniture and elegant Brussels carpet. All new pianos . . . not a stick of old furniture in the place."

By November the President was dead.

In the crisis the Board acted as one man. They had had four months to observe the energetic little woman with the combination of Yankee "drive" and southern charm. They had a feeling that anything Luella St. Clair started would be finished. In a statement that shattered all precedent at Christian College they declared that a woman was the proper head for a female institution, and that Mrs. St. Clair, as president, was not to be looked upon as a substitute, but as "one eminently fitted to fill the office."

Academically, this was an exaggeration. Educated in the public school of Virden, Illinois, her birthplace, Luella Wilcox was the only girl to finish in the high school's first graduating class. She was valedictorian. Progressing to Hamilton

College in Kentucky, her mother's home state, she was graduated after one year. It was when she returned the following year to edit the college paper that she met, and in 1886 married, the young mathematics instructor, Frank St. Clair. He was a graduate of Bethany College, West Virginia.

With him, she taught English a year, but her most recent experience had been as a country school teacher in the mountains of Colorado. Perhaps those three winters of breaking trail each day on horseback contributed an intrepid quality which was to serve her better than any Master's degree. Too, she had the tenacity of her Scottish mother and the Irish wit and faith of her father.

Just turned twenty-eight, the dazed young widow probably was not aware that she was one of the first woman college presidents in the United States. As she signed the usual contract for lease (at $10.50 per girl) she was fortunately not aware that 1893-94 was to be a year of bank failures and national panic. She only knew that school was in progress, and that somehow she must finish what she and her husband had started. She submerged herself into the renascence of Christian College.

Not since John Augustus Williams had there been such innovations. By the end of the first year she had launched a college magazine, organized an active alumnae association and installed electric lights. She had doubled the faculty and done away with the old public examinations. She had added a kindergarten, a college orchestra, a branch of the new YWCA movement, and an Elizabeth Barrett Browning Society to compete with the exclusive Martha Washington. And she had discarded the bonnet for "a becoming hat."

These three little words in the catalog stood for a drastic metamorphosis in student appearance while the new president sought the perfect substitute for those "back-country" uniforms. By the end of the first school year she had found it: the academic cap and gown. This doleful black woolen costume currently used at Smith and Vassar was to become a familiar sight on the streets of Columbia. Whether or not the college girls agreed that the three-cornered mortar board with two dangling tassels gave "a certain intellectual expression

Luella St. Clair Moss
1893–1897
1899–1903
1909–1920

"The Line" on the way to church

"A New Look" in college girls

Del Sarte group

ank P. St. Clair, 1893

Mrs. W. T. Moore, 1897–1909

vy Chain, 1903

The Auditorium

Rogers Gateway

uella St. Clair Hall

Chapel window

Mermaids of 1919 open new pool

Gymnasium Class, 1903

Beyond the elm — no man's land

Left: W. T. Moore and Journalism Class, 1902

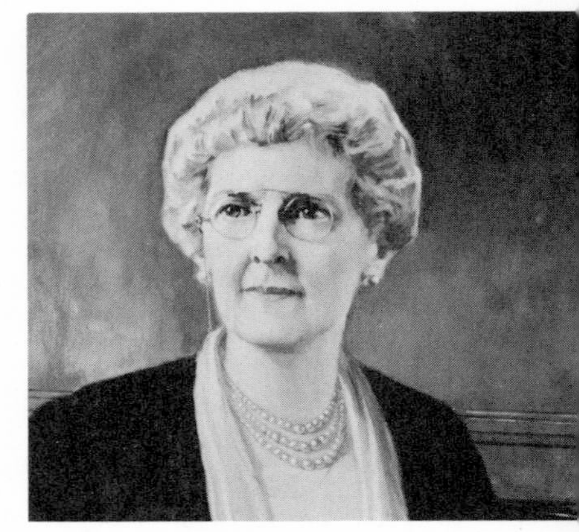

Mrs. Marion W. Hertig saw to it that . . .

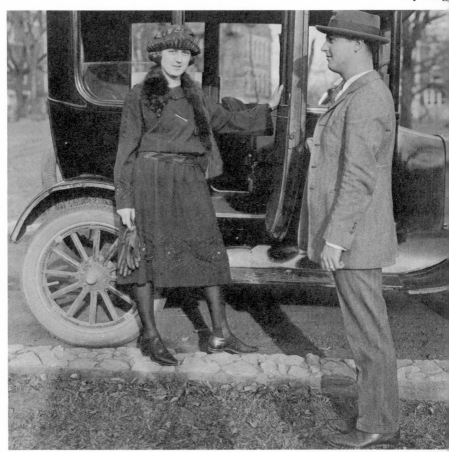

boy met g

to the face," they soon found that it was not necessary to wear all the customary petticoats under the voluminous folds. And the huge sleeves, held at an angle as one passed young men on the way to church, were convenient for receiving notes.

The rewritten catalog of 1894 in format alone reveals the changes in Christian College. After forty-two years the catalog has been reshaped into an oblong booklet, 5½x8½, with actual photographs. These first real views of the College record the chapel with one hanging lantern and childish desks, the original "study" with a closeup of the new golden oak and the brussels carpet, The Old Elm with its huge protruding roots, the front campus—a pasture of tall grass with a horse grazing. A dining room scene shows the vaunted electric lights dangling from cords and covered with crocheted shades; napkins arranged fanlike in a glass. A typical bedroom has lace curtains, tall window-plants in cans, turkey feathers in a wall holder, and a standing easel supporting the painting of a plump cherub. "Christian College Avenue" turns out to be a country lane with picket fences. A picture of the fine stone Christian Church under construction is also included.

The woman's touch is everywhere in the catalog. Plain Mrs. Lizzie Soule is now listed as Mrs. Elise Soule; china-painting has come into the curriculum along with mandolin playing; from now on each girl will be required to bring to college her own monogrammed silver napkin ring.

Under "Discipline" are those same admonitions set down by President Rogers, but everything is more mildly expressed. Though "the penalty of a clandestine correspondence is dismissal," the old rule about all communication with young gentlemen being forbidden is tactfully omitted. The stress placed on daily attendance at morning chapel by both teachers and students suggests that this rule was becoming difficult to enforce. And for almost the first time in a catalog there is some light shed on the feelings of the faculty: "Such duties as escorting young ladies on walking expeditions, keeping study hall, etc., are common burdens, and every teacher must bear an equal share."

From an historical standpoint, the monthly *Christian Col-*

lege Chronicle was among the most important of President St. Clair's innovations. Inaugurated as a magazine in which students might perfect their composition, it recorded more and more of college life as its volumes continued. Interspersed between conventional essays and such tidbits of filler as "For fifty years no smoker has graduated from Harvard with the honors of his class," are glimpses of campus life at the turn of the century. The M.S.U. boys serenade with a selection called "Galilee." "Professor Pannell's genial countenance is occasionally seen in chapel. . . ." (Evidently the good professor had not reformed much since the days when President Rogers prayed over his non-attendance.) "The hygienic slop jar for the first time in the history of Christian College finds a place in the students' rooms." The Del Sarte pupils entertain the public with "tableaux vivants." The president of Missouri University shows stereopticon slides on "The Amusements of the Romans." The ladies of the Christian Church send chocolate cake for dessert.

The schoolgirl's calendar included "merry wagonnette parties" in the fall to gather leaves, bobsledding in the winter, and in the spring "the same Uncle Charley who cleaned the campus in mother's day, heaping the leaves into piles and clearing the garden for another year's service. This task is followed according to annual custom by the black man with the whitewash which he splatters on fences and posts."[1]

The *Chronicle* shows much concern with the status of women: Miss Rockefeller is learning to type; a certain authoress reads her stories in public; another has gotten a divorce. "Can College Girls Stand the Emotional Strain of Going to Matinees?" asks an editorial, hotly debating Dr. Richard Dewey's verdict that such entertainments are too hard on the feminine nervous system. A journalism class visiting the plant of the *Columbia Herald* is photographed as "new women in search of a new sphere."

But the most significant interpolations in the *Chronicle* are promotional: "Pres. Harper received $175,000 from John D. Rockefeller as a New Year's present to the University of Chicago." "Robert M. Stockton of St. Louis has donated a beautiful gold medal" to Christian College. Letters from prominent alumnae are printed. Little acorns, which the college-president-editor of the *Chronicle* already saw as great oaks. Great buildings from gold medals grow. It was no accident that a decade later Mr. Stockton was to be the donor of Christian's academic building.

These were little womanly touches, but the touches of one particular little woman. Not the sweetly sentimental widow who looked at the world with candid blue eyes under frizzled blonde bangs. Rather, an aggressive courageous spirit, a champion of women's rights, a planner with vision, a fighter determined to win. Trustees Bright or Dorsey, had they read the first years of the *Chronicle,* could have forseen some of what was in store for Christian College.

In between promoting the College and balancing its books this remarkable woman-president found time to be herself. Rapidly she took her place in Columbia society, reading her paper at the literary salon of the day, Miss Emma Willis' elegant home, *Le Refuge.* To the schoolgirls who admired the swish of her moire train as she swept to the table, she was lovely. And though the College without a Papa began to lose some of its family aspect, she drew her pupils very close as she read to them in the library at night under the dim portraits, or sat sewing with them in the newly formed "Dorcas Club."

Her lonely moments she kept to herself and though outwardly independent, she had her secret crutches. The smallest and strongest of these was her daughter, Annilee. The very sight of this sunny child so dignified in her miniature cap and gown, practicing her "piece" for the Cannie Russell Society, provided her mother with the lift that meant going on to another day. And whether or not the novice President could have turned in a successful financial report that depression year without the sound advice of her father is a question.

Seymour Borden Wilcox was a New Yorker by birth but had gone into the shipping business in St. Louis during that city's early river traffic days. Removed to Illinois before the War—in which he was a southern sympathizer—he had prospered in real estate. Now bringing to his daughter his long practical experience, he advised her sagely, and she leaned on him as her closest confidant and friend.

The faculty was an additional support. Enlarged from nine to sixteen it was the strongest in years, and the first to have its qualifications well publicized. Apparently at least ten of the sixteen had college or conservatory degrees. The two M.A's on the faculty were, as usual, the science professor, William Buckner, and the teacher of philosophy and religion, W. S. St. Clair. Will St. Clair, who had come to Columbia with his brother, Frank, was so affable that when anything needed to be attended to it became a college slogan to say "Professor St. Clair will do it for you." He later became Mayor of Columbia. His wife, Louise, taught piano. A cosmopolitan flavor was added to the group with the engagement of two Canadians: Agnes Hull Simpson, who taught Elocution, and Lucille Dora. "Miss Cute" Dora, as the girls called her privately, was to add spice with certain eccentricities, and the chatty columns she contributed to the *Chronicle*. Mrs. Soule, recently returned from art study in Baltimore, Anna Heuermann, musician and teacher of German, and blunt British retainer, Professor Pannell, also lent color. Then there was the usual sprinkling of former graduates, local talent, and University products. It is true that only half the faculty taught arts and science courses and that the curriculum was leaning rather heavily towards the fine arts.

This tendency was perhaps unconscious, for in her first Commencement address the young President pleaded for substance rather than shadow in female education and referred to Christian College as "a Vassar in this garden spot of the West." The papers described her and her speech with superlatives. ("She is undoubtedly the ablest president the college has ever had," said the Kansas City *Times*.[2]) Modesty did not prevent Luella, as managing editor, from reprinting such statements in the *Chronicle,* for she knew the value of advertising. As she handed the girls of her first graduating class their diplomas, she confessed that she would never feel quite the same about any others as she did towards the class of 1894. That night she breathed a little prayer of relief and for once tried not to think. Not back into the irretrievable past, nor ahead into the future, and the long hot summer to be spent in storming Missouri for students. . . .

The second year was a settling down. As always, after the ending of uncertainty brought on by a change in administration, enrollment started to rise. Professor Buckner, a strong right arm of the faculty, had also spent the summer in recruiting. Mrs. St. Clair now took over the bookkeeping, in her father's winter absence, and was proving herself not only competent but astute. In the mid-Victorian study where J. K. Rogers had filled ledgers with his methodical entries, she wrote away on hers. But often she would put down her pen, her head full of schemes. Driven by the same necessity of keeping the school alive, she was to be a more daring financier; more concerned with raising money than keeping it. She was never to have his respect for books that balanced.

Life was just becoming normal when the second tragedy struck. Almost before Luella could reach him, her father died in New Orleans. The shock was severe, for its ebbing left the knowledge that now she was indeed on her own. Work was the answer. More work, more worry, more plans. More speeches to church gatherings, more papers at ladies' clubs, more addresses before the State Board of Education. These early speeches were illuminating guides to their author. A bit schoolgirlish, ornamented with "thees" and "thous" in the fashion of the day, they were nevertheless clearly outlined, logical, documented with scholarship, and climaxed with a certain emotional impact. There was no redundance, covering up fuzzy thinking. The author seemed to know in writing, as in life, exactly where she intended to go.

More traveling became necessary, more conferences, more burning of midnight oil. It was imperative to be seen everywhere, to know everyone, always to be at the right place at the right time. When visiting dignitaries came to Columbia—whether the earnest ladies of the W.C.T.U. or the gentlemen of the Missouri Press Association—it was important to entertain them as lavishly as possible.

It was quite natural, for example, that Mrs. St. Clair should be on hand in January, 1896, to welcome the dean of the new Bible College of Missouri. Fifty leaders of the Disciples of Christ were in Columbia for the reception and dedication, including T. P. Haley, J. H. Garrison, D. O. Smart. University

President Richard H. Jesse was an inaugural speaker. Dr. Jesse, in his expansion program, had fostered this idea of a non-denominational institution for higher religious training as an adjunct to the state university. The dean chosen, Dr. William Thomas Moore, was distinguished as a clergyman, cosmopolite, author, and journalist.

Dr. Moore looked even older than his sixty years, with his flowing white beard and tall thin stature. An American, he came directly from London where for ten years he had been pastor of the West End Tabernacle and editor of *The Christian Commonwealth.* He had been in Columbia before, for in 1872 he had preached the Baccalaureate sermon at Christian College. Emma Frederick Moore, his second wife, was twenty-seven years younger; a stout, handsome woman with a beautiful complexion and a determined, blue-eyed gaze. Obviously accustomed to moving in an international set, she was none the less gracious in her response to the small-talk of this small-town receiving line.

Wellesley, the East, London, editors. . . . Luella St. Clair, with her thirst for culture, was prepared to be impressed. As the eminent doctor held her hand in greeting, she refused to notice a sententious quality in his tone or be taken back by the remarkable length of his beard. She and Mrs. Moore found each other instantly attractive, as if the newcomer had said, "Why, here is a person worth knowing, even in the provinces!" And she, "Here is a woman, like myself, who means to go places." Luella went home strangely stimulated and wrote: "Tonight . . . I met Dr. Moore and his charming, intellectual wife. She is a Wellesley graduate. . . ." It was the first sentence in a new chapter of her life.

If all her diplomatic activities were important to the welfare of the College, they were also supremely exhausting. Always in the shadow of the brilliant Mrs. St. Clair who was rapidly becoming so well-known in the state and "the brotherhood" walked Luella Wilcox, the conscientious schoolteacher. Always there were the onerous duties of the chapel, the classroom, the girls to discipline and soothe and inspire. Culture and character-building, President St. Clair took with equal seriousness. She truly loved poetry and music and sought to make both a part of the nature of her pupils. She was ambitious to enlarge the music curriculum. With her talent for putting ideas into acts, she managed to secure the gift of a $1000 grand piano for the student winning a graduation competition. This contest-recital, held each June in the Hadyn Opera House, was to become one of the thrills of remembered school life.

She was the first president since the stormy days of Williams, Shannon, and Caleb Stone, to be concerned actively with politics. Like any good teacher, she communicated her excitement to the girls, who campaigned violently on the campus, wore buttons for Bryan, and made speeches on free silver or woman's rights. On this subject she was passionate. Her concept of woman's place was almost as heretical to some of her contemporaries in 1896 as it would have been to John Augustus Williams. For years she told her girls that on the day women got suffrage they could have an all-school holiday. "Club women" was a new phrase she began to use.

She threw herself into life as only a woman can. She put on an armor of optimism. The cracks in the college walls, the paint already peeling, the debts falling due, the needed sidewalk and the predicted droughts—beat upon her optimism and fell back. She forced herself to look ahead, always into next year, to bigger enrollments, more tuitions, new buildings. The more she drove herself the more the tensions mounted. Still she controlled the sweetness of her voice, although a tight line sometimes showed around her mouth, and a ridge across her forehead. It was only when she looked at her daughter that she knew why the game was worth the candle. Sometimes a feeling of aloneness swept over her and she longed to gain relief by pouring her troubles on Annilee's nine-year old head. It had been so long since she had had someone to lean on! It was the yearning for companionship which attached her so completely to Mrs. Moore, for since their first meeting the two had become almost inseparable.

The Moores lived just three doors away, in Jerry Dorsey's old home on Christian College Avenue. It was pleasant to stop there for a daily chat, to unburden oneself of college cares to one not connected with the school, to ease some of the strain of those swift days racing towards graduation. It was a test year to Luella. The "big class of '96" was to be the largest graduated since the beginning. Patronage was definitely allying itself behind her as president. The fiscal report which she must hand to the Board that July was, for the first time in the panicky nineties, encouraging. As soon as Commencement was over, she promised herself, she would get to work on plans for expansion. She set a deadline: the fiftieth anniversary, 1901. In her mind the word JUBILEE began to take shape in large, golden letters.

Meanwhile she was weary, and there was no rest from the long hours of being her own bookkeeper. As she grew more frail, the little President found strength in the heartiness of her friend. Sometimes Mrs. Moore would come over and help her in the office. Increasingly Luella deferred to the advice of the other, who had once managed a school for girls in New York City.

It was in November, 1896, four years to the month after death struck Frank St. Clair that it reached for his widow. A severe case of *La Grippe* became double pneumonia. There being no hospital in Columbia, the doctor summoned a trained nurse from St. Louis. It was Mrs. Moore who took charge of Annilee and Mrs. Moore who took over the duties of the president's office. In the crisis when the nurse called to the doctor that his patient was dying, Luella herself heard and became vaguely aware of the struggle. It was remembering Annilee that brought her through. But her nerves were shattered. Convalescence was slow and she seemed unable to drive herself any longer. Even before the physician told her, she knew her choice. Either she must take a year's complete rest or face the fact that she might never be able to work again.

March 8, 1897, she turned in her resignation, to be effective July 1st. Her note to the trustees contained a postscript.

> This resignation . . . is conditioned upon the acceptance by the Board of Mrs. W. T. Moore as my successor in office, elected in the usual way and for the usual term of lease. . . .

Upon reading this Messrs. Lenoir, Hurt, Kirtley and Dorsey, officers of the Board, looked at each other with some doubt. But there was no dissension in the trustees' feelings toward the outgoing president. In the most complimentary vein they had ever attempted, they expressed appreciation of "the brilliant gifts, earnest labors, wise management, and almost unparalleled energy which has characterized her administration. . . ."

If the furniture Mrs. Moore had brought from England seemed too small for the parlors of the old building, Dr. Moore's 5000 books more than filled the shelves of the study. The catalog publicized his as "one of the finest private libraries to be found anywhere." The new administration opened without incident, except for the student who fell out of the second-story window while her mother was unpacking.

Long letters came from Luella from Italy, France, England, as she toured the galleries with her sister, Maxine Miller. By winter she had rejoined Annilee in New Orleans and was enrolled in Tulane University. She wrote of taking walks in Audubon Park, of growing much stronger and thinking daily of her old tasks at Christian College.

Letters went from Mrs. Moore. Dr. Lenoir had resigned from the Board, and Mr. Dorsey as treasurer. Enrollment was down. The dormitory wings were in such bad condition as to be dangerous and water was standing in the cellar. The trustees simply must find a way to finance a new building. It would be pleasant to talk it all over with her. Why didn't she bring Annilee back for school and spend the next fall on the campus? There were also letters from members of the Board. It was as "financial secretary" that Luella St. Clair returned to Christian College in the fall of 1898. The arrangements were for her to visit the Christian churches of the state in an attempt to raise $50,000. Meanwhile the Board voted to borrow $15,000 and start building.

The two women went deep into plans for a greater Christian College. They conceived an Elizabethan building of pressed brick and white Bedford stone, with a round arched entrance. It would have administration offices, parlors, library, art, and kindergarten facilities, a dining room, and three floors of dormitory rooms *en suite,* with baths at the end of each hall. They chose a woman architect, Mary Hale, and contractors who understood the urgency of a deadline. Building commenced in March, 1899. It had to be ready for occupancy by September.

It was soon apparent that there was no money to pay for it. Of the $15,000 borrowed, nine represented old debts. To initial contributions of $5000 each from Mrs. St. Clair and Mrs. Moore the churches had added nothing but their good wishes. For at least the third time disaster faced the College. But the sums needed were too great, now, to be supplied by a Dr. Lenoir reaching in his office vault.

The solution came in the form of two startling facts: In April, 1899, the Board announced the election of Mrs. St. Clair as co-president of the College. On May 9, there was recorded in the Boone County courthouse a deed of sale made out to Mrs. W. T. Moore and Mrs. Luella St. Clair for "that portion of land . . . known as Christian College." The terms were those proposed either by the ladies to the Board, or by the Board to the ladies. (Later accounts differed.)

> We propose to assume all indebtedness of your corporation amounting to . . . $9,500 . . . and within one year from this date to expend . . . at least $15,000 in the erection of new buildings. . . . As soon as we shall have complied with the foregoing conditions the Board of Trustees are to convey to us the present college grounds.[3]

The co-presidents further agreed, and posted $5000 bond as warranty, "to continue personally or by our agents the management and operation of the school . . . for a period of at least ten years" and to give the trustees option whenever they should decide to sell.

The scheme sounded like a conception of Luella St. Clair, who was always willing to plunge and know that the pennies would fall from Heaven. It initiated years of finance typically feminine in its involvements. The word "sale" was not publicized but in an official statement the trustees eulogized the "two noble women" who had "taken over" the obligations of the College. It was, they emphasized, only a relief measure to finance improvements until the trustees or "some larger body of the Christian Church" could redeem the school. It was hinted that the church would prove itself a wise investor to buy Christian College which meanwhile would continue on the same lines inaugurated by "its wise and beneficent founders." These gentlemen were probably squirming in their graves, for the charter had specified that Christian College should be the property of its corporate body of trustees or their successors "in perpetual succession."

The present trustees, having violated the spirit of their charter, became punctilious about its wording. They sidestepped the clause that "no debts must be contracted on the property" by securing an amendment from the Legislature. A year later, in a blunt recollection to the Board, Mrs. Moore was to describe the sale transaction differently: The Board "all knew," she said, "that the placing of the College property in the name of Mrs. Moore and Mrs. St. Clair was considered by all concerned as a matter of expediency for the securing of a loan to assure the completion of the present new building."[4] (Is there a small private college whose administrators have not faced the choice between bankruptcy and expediency?)

All of this finagling was *sub rosa,* a sort of undercurrent to the busy hammering of the workmen. Workmen were all over the place, sometimes a hundred at a time. That summer of 1899 the old elms and oaks were shaken out of their holiday quiet. As the west wing of the old dormitory was pulled down, the north wing of the new structure rose in front of it. This much was ready by September, except for connection with the heating plant. The ever-increasing student body was stowed away in the new wing and the part of the old building still standing.

"Of course the inevitable trial of our strength and patience came," wrote Luella years afterwards.

> With the delayed shipment of radiators for our new hall a severe cold spell in September caused a telegram to be sent to Chicago to ship by express fifty oil stoves to Christian College. They were to relieve the discomfort of the shivering girls. The students were at liberty to replenish the big lamps of their stoves. We used more than a barrel of oil a day. With oil impartially spilled along the line of march of the vestal virgins, even upon the temporary wooden steps of the new building and the hallways, only a protecting providence (He would

> have had little help from our town fire department) could have prevented the starting of a disastrous fire.
>
> However, we survived that hazard and others. The noise of the building operations might jar upon the harmonies of a sonata in the Music Hall, or the reading of a sonnet by a teacher of English; students might be cold, uncomfortable, or in crowded quarters, but everybody was happy. Hope was in the air. Growth was in progress. . . .[5]

Daily she would stand as the girls came from class and command each one to carry a brick. Thus the work sped, and the Christmas holidays saw the building complete and occupied.

No one took a livelier part in this triumph than Annilee. Almost twelve now, she was a frail child who had suffered two serious attacks of inflammatory rheumatism. But her steps were swift and her hands eager as she dashed back and forth, carrying their possessions to the suite on the first floor of the new hall. She sniffed the clean painty smell as she hung her mother's dresses in the closet. She begged to fold away the linen handkerchiefs and the kid gloves. With a grown-up preoccupation, she frowned as she tried her small desk first one place, then another. The first night in their new home she was too excited to be tired.

"Oh, Mother," she said, "Isn't it wonderful that we have the new building you've prayed for!"

But the holiday joy was short. The Christmas ornaments had just been packed away when the third rheumatic attack came, more cruel than ever before. By the 5th of January a small coffin lay in state in the parlor of St. Clair Hall. The last service was held there. In town, the stores closed for one hour.

The little campus was devastated. The dazed mother went ahead with long-scheduled plans which suddenly seemed not to matter. She had fulfilled the terms of the contract. This fine three-story building with its frontage of 229 feet, a building "unequaled by any school for women in the southwest," according to the catalog, was legally half hers. She would have given weeks of the money-raising that went into it for one more hour with Annilee. The dedication of "St. Clair

Hall" was for her an agony. Named for her husband, it would ultimately come to be regarded as honoring herself. Actually, to her it always meant Annilee. Later she found relief, in her own fashion, by writing in verse, "The Little Girl's Gone Away."[6]

This time she allowed herself no respite but submerged her grief into work. In answer to the Whys that would come she gradually evolved a conviction: what she could no longer do for one girl she must do for many others. From now on she would live, eat, think only for the College. She dusted off her dream of a Jubilee—a great, semi-centennial celebration. She and Mrs. Moore went to work on plans for a new chapel building.

But the fiftieth anniversary was too near. The best they could do by May, 1901, was to announce that "before another Commencement" there would be a fine stone chapel adjoining St. Clair Hall on the west. The Golden Jubilee would be postponed until May, 1902, declared the society of alumnae, whose president, Mrs. Camilla Switzler Branham, had been busily sending out letters. Indeed, the new auditorium —"Alumnae Hall"—would be necessary to accommodate the crowd. She suggested as projects, meanwhile, a cathedral window or a pipe organ. Instead of the Jubilee an interesting announcement was made at the fiftieth Commencement.

"It will be remembered," reported the papers,

> that two years ago the trustees of Christian College made over the property to Mrs. Moore and Mrs. St. Clair, on condition that they would erect new buildings. . . . These two women, out of their own private resources, have . . . provided $75,000 in improvements, making the whole property worth, in round numbers, not less than $100,000. They have now re-deeded this splendid property back to the trustees to be held in trust by them for educational purposes, for all time.[7]

According to the *Chronicle,* when Elder Winders made the announcement "the walls of the old church rang . . . as the multitude came to realize the Christian grandeur and importance of this munificent gift to C. C."

Privately, there were other motives for this reconveyance. Did the two donors foresee an instance where private ownership would be a barrier? Were they recalling the advantages of having more shoulders to carry future debts? Or was even "this splendid property," as of old, a "hot potato" which no one wanted to hold for long? Too, there were strings attached to the gift. The deed stipulated that W. A. Bright, party of the second part, was to hold the property in trust for the two women during their lifetime, only upon their death conveying it to the third party—the board of trustees.

The summer of 1901 was a never-to-be-forgotten drought. The ground parched day after day under a pitiless sun. There were no crops. The two women worked hard, and Luella traveled in the interests of the College. That fall, to her frank astonishment, school opened with a full enrollment. She had devised a bond-selling scheme for raising the $25,000 goal. William H. Dulany, of Hannibal, Missouri, purchased the first $5000 scholarship bond by which "one worthy, white . . . girl" would be educated each year. Rowena Dozier Mason bought an annuity bond establishing a scholarship after the death of the donor. Other donors were Benjamin F. Lowry, Frank Coop of Southport, England (a relative of the Moores), Mary W. Campbell Haley and Amanda C. Graves. The three women were Christian College alumnae. A committee headed by David Anderson Robnett solicited funds in Columbia and elsewhere.

Although there was no stone chapel by Commencement, 1902, the money was subscribed and building had begun. In the *Chonicle,* Mrs. St. Clair hopefully proposed that "a great alumnae reunion" be planned for 1903 co-incidental with the proposed St. Louis World's Fair.

As she confessed later, "A building always costs more than the most generous estimate." The new plans included a gymnasium, enlarged art department and library, besides the auditorium seating one thousand. (This was advertised as "the handsomest room of its kind connected with any school for women in the United States.") Topping this was a feminine innovation: a roof-garden "built like the deck of a steamboat" with a system of awnings to provide shade and "growing plants, chairs, settees and hammocks to invite students to open air life."[8]

It was a long way to the roof, however. Maurice Wightman, who was reared on campus, can point out where one shade of brick ends and another begins as work on the auditorium would halt for lack of funds.

"This regeneration of Christian College," wrote the *Statesman,*

> is one of the three most important events in the life of Columbia within thirty years, the other two being the rebuilding of the University and the securing of the railroad. . . . The new college will be the finest of its kind in the west.[9]

The old main building, its wings and third floor removed, was restored to its 1851 exterior except for a covered runway from its second floor to St. Clair Hall. "The Bridge of Sighs," music students called it, as they trudged to one of the thirty-two newly soundproofed practice rooms into which the "mansion" had been divided.

Life was full of "firsts" in the new college at the beginning of the new century. The first telephone was installed in 1899. The first Ivy Chain was formed by the class of 1900.[10] Miss Lucy Laws, the English teacher who had studied under John Augustus Williams at Daughters' College, wrote the oration and supervised the planting of those vines which would cover the walls of St. Clair Hall. For the occasion Dr. W. T. Moore wrote the Ivy Song which is still sung. The class day staff, a polished thorn cane with one gold band for each Commencement, had originated in 1896 and was already a tradition along with the white silk graduation caps and gowns first worn then.

The first Christian girl to become a beauty queen was Allie Locke Morris, selected by the St. Louis *Globe-Democrat* as the second most beautiful woman in the Louisiana Purchase. (She was chosen for her perfect eyes and pompadour.)

"In the annals of history no single year has recorded the triumphs of 1901," claimed an editorial in the *Chronicle:*

> The dirigible balloon, wireless telegraphy, the practical submarine . . . the mile-a-minute automobile . . . the Baldwin-Peary race to the north pole, are the dreams of science realized.

It was the day of the Gibson Girl, the mutton-leg sleeve, lawn tennis, "The Rosary," "A Bicycle Built for Two." As spring of 1903 came on and the auditorium building neared completion, the word "Jubilee" was not mentioned, but a gala dedication was set for June.

The trustees of Christian College were electrified when in April Luella St. Clair informed them she had accepted the presidency of Hamilton College. They drafted a note to the principals which fairly sputtered. Her resignation might jeopardize the building program! How could one partner resign without consulting the trustees? They should be able to choose the new president if there was to be one. It was time to clarify their rights!

The three-page answer they received was a masterly example of the iron-hand-in-the-velvet-glove. They were reminded that, according to their own legal deed, the two women were lifetime owners of the College, bound only to insure its continued operation. Moreover, though the support of the honorable body of trustees had always been invaluable, if any of those trustees felt they could no longer continue under the circumstances, perhaps they could be replaced. . . .

The ten men were no match for two determined women. Tersely they replied that, as far as they were concerned, the incident was closed. It was not the last time they were to regret their mess of pottage.

The auditorium was opened in March, 1903, with an eighty-voice rendition of Gaul's oratorio, "The Holy City." It was to be dedicated at the fifty-second Commencement with a week of events including an operetta, "The Courtship of Miles Standish," Shaw's "Candida," and the graduating class for the first time seated on this stage. But again for Luella St. Clair, success was empty. As she looked out over the opening night audience in full dress and watched the two hundred lights begin to glow, tier on tier, secretly she tasted the bitterness of retreat. It was a magnificence she had created, but was not to enjoy. It was a triumph built on disharmony, disillusionment and a broken friendship.

The first years without her the school ran on gathered momentum. A board resolution called 1904 "the most successful scholastic year in the history of the College." It was a Golden Age for Christian College, as even the students of that decade seemed to realize.

What were they like, these twentieth-century college girls? They arrived at school provided with "a Bible, umbrella, overshoes, laundry bag and all necessary toilet articles." Mary Young McCaskill '08, recalls:

> All new students wore a blue satin ribbon pinned on with CHRISTIAN COLLEGE on it much as an entry at the State Fair. As we traveled from Kansas City to Columbia new and old girls boarded the train at every stop. . . . There was much squealing, laughing and embracing.[11]

Once over the stile, underclassmen were not allowed off campus without a chaperon. "Dressmaking and dentistry must be attended to at home," said the catalog. On one Monday a month (once a week for Seniors) gentlemen callers could spend an hour in St. Clair parlor while Dr. Moore traversed the corridor and glanced in the mirrors which hung strategically at either end.

The parlor did not encourage informality: figured carpeting, baroque radiators, pictures above pictures, sofas placed cat-a-corner and smothered with pillows, three-legged tables covered with a doily and supporting a statuette or fern. Brave was the young man who entered this clutter to deposit his umbrella in the majolica "stand" and himself on one of those weird and wonderful wicker chairs. Yet he did, and because young ladies were granted special permission to see a fiancé, many a girl quickly became engaged. The College was something between a nunnery and a marriage-bureau.

Incoming mail was still inspected. Flowers from gentlemen friends, if delivered at all, were placed in the parlor where the girl was allowed to look at them. The catalog ruled:

> The School has no public telephone, that in the office being . . . for business purposes only.
>
> No lamps, candles, matches or cooking utensils allowed in rooms.
>
> Morning chapel services are an essential part of the college course.

Daily exercise in the Gymnasium is *required* of each student.

For "gym," girls wore navy serge skirts or baggy bloomers, and a middy blouse, and tied their hair back with a large bow at the nape of the neck. Basket ball contests with neighboring high schools and the university girls had taken the place of the "hotly contested" bean-bag games of ten years before, although it was true that the long-awaited gymnasium underneath the auditorium had a roof height more suitable to bean-bags than basketballs. They now had school "yells":

Boom-a-lack! Boom-a-lack!
Bow-wow-wow!
Chick-a-lack! Chick-a-lack!
Chow-chow-chow!
Boom-a-lack! Chick-a-lack!
Who are we?
We're the girls from old *C. C.*

According to season, girls skated or boated in the new lake constructed in 1904 from the pond at the back of the campus. Swimming was advertised but probably not much indulged in; it was more fun to row out to the "island" for picnics, especially with a young male teacher at the oars.

Other picnics, well chaperoned, took the girls along Providence Road to Rollins Springs or on the annual "camp fire." Also with chaperon they could attend church group "rink parties," visit the Farmers' Fair at the University, or watch the traditional arrival of the engineers' Saint Pat. For town concerts, rare visits to the theater in St. Louis, or Sunday night Christian Endeavor, they still wore cap and gown. They even wore cap and gown to the first football game they were allowed to attend, in 1908, and as they marched to their special grandstand the M.U. boys stood at attention.

Football scores were important. "We went down to Broadway to hear the fate of the TIGERS and how heavy hearted were we as we returned to the prison," records the *Chronicle*. Victorious games were often followed by night raids on the campus, which girls were forbidden to watch, since the boys were "en négligé." These night-shirt parades almost replaced serenades as a way to get acquainted. One famous episode involved some University boys trying to drag a cannon up the front steps of St. Clair Hall. Hollows in the stone still mark where it bumped its way down when they were discovered. Another night as the boys pressed close with their torches, calling "Throw down your cards, girls!" genteel Miss Laws heard and misinterpreted the word "cards" as "garters." Her subsequent lectures in chapel amused the girls, who never set her straight.

University "frat men" probably inspired the three secret sororities at Christian. From upstairs windows girls gazed out over "No Man's Land" to the fraternity house across Rogers Street. Or they ostensibly studied their Latin in the hidden seat made by the roots of the big elm tree. (Latin translations might be free, as they changed the college motto "Not to be ministered unto but to minister" to: "Not to be a minister, but a minister's wife.")

Actually, they were getting as near as they dared to "the crack"—that fatal line in the sidewalk formed by the roots of the elm tree which had replaced the tree itself as boundary. Only the Seniors could go beyond, for a timid attempt at self-government in 1904 had resulted in Senior Privileges. Though shopping was frowned upon, they went in groups of four to buy high-buttoned shoes at C. B. Miller's and phosphates at Tilley & Hatton's Drug Store. The drug store was perhaps the source of the forbidden Allegretti chocolates and Beech-nut gum whose wrappers dotted their albums. Harris Café was a popular rendezvous, being in direct route to the University.

But the campus had its simple pleasures. The Hallowe'en party in the gym, an "art feast" in the new studio, formal At Homes and riotous "mock weddings." Dressing like a man was a time-honored amusement and college girls would have their pictures snapped in trousers and derby, one arm around a girl companion. Kodaks were popular accessories. Another favorite pose revealed lifted skirts, black stockings—and legs!

Even schoolwork was not bad, except for the pencil-chewing days in April when Junior and Senior essays were due. Then the new library with its wrought-iron balcony, window-seats and Dewey decimal system was much in use. (This was the large room off the corridor between St. Clair Hall and the auditorium.) It was fun to draw from the plaster cast or bake one's own pottery in the kiln of the art room at the foot of the basement stairs. Oil-painting tended towards canvasses of flowers, pedestals and fountains.

Even home economics was glamorized with the new Department of Domestic Science in the basement. Though sewing had always been encouraged, 1904 was evidently the first year cooking was taught. A student reported to the *Chronicle:*

> The collection of dainty utensils placed side by side in the drawer alloted to each girl, the beautiful range and the handsome dinner set, with sparkling new silver . . . all aided in making our vision of tempting viands—which *we* had prepared . . . real.

The "Cooking Girls" were regarded with respect, as being able to prepare and serve to their principal such a menu as the following:

Caviar on toast
Veal croquettes
Saratoga chips — Cream cauliflower
French peas — Olives
Biscuits — Chocolate
Shrimp salad
Pistachio cream — Cake

Food was a tremendous concern. At the cry "The apple man is here!" girls would come running across the campus carrying a shoe-box. Crackers, apples, and ginger snaps were hoarded snacks, while ham sandwiches, chocolate cake and fudge made a party.

Happy memories were the "Annie Fisher Feasts," recalled Mary Young McCaskill:

> Annie was a colored cook who delivered in her ramshackle buggy, the most delicious chicken salad, beaten biscuits, maplenut ice cream and many other delicacies dear to the heart of a college girl. These were enjoyed by the gang often by candle light.

Aside from rising bell at 6:15, even the routine was fun. The rigid inspection of "the line" when the queer angles of mortar-boards would bring to light crumpled paper wads, handkerchiefs, "rats"—astounding devices to keep the pompadour from being crushed. Those two high spots of the day—luncheon and dinner—when mail was distributed from a basket: the suspense of the carrier's approach; the thrill of a letter by your plate.

Monday morning was cleaning day, when students in dust-caps exchanged brooms and shook out rugs and no one could walk through the halls in safety because of the boxes. The girls were proud of their suites: the sitting room with desk, dresser, pillows, pennants; the bedroom with washstand, table, photos and books, and two iron beds. These "downy cots" were supposed to be occupied by 10 P.M. But after lights the real fun began. Out of the closet came the chafing dish, and an umbrella to be held over the transom so that no glow would escape. A bit of butter, stolen from the table, was as indispensable to Christian College fudge as the smothered giggles. "Cook over a candle until you are sure there is a teacher at the door. Then hastily fling the whole apparatus in the closet with five or six girls."

There is another recipe, for KISSES:

> To one piece of dark piazza add a little moonlight, take for granted two people, press in two strong hands, one soft one. Sift slightly two ounces of attraction, one of romance, add a large measure of folly, stir in a floating ruffle and add one or two whispers. Dissolve a half dozen glances in a well of silence, dust in a small quantity of hesitation, one ounce of resistance, two of yielding. Place the kisses on a flushed cheek or two cherry lips and set aside to cool. Warranted to succeed in any climate.[12]

These souvenirs in albums recorded an exuberance which existed perhaps in spite of Mrs. Moore. Some girls complained that "she had eyes in the back of her head." They were sure that she opened their mail and read their memory books. She would go down the line, they vowed, looking for caps at a rakish angle, and jerking them roughly into place—point exactly above nose—with little regard for the huge hatpins. They remembered her sitting in her office, "number five," watching down the walk for approaching offenders. The miscreant who was called on the carpet there remembered how her eyes protruded as she scolded.

Other girls, perhaps less mischievous, recalled her as jolly and sympathetic. They thought of Dr. Moore as a pious oldster who devoted class time in "Bible" to lecturing on the dangers of attachments with young men. One Columbian, caught on campus in a youthful escapade, was led to the study where Dr. Moore made him kneel as they read the Bible and prayed.

Dr. Moore would invite the girls into his library to chat, giving them candy, though the rules forbad sweets oftener than once a month. Here met the sixteen pioneers of his Journalism course and pecked furiously on the tall typewriter, putting out "The Rag-time Gazette." According to Hearst's *Chicago American,* in the spring of 1902 journalism was:

> a radical departure from the courses of study heretofore pursued in female colleges. . . . Christian College is the only school in the United States that has now in practical operation such a department. . . . The only two schools in the U. S. that claim to teach journalism confine their work almost entirely to the correspondence method.[13]

Perhaps it was Dr. Moore who was responsible for the school's first national publicity. The January, 1903, *Ladies' Home Journal* had a survey asking college girls all over the country whether they would prefer to be men or women. Christian College was the only school in the mid-west asked to participate, and the answers of the girls drew much comment.

There was no doubt but what Dr. and Mrs. Moore had important contacts and the *savoir faire* to pursue them. Mrs. Moore secured a gift from Miss Grace Dodge of New York, a prominent early welfare-worker with whom she had once been associated. She went to see Andrew Carnegie, who agreed to give the College $25,000 if the trustees would raise an equal sum and pay the existing debt. But the Board was cool to her suggestions. The improvements of her administration continued to be the necessities: a deep well, with water tower and tank, a brick addition to the power house with a new dynamo for increased lighting facilities, a new stable, fences, granitoid walks, a washing machine and mangle in the laundry.

Of the fifty-seven teachers Mrs. Moore hired, thirteen had a background of advanced training in Europe. These were nearly all teachers of music (with whom her staff was overbalanced). Professor G. L. H. Buddeus was the most distinguished of these. A graduate of the Royal Conservatory at Leipzig, he had studied and taught abroad for eight years and had toured Europe as a concert pianist. Another had been soloist with the Chicago Symphony Orchestra. Unusual faculty for a small school in a small mid-western town, they served to increase the musical reputation of Christian College.

As the fine arts increased, the academic emphasis had decreased, notable science teachers for the first time being lacking. Languages dominated what academic courses remained. The new Department of Domestic Science was well-staffed and there was a rather unpopular teacher of "Gymnastics," Miss Florence Heath.

Almost no southern influence remained under Mrs. Moore unless one counts the graduates of Missouri University who were usually recruited for history, languages, and the preparatory school. These were out-numbered by easterners from Massachusetts, New York, Philadelphia, Ohio, and Michigan, with several graduates of the University of Chicago. But few of them stayed long enough to affect Christian College. Only Miss Laws and the beloved Miss Cauthorn, Professor Buddeus, and Mrs. Moore's niece, Mrs. J. M. Frederick, who acted as secretary to the college and ran the business office.

If there was marked faculty turnover there was also internal unrest. There seemed to be continuous trouble with the servants, some of which reached the newspapers and the court. And under the rigid discipline there was an uncommon amount of mischief brewing. It exploded in 1908 after a Missouri football victory over Texas:

> Excitement ran high, and the boys wanted to celebrate that night. They asked . . . to bring fireworks into the grounds and invited us to join them in the fun. Mrs. Moore . . . refused. This kindled resentment, so they

> came, 300 strong, and entered the dormitory by . . . fire escapes, then marched lockstep throughout the building.
>
> The student body and teachers were in the gymnasium having a taffy-pull in fancy dress. Needless to say, we were in a rebellious state of mind and it took considerable quieting to handle us.
>
> When the noise ceased and we were allowed to go to our rooms, nearly every girl discovered some object missing—carried off as trophies.[14]

(These objects were mostly undergarments, for the student laundry had just been distributed. The more daring raiders carried these to church the next day and tried to identify the girls by their name-tapes!) The boys stormed the kitchen, where the cook was still making taffy. As they reached for the candy, the cook poured boiling taffy over their hands, burning some badly. When Mrs. Moore, furious over the break-in, went to the University and threatened to prefer charges, the administration replied that they would countersue for the boys having been burned. The whole affair was dropped, but it explained a trend. For two years girls had been withdrawing from Christian College.

Meanwhile, Luella St. Clair's term in Kentucky had lengthened into six years. She had re-established the old seminary as a two-year college affiliated with Kentucky University (as Transylvania was then called). She had doubled enrollment, purchased new real estate, improved old buildings. The news came back to Missouri through many channels. In return, she got disturbing reports. Her sister, Maxine Miller, wrote of bills unpaid, creditors hounding. Then, after the fracas of 1908 almost one-third of the student body withdrew. Fate, in the form of severe arthritis, prevented a further denouement. "Mrs. Moore, who was now a chronic invalid and who had put practically all of her money into the college for the last ten years, was granted a yearly annuity by the trustees," according to official statement.[15] She resigned. An urgent request was sent to Luella St. Clair.

In June, 1909, she returned to Columbia and for the third time was elected president of Christian College. This time her old friend, Mr. Jerry Dorsey, was not at the station to meet her when she stepped down, the same frail, "spirituelle" little figure under a becoming hat. But was she quite the same? Drought, disappointment, money-raising, were old stories to her now. She had the techniques for dealing with them. Had she also, when occasion called for it, a certain stubbornness? People had not remembered that under her mild, round eyes, her jaw was so firm.

Her return, as her first contact with Christian College, brought innovations. From this date the *Minutes* of the Board in the big ledgers were typewritten. The first college annual appeared in 1910. "The College Widow," named by humorist George Ade, replaced the defunct *Chronicle* as the best record of student life. In it we see the students for the first time as individual faces. And we read of further innovations: State clubs, the Dramatic club (Mary Arden), baseball, horseback riding, a Junior Prom (still without men), an Honor Roll, an Athletic Association. The class day staff is now filled with gold rings, and succeeded by a gavel. The annual class gift is inaugurated. Christian College now has a hymn—"When far from the reach of thy sheltering arms . . . ," written by Louise Darneal '09. The valedictorian no longer reads her essay, but delivers an oration. Sunday morning is still the time when girls are most apt to fall sick, a university "cousin" is still convenient, but now girls are sneaking into afternoon movies and irreverently referring to their three-cornered caps as "peanuts."

The President's return and 1910 also brought the first reference to Christian as a "junior college." This was a concept she had already used at Hamilton. It was a new title in the academic world, introduced just before 1900 by President William Rainey Harper of Chicago as he surveyed the breach between the first and second two years of university training. To American education, trying to find itself, were posed three questions:[16] (1) "Shall the . . . University have its legs cut off," — consist of only the last two years of specialized training? (2) "Shall the four year high school be stretched?" (3) "Shall certain American colleges have their heads cut off?" Actually, all of these things were happening in the United States. Christian College, like most denominational schools which had commenced with a liberal-arts plan and now found it difficult to keep honest four-year standards, fell into the third category. However, it is possible that Luella St. Clair overlooked some of the philosophy and rather seized on the idea of something new when she first used the term at Christian in the catalog of 1910.

So far, it was a name only, for educational requirements seem to have been changed little from President Oldham's curriculum revision of 1889. Mrs. Moore had dropped Kindergarten and primary school in 1907. The complete course at Christian College was still regarded as requiring four to six years, but now Freshmen and Sophomore classes were frankly listed under "Academic" (high school), with Junior and Senior classes under "junior college." The B.L. was still given upon completion of the junior college literary course. The degree B.M. was given in music, with at least four year's work prerequisite to graduation. In addition, there were post-graduate courses in music, art, and oratory—all granting diplomas! Boarding students might range from age twelve to twenty-one and even a few men were enrolled as day pupils in languages, elocution, or music. Academically, it was a hodge-podge, but the President was interested in the academic now chiefly as it related to her main theme: expansion.

Immediately upon her return she had written to Andrew Carnegie and found that his offer was still good. He would contribute $25,000 if the trustees could equal that amount in an endowment fund and clear the existing debt of $10,000. This was the sum remaining from the original $43,000 incurred by the two women when they started their building program in 1899.

Under her leadership the Board felt confident. In only three months—by the fall of 1909—they were able to record the statement that once more Christian College was free from debt. The necessary $25,000 endowment was the gift of one trustee, Robert M. Stockton, on condition that the building be a memorial to another, Jeremiah Spires Dorsey.[17]

Plans were drawn for the new academic building, directly in front of the chapel of Oldham's day. It was to be three stories, brick and stone, 122x92, connected by a covered "loggia" with the east administration wing of St. Clair Hall.

Eleven classrooms were included, chemistry and physics laboratories, an office and a YWCA cabinet room. "A splendid gymnasium 90 feet by 42 with running track and full modern equipment" was designed on the north, and above it a large study hall connected with sliding partitions to a Gothic chapel seating four hundred. (That sloping track along the gallery of the gymnasium was to become a curiosity in later days.)

But there was one legal slip between the cup and the lip: the question of ownership. The Carnegie grant was available only if the College were owned by its trustees. In April, 1910, Luella St. Clair signed a quit claim against "the property known as Christian Female College." The trustees agreed to purchase her half-interest with yearly payments equal to the annuity paid Mrs. Moore. Thus, at a price, they went about buying back their birthright. Old Elder Allen could rest easier in his grave.

As Dorsey Hall began to rise, Luella picked up the other thread her exodus had dropped—the Golden Jubilee. It would have to celebrate the sixtieth anniversary now. Feverishly she put those around her to work communicating with all known graduates. Their names and addresses (879 living and dead) were published in an alumnae directory. Marion Hertig, the new English teacher who seemed to appreciate the occasion, wrote letters to former valedictorians, asking them to speak, to winners of the piano contests, asking them to play. Jubilee gifts were announced: $400 for the library, oil portraits of the presidents and their wives for the halls. A solid week of events to precede Commencement included the dedication of Dorsey Hall, unveiling of the chapel window, an alumnae banquet at the Columbia Hall. The conductor on the M-K-T "Katy Flier—the fast train to Columbia," dusted off the green pullman seats in anticipation of unusual business. On May 23, 1911, when three generations of alumnae met under the broken branches of the old Elm, Luella knew that the Jubilee was at last a fact.

The President's lawn-party that evening was a brilliant success. (Japanese lanterns, orchestra in the background, perfect weather for the 500 guests.) But it was only a prelude to the sentimental reunion of the next morning. Some of the audience that crowded the new chapel then could remember back to the early days of Columbia and the Victorian age of women. Elizabeth Cooper Pollard '54, the oldest alumna present, thought of that second graduating class. How handsome and intense President Williams had been, and how solemn when he gave them their Bibles! This vaulted hall, where the two-room cabin had stood, was as foreign to her picture of Christian College as its woman president would have been to Williams.

Jennie Robards Rogers, of the same class, was thinking of a later president whose portrait now stood ready to unveil—the stern but gentle man who was her husband; and of a little old building, in the background now, which they had once struggled so desperately to keep open. Other Jubilee visitors may have been in the audience that morning: Henrietta Pearre Wilkes, the "Miss Nettie" of broomstick fame; former President Bryant. And perhaps because there was so much of the past, there was an unseen presence—waiting.

A small granddaughter presented the Rogers portraits. Then the alumnae roll call began, and necks craned as Mrs. Rogers was the first to stand. Answering for 1856 was Regina Victoria Royall Broadhead; for 1858, Narcissa Bradford Dyas. The roll call for 1861 summoned Mrs. Richard Shannon, the Elizabeth Lard of Civil War days. Her father, Moses Lard, had been one of those first voices to cry out in the educational wilderness west of the Mississippi. Beside her sat her husband, son of founder James Shannon. He claimed to be the first pupil ever enrolled in the primary department of Christian, having been taken by his father to the opening session in 1851 when he was a little boy.

"And this is the little boy," she remarked, patting him fondly. The audience looked at the white-bearded man and laughed. Then she grew serious. She could not think of her schooldays without remembering the black shadow that had seemed to fall over her girlhood when her father told her the College might be closed. She could almost feel the weight of it now. . . .

"Hardships were many," she began with difficulty. "I roomed in the attic of Christian College with six other girls.

. . . But there was never a complaint. . . ." Her voice quivered, she hesitated, and sat down. Her drooping head showed that the interruption was critical. A physician hurried up from the audience. But even as she was carried out it was clear that she had expired.

For a moment the crowd sat stupefied. The warmth in the room was snuffed out. It seemed that the Jubilee for which so much preparation had been made was to end in tragedy. The audience commenced to stir. Then Luella St. Clair arose. Never had she looked more fragile—or more firm.

"The passing of our dear sister," she began, as the murmur ceased, "is not a dreadful event. It is the most beautiful thing that could have happened. For Mrs. Shannon, this was not only a Home-coming, but a Home-going. It is therefore not an occasion for lamentations and tears. . . . The portals of glory have opened and a Saint has entered in. . . ."[18]

The audience relaxed. And Luella St. Clair had at last won a bout with Death.

Such was the triumphant ending to the story of the little widow who put her thumb in the dike. That November, under the light from the stained glass window dedicated to Annilee, Luella St. Clair became the wife of Dr. Woodson Moss. The College physician, he was of a prominent Columbia family, and the room was crowded with civic and social élite. It was Mrs. Hertig's first official duty to escort the girls to the wedding, and see that they preserved their decorum as the new college father kissed each one. These irrepressible creatures had presented the bride with a large jewelled watch, in deference to her habit of pausing in chapel to borrow the timepiece of the nearest male.

For the heroine it was a new chapter, but for Christian College it was a continued story of prosperity and growth. In 1912 President St. Clair-Moss secured funds from trustees, alumnae, and friends to erect a stone gateway entrance to the campus as a memorial to Joseph Kirtley Rogers. This landmark was dedicated at Commencement, 1913. Another landmark passed in 1914 when the three-cornered cap and black gown were discarded for skirt and shirtwaist or a Peter Thompson middy suit. But 1914 brought a new tradition: the May Queen, with her pageantry and trumpeters. Hazel Davies, the original queen, wore a gown rented from a St. Louis costumière. A tradition peculiar to St. Clair hall was born in the school year 1915-16 when "Hop Alley" was named. John Davis Clarke, one of the original occupants depicted in the 1916 annual, recalls:

> In those days we were required to be ready for bed by 9:45 when the corridor teacher came by and said "Good Night." The lights were turned off and only the fire escape lights in the halls were burning. Since we were down the west wing we would slip into each others' rooms . . . with great excitement, fearing we might be caught . . . Ruth Simon of Webster Groves gave the name 'Hop Alley' after a notorious section in St. Louis since we too were ignoring the Law.[19]

(The Hop Alley of St. Louis was "Chinatown," near Eighth and Market, named for the opium or "hops" reputedly sold there.)

In 1915 the College purchased the two bungalows which the sororities had built on the west campus three years before. A Greek letter society, Beta Sigma Omicron, had appeared in 1899. Eta Upsilon Gamma, national sorority founded in 1901, originated on the Christian College campus.[20] Phi Mu Gamma followed, but did not own a house. The sororities were a source of unparalleled happy memories for members and for years fostered most of the social life of the College. But to those excluded they brought discontent. Their "rushing" became more vigorous than that which went on at the University. The feeling of competition they created spread to every other school function, causing increasing malice. Thus, 1915 was a year of controversy and the President was regarded by many as unforgiveably high-handed when she asked the sororities to disband. In their place she substituted the Twelfth Night Club, an all-school organization whose aim was "to crowd twelve nights of revelry into one." It was Mrs. Hertig who marshalled the girls into a grand march around the gym at the first party and placed the ringed thorn-staff in the hands of Portia Penwell, first president.

The First World War halted building, but boomed enrollment. The girls knitted, rolled bandages, rode floats in Liberty Loan parades, and admired their militant president, who was the only woman in Columbia to make war bond speeches. As in any war there were so many engagements and elopements that someone suggested "Here Comes the Bride" be the College hymn. They adopted war orphans, raised money for the Armenians, succumbed to the national 'flu epidemic so that school had to close early. To them the Armistice was the night of a big parade, downtown, and a dance in the gym —without men!

The postwar era was athletic-minded. As the President remarked, some students who had never seen a bathing suit chose their college on the basis of whether it had a swimming pool. So in 1918-19 she campaigned successfully for $25,000 to build the natatorium. She was determined that Christian's pool should be the largest and most beautiful connected with any institution in the Middle West.

Along with this physical expansion the President had been building for the College a legend: the symbol of "the Christian girl" as a being set apart, a little above any other. She contended that in a train car full of girls coming to school, "the Christian girl" could be distinguished by her well-bred behavior. Others might be conspicuous or loud, but not her girls. It became a local belief that "you could always tell a Christian girl" from others on the streets of Columbia. It was a tradition abetted by Miss Laws, who had a firm conviction that a young lady's best assets in life were a good rearing and a pair of fresh white gloves. Although the ladylike symbols have been discarded, the local sentiment still persists, as any Columbia taxi-driver will tell you.

It was quite true that wherever Mrs. Moss went she unerringly sought out the daughter of the town's leading family to recruit for Christian. President Jones of Missouri University often told her, "I envy you your alumnae." To quote one girl who grew up in a representative Missouri town, "I always heard, Christian College gives you the polish that never wears off." Thus far, the legend was a fact.

Gentility was no affectation with Mrs. Moss. She had a real need of being surrounded by "nice" people, a distaste for the vulgar or coarse. She was completely at home in distinguished company. If, as she stepped out the door after a University function, the Governor of Missouri halted his black limousine to inquire whether he might drive her home, she accepted such deference as her due. In return she had a sense of *noblesse oblige,* time for the thoughtful gesture. To a faculty member's housewarming she sent a dozen yellow roses. For a former student's marriage she selected some of her own wedding silver. "In fifty years," she wrote, "pass this on to another Christian College bride."

Hers was a talent for intimacy with the human race. Women as well as men, janitors and students, all found themselves charmed and engaged in her interests. This was perhaps her great secret of raising money. She could appear before a banquet, speak thirty minutes, and leave with $10,000 in pledges. Known for her witty repartee, she appreciated humor in others. She laughed when Walter Williams, dean of the University of Missouri school of journalism, introduced her as "Luella St. Clair-Moss, a steam-engine in petticoats."

She firmly believed, as she had said once early in her career, "that a woman's chief glory, next to cultivating her heart and mind, lies in society and its functions." It is true she meant Society in its highest sense. Her students became civic leaders just as those of J. K. Rogers had found their outlet in the church and the home. Her most famous graduate typified her training. When Artie Mason Carter, 1900, honor student in piano at Christian, founded the Hollywood Bowl in 1922 her motive was to bring great music "to every Tom, Dick and Harry" at a price he could afford.

When Luella St. Clair-Moss said that "Christian College has put itself upon the high plane of being a finishing school for young women," it was not the same high plane to which L. B. Wilkes and J. K. Rogers referred. Still she considered herself an intellectual and chose for her official portrait one in cap and gown. But she always retained a conception of Christian College as a preparation for the great eastern schools she so admired.

In 1913 when the old A.B. degree was discarded for an A.A. (Associate in Arts) carrying sixty hours' credit and enabling transfer to the University as a Junior, she considered it "a strong and dignified forward step." Indeed, Christian College was again pioneering in education as it became one in the first handful of junior colleges in the United States.[21] Luella published "An Open Letter to Parents" describing the advantages of the junior college system in general and Christian College in particular and printed "An Officially Standardized Junior College" on the title-page of the catalog. Standardization had become increasingly important in the educational world and Luella, alert to trends, saw this. However, she saw it as one of the improvements a modern school must have, like running water in the rooms.

To Christian it brought immediate changes for the better. The required classroom facilities had been met in Dorsey Hall. In 1914 an expanded library, for the first time independent of the fluctuations of presidents, was established in the large hall next to Dorsey chapel.

Standardization also meant the doom of the finishing school concept where poise, social accomplishments, and being a lady mattered most. Luella was beginning to see that these were not enough. Emerging from the cocoon of the war years was a creature she did not wish to recognize, even through the distance of her lorgnette. "Flapper" was the horrid word. Being a lady did not have the old appeal to these shorter-skirted, slang-speaking girls. Culture and refinement were no longer the criteria on which high school graduates chose their colleges, or high school principals advised their students. And though she used it glibly, neither did she truly understand the language of "credits" and "hours" which was becoming the be-all of the educational world. Perhaps it was because she was beginning to feel, for once, inadequate that she tried in 1916 to resign. That failing she looked around for an interpreter. Edgar Desmond Lee was the young man she chose, over-riding his objections that he knew little about girls or church conventions. He did know about professional education, however. With him beside her she could go ahead, continuing to promote Christian College in the way she knew best—building.

During the war years girls had been crowded out of the dormitory into houses up and down Christian College Avenue.

When the Missouri Movement, a fund drive by the Christian church to aid its six affiliated colleges in Missouri, was inaugurated in 1919 she entered the campaign eagerly, seeing it as a way to get a new dormitory. Trustees W. A. Bright and D. A. Robnett led in the giving, with a heartening response from others of the Board, Columbia, and Boone County.

Her sister Maxine had furnished the dormitory plans, adapted from a hotel building in Mississippi. Luella herself served as contractor, keeping the accounts, working with the building superintendent, and, as she recalled, "finding some way to pay the workmen on Saturday nights." It had seemed wise to include the new home economics department and conservatory of music on the ground floor, although she still dreamed of them as separate buildings. Missouri Hall, flanking Dorsey on the east, was completed in 1920 at a cost of about $175,000 including furnishings. It housed 110 girls and was named "Missouri" for donors all over the state. It was the eighth building she had helped to place on campus, a total investment of $500,000. Her work done, and once more a widow, Luella St. Clair-Moss resigned after twenty-five years of college service.

It was a victorious resignation. The trustees elected her the first president emeritus of Christian College. She was able to say: "It was with great joy and pride that I turned over to my successor . . . the most complete and up-to-date junior college for women in the Middle West." A simultaneous victory, to her who had worked so long for it, was that a month later women received the right to vote.

The last chapter of her life does not belong here. But since in its distinction it cast a definite glow on Christian College it should be summarized briefly. In "retiring," Mrs. Moss did what she had always told her girls a woman should do: turned her talents and energy into public life. Only two years after women received suffrage she ran as Democratic candidate for Congress, the first woman in Missouri ever nominated for a national office. She traveled vigorously, made two speeches a day, was the first known candidate to write newspaper articles, and ran on the issue of tariff alone, fearing her educational qualifications might prejudice the rural constituency.

In her own community she helped to found the Tuesday Club, the Readers' Club, served as president of the D.A.R., was the first woman elected to the Columbia Board of Education. Her state-wide activities included: 1925-1927, president of the Missouri League of Women Voters; 1929-1931, president of the Missouri Federation of Women's Clubs; 1933, first woman member and in 1935 president of the Missouri Library Commission, to which she was appointed by Governor Park. Twice she was a delegate to the Conference on the Cause and Cure of War, in Washington. She served as a Missouri representative on such divers national boards as the League of Women Voters and the World's Fair Committee. In the church she had the reputation of being the finest woman speaker in the brotherhood and the signal honor in 1929 of being elected vice-president of the International Convention of the Disciples of Christ.

Although she had always been too busy educating others to amplify her own meagre academic training greatly, she was in 1937 the only Missouri woman to hold honorary membership in Delta Kappa Gamma, national honor education society for women. In 1937 Culver-Stockton College awarded her the honorary degree of LL.D. Her name is in bronze on a tablet in the Missouri State Capitol listing the women "whose courageous work opened the opportunities for complete citizenship to all the women in the state;" also on the National Roll of Honor in Washington, D. C. "for service in the field of education; [and] in helping to secure equal political status for women." Undoubtedly one of the outstanding women of her day in Missouri she was the most distinguished woman educator in the history of the Disciples of Christ.

But always, dearest to her heart was her connection with Christian College. For fifty-five years their lives were so entwined that neither would have been quite the same without the other. She had continued on the board of trustees and would attend meetings till the week before she died at eighty-two. By then the trustees she met with were the sons of those men she had cajoled, fought and inspired.

To some it was sad that Mrs. Moss outlived her generation. Probably not to herself, who had always waded into life with zest, unmindful of the breakers. One day the doorbell rang at the apartment of Mrs. Ethel Estes. There in the lobby stood Mrs. Moss, in furs and marcelle, clutching her familiar little mesh bag.

"Laura, dear," she said, peering into the half light, "put on your hat. I've come to take you to Christian College Club." Ethel did not know how to say that her mother, Laura Barton Robnett, had been gone from Columbia for twenty years.

For the funeral of Luella St. Clair-Moss the minister chose as his text: "Stir up the faith and fire that is within you." If, in those last years of her life, some of the fire had gone out, a warm glow had remained. In "Sunny Corner," her suite in Missouri Hall, she would laugh at her own belated efforts in home economics as she brewed tea for any of her 3,000 daughters who happened to return. She liked to look out at the entrance gates, where she could so clearly remember a stile. The old Elm had been cut down in 1925 and she did not let her eyes linger on the hillock where it had been.

Like a Pharaoh she lived in the midst of her own monuments, and when she left, they remained, her contribution to Christian College. Twenty-five years of expansion, recorded in brick and stone.

VIII

THE DEMOCRAT AND HIS DILEMMA

1920-1927

It is surely a higher thing to do honest and thorough work in a lower field than to fall short . . . in a higher field.

—WILLIAM RAINEY HARPER, 1900

THERE WERE MOMENTS when the ninth president of Christian College felt himself to be "a small dog in high rye." Such folk expressions came naturally to Edgar Lee, who was never ashamed of his beginnings as a farmer's son in Laddonia, Missouri. Candor and humility were also a part of his charm.

His good looks perhaps appealed more to Mrs. Moss when she hired him in 1918 as professor of history and the next year made him her assistant with the title Vice-President. More than six feet tall, dark-eyed, handsome, with a genial boyish smile and a warm handclasp, he stood out in any crowd. His hearty, slightly twangy voice and booming laugh went with his stature.

As a student he had been persevering rather than brilliant.

When he had finally saved enough money by teaching in rural schools to enter the University of Missouri at twenty-five he promptly completed his A.B. and his M.A. in education. The wife he met there, Bennetta Barkley of Mexico, Missouri, was a talented musician and a Phi Beta Kappa, factors also considered by Mrs. Moss. But it was his nine years' experience as superintendent of schools which she needed, for he could speak the mysterious language of those public school men who were claiming more and more of her potential students.

Even with two years' background as her "right-hand bower" (so the girls characterized him) the new President was baffled by his predecessor. For example, he had found all the records of the College kept in shoeboxes. Mrs. Hertig's assurance that Mrs. Moss had always been able to find what she wanted did not deter him from purchasing the first filing cabinet.

Then there was the debt. The trustees had made it clear, as stated in Lee's inaugural speech of 1920, that Mrs. Moss would continue to direct the finances of the College. It was she who sat in on the board meetings and she to whom that group of local business men listened with respect. It was she who had incurred but he who must pay the debt of $135,000 on Missouri Hall as well as the galling yearly annuity to the two women who were former presidents. As the first president of Christian to receive a salary rather than the income from leasing the college, Lee would have little opportunity to get rich or retire on his profits. With no chance for physical expansion in sight he echoed Augustus Williams' old theme of quality rather than quantity and turned his attention to the academic.

Here was a tangle to dismay the professional educator. Christian College still had post-graduate courses in anything from china-painting to oratory. It still had a high school but with so few pupils that it had been "warned" by the accrediting association.

Lee saw the importance of meeting the standards set by the University of Missouri. Missouri's President Jesse in 1893 had made the first attempt to define colleges in the state.

Two years later Missouri helped to charter the regional accrediting agency, The North Central Association of Colleges and Secondary Schools. Missouri was first in the nation to correlate private junior colleges with the state University, which since 1912 had published an "approved" list.

So for Christian College to follow the University of Missouri was no longer a matter of tradition. To be approved by Missouri now meant to be academically respectable in the Middle West.

Because Lee understood this, the educators at the University were relieved to see him. Now on their visits of inspection to Christian, instead of being embarrassed by the feminine answer of a five course dinner and vocal solos they would get a direct response to their question: "Are you able to be approved?"

"Are you approved?" It was a simple, direct question which could be answered by a simple, direct man like Lee. It was a question which had already meant death to neighboring women's colleges unable to make the transfer from old ways to the new. It meant unequivocal hewing to a line: so many hours of prescribed courses; instructors with not only a Master's degree but so many credits in professional education. Lee saw what must be done, but it was another thing to do it.

All around him were the women. The genteel retainers and the talented young lady assistants with no degrees. Robert Abram and Henry Laudenbach were the only men who joined him on the full-time faculty. There was "the great triumvirate": Mrs. Moss, with her lorgnette; Miss Laws, with her white gloves; Miss Hall, whose province was the green carpet. There was Mrs. Hertig, with her velvet throatband and her iron hand. The classical Mrs. Lisenby; dramatic, distracted Miss Trappe; Miss Potts—strong individuals all, but who would unite if threatened. And there was scarcely any "professional education" among them. There was his own wife, an ambitious, outspoken woman who had definite ideas on every subject. Women were everywhere, with their illogic, their intrigue, their incredible ways of doing things—their femininity. The just-turned-forty male President felt hemmed in, almost smothered by petticoats.

There were other things that bothered Edgar Lee, because he was a man, and the very essence of a democrat. When he first came, he and Mrs. Moss had not seen eye to eye on the subject of the Honor Roll. A chapter of Phi Theta Kappa had been organized in 1918. This honor society would become, under Christian's leadership, the national junior college equivalent of Phi Beta Kappa.[1] To Mrs. Moss it was a symbol of modernity, rightly carrying prestige. But if one of the loveliest girls in school, who came from one of the nicest families, did not actually have grades that warranted inclusion, couldn't the boundaries be broadened a bit? Why wound feelings, and alienate influential patrons? He had retreated from her question, as shocked as she was dismayed by the feeling that this young man had a great deal to learn about life.

And the student government was that in name only. Secretly Lee termed it "phony." Initiated in 1914 by Mrs. Moss as another concession to progress, it consisted of a student council chosen by the faculty and politely voting as the faculty suggested. These girls, satirized in the annuals as "the good and pepless," were scorned as spies by the rest of the students who provoked them into more and more vindictive punishments. Actually, discipline had changed remarkably little since the autocratic days of J. K. Rogers.

But times had changed. Here were 160 girls from fourteen to twenty, sheltered, shut-in, chaperoned, in one of the most unrestrained periods of feminine history. Here was the most difficult period of youth—adolescence—in an era which was itself adolescent: the ebullient twenties, postwar years of crashing conventions, crashing convictions, soon-to-come crashing stock-markets. Trying to crowd all this steam into one eighteen-acre box was bound to lead to one inevitable result. Lee had felt an explosion building up ever since he came.

The students came from a world, and were surrounded by a world of jazz, gin, prohibition, one piece bathing suits, and The Charleston. Texas Guinan, F. Scott Fitzgerald, Rudolph Valentino, were the headliners in their papers. "Jada," "How Dry I Am," "We Won't Be Home Until Morning," were the songs which came through the earphones of their crystal sets. "Three Weeks," and "The Sheik," were the novels they smuggled from under their pillows when the lights went off at 9:45.

At Christian they were wedged into an artificial world of rising and bedtime bells, daily chapel, once a week movies, chaperoned shopping, and no bridge-playing. The spinster guardians of Christian College were still trying to keep them from spooning in a hammock in a day of necking in flivvers. Only Mrs. Hertig seemed of their world. Occasionally, in the alumnae magazine she edited,[2] she would include such a filler of college humor as:

> Let me park in a car by the side of the road
> And be a friend to Man.

Outwardly, like most nice girls, they conformed. They wore the required bloomers to gym (pinning back the legs), but they also wore georgette "teddies" underneath. They probably said "Yes ma'am," but they also said "keen," "classy," "tough," "hangover," and "Whoop-ee." They bobbed each other's hair and experimented with peroxide. They made Clara Bow spit curls, or practiced the vamp glide of Theda Bara. Rouge and "paint" on faces were still new enough to be controversial, and one wit advised all those called before the student council to wear waterproof mascara.

The yearbooks of the twenties show faces suddenly more pert, more provocative, more contemporary. Doubtless the advent of lipstick did more to change women's appearance than any other one thing. Girls wore fur neckpieces in their yearbook class pictures. Middies were going out; satin dresses were seen on campus; the first sweaters were coming in. They took snapshots of each other clasped in ardent embrace, with skirts above knees, or pretending to smoke. They "dolled up" to go downtown afternoons, and secretly met boys over a "Home-made" at Jimmie's College Inn. To go to the University campus was still forbidden, but they found many supplies they had to buy at the Missouri Store nearby, and classes in the Bible College across from the quadrangle were strangely popular.

Kissing was not unknown to the parlor, but dancing was

still a girl-with-girl affair. New Juniors were told by the Seniors that the college charter forbade "any man holding a girl in his arms within the walls of Christian College." This was as firm a tradition as hot biscuits for breakfast. Rebellion was rising at the open house "mixer" each spring and fall when properly invited university boys were herded into the gymnasium, greeted by girls who frankly inspected them for fraternity pins, offered punch and cake, and allowed to *listen* to the band—but not to dance to it—until the lights blinked time to go home.

Dancing was a moral issue of the day—and not only at Christian. The dean of women at the University, Miss Eva Johnson, witnessing "the shuffle," and the "cheek to jowl" at the Daniel Boone hotel in 1921, sent for the proprietor and requested that "dances which tended to sinuosity . . . be not indulged in any more by students of the university." A *Tribune* item of 1922 states that such "gyrations" as "suggestive wiggles, jerking and shaking, cheek-to-cheek positions" and similarly objectionable postures had been popular in Columbia for several seasons.

> "Stays" have been abandoned as an impediment to free . . . motions of the body. Any girl who has the propriety to wear them and insists on retaining her self-respect and modesty is called "old ironsides."

And old Mr. Venable, a Columbia dancing master for more than forty years, averred:

> If I had a daughter who would dance the present day dances I would turn her across my knee. If the good men and women do not do something to stop it I tremble to think where it will lead. . . .[3]

To Christian girls it led to being campused, if caught, for the most flaming of their youthful escapades usually involved either stealing to fraternity dances or riding in a car. Having ridden in a car at night could mean expulsion, while the penalty for smoking (which was so new a vice as not to be mentioned in the rules until 1933) was six weeks' confinement to the campus. With this challenge, girls went to the most elaborate lengths to try it, stuffing door cracks with towels and blowing cautious puffs through wet wash-cloths.

It took courage to let fresh air into this atmosphere, but the new President was determined to do it immediately. His aim, he announced publicly, was to have "government of the students, for the students, by the students." He assembled the student body and, to use one of his favorite expressions, "put it up to" them. He was willing to try a real system of student government, where elections would be private, where students would make the rules and decide on the punishment for infringements. It would be the end of strict chaperonage. It would also mean, he pointed out, that he was putting his future reputation as a college president into their hands. Mrs. Hertig warned him of the danger of turning so much power over to young girls. But they loved him for it.

"We won't let you down," they promised. The catalog of 1921 records Lee's first reform:

> The executive committee of the student government association is elected annually by the students. This committee then chooses some twelve or fourteen additional members from the student body, and this entire group serves in the capacity of a student council. All questions of discipline are controlled by this council, in co-operation with the executive committee of the faculty.

Though the revolution took several years, and it was some time before a girl would serve on the SGA without trepidation, they seldom did let him down.

Another way he saw to handle steam was to harness it. Mrs. Hertig had tried this years before when she started the annual vaudeville. Such hilarious shows as Hi Jinks or All Aboard occupied the girls for days, giving them a chance to cut loose and be their most silly, energetic selves. But only the more lively participated. Group activities were few or sedate: the Hallowe'en party, the fall wiener roast at Vandiver's or Shepard's farm and the snake-dance home past the fraternities, the Christmas bazaar, Sunday School, teas, and the open house which had replaced the old Martha Washington reception.[4] The YWCA and the athletic association were almost the only active organizations. Twelfth Night had removed the competition of the sororities but it had not done away with a few girls being the social arbiters while others were lost in the background. No wonder that schoolgirl energy burst out in the third floor feasts after lights, barnyard noise contests, hazing, complaints about the food, and really bitter rivalry between the Juniors and Seniors, culminating in a battle to hoist class colors from the auditorium tower.

Lee's second reform was to channel this energy into more organizations. By the end of his second year there were nine major campus organizations, forerunners of the twenty-four at the end of his administration and the thirty or more which exist today. One of the most notable was the sextette founded in 1920 by Anna Froman; an outstanding group of precision trained singers, it soon became a touring attraction and continues, as today's double sextette, to be a top advertisement for the school.

From the variety of other clubs—languages, art, science, League of Women Voters—each girl was expected to choose at least one. Lee worked out a point award system for participation with fewer points available to those whose grades fell below M. Scholars as well as "queens" became campus leaders and even the shy girl found herself entering into activities and "developing a sense of community service which she takes out of school with her." "The college community," was a favorite concept of Lee's; "a laboratory where interesting experiments in self-government are carried on with president, faculty, and students as co-workers."

All of these movements toward democracy were consolidated in a tiny but historic publication in 1925, the first student Handbook. Its flyleaf contains a "grant of power," signed by the President:

> The faculty of Christian College believing that the gradual development of . . . self-government among the students in matters that relate to their conduct . . . has been for the welfare of the college, hereby grants to the Student Government Association . . . the right to enforce the prescribed rules and regulations. . . .

These rules follow, and the very fact of their printing here is significant. From 1851 until 1916 the rules were always carried in the college catalog. This was the best source for a picture of changing manners and morals. The sixty-fifth catalog (1916-17) suddenly dropped them, with the statement: "Student government regulations and house rules for resident students will be furnished upon registration." In whatever form these were furnished, no complete copies have survived, so that this 1925 printing represents the filling of a ten year gap. The Handbook was to continue and expand until it contained all the social information about Christian College.

It is difficult to believe that some of these rules represent a new leniency:

> All first-class Columbia mail will go through the office of the Dean of Women. All other communications are expected to be held over the telephone or in person, not in the form of notes. . . .
>
> No girl is allowed to go to the Western Union Office, the barber shops, to any doctor's or dentist's office, or upstairs in any office building except with a chaperon. . . .
>
> No demonstration is allowed during serenades. . . .
>
> All window shades must be pulled down when the lights are on. . . .
>
> There shall be no playing of Victrolas [during quiet hours].
>
> Electric curling irons may be used in the rooms. . . .

Girls were allowed to go downtown alone each afternoon to approved eating places, shops, and beauty parlors, but they must wear hats and gloves. They could now talk three minutes to a young man on the street and he could walk them home. In dating, each girl must register the name of her escort with the dean of women. Then she might go to a picture show with him on Saturday night, or receive him in the parlor on Sunday evening. Only seven engagements on week nights were allowed during the year, though special permission could be obtained for "worth-while" cultural events. Any girl out after lights had to say a personal good-night to the dean of women.

By two years later in the Handbook revision of 1927, dinner and show dates had been extended to Wednesday and Thursday afternoons and Friday nights, as well as weekends. One still could not drink a casual coke with a boy one met on Broadway. This favorite Columbia preoccupation of "jellying" had to be arranged in advance for Christian girls, which removed much of the charm of a "jelly-date." But they could take part in such co-ed activities as a style show at the University. And daily chapel became "assembly," held only twice a week.

Lee's expansions of freedom—student government, a true honor system, the vanishing chaperon—soon paid off in enrollment. By 1925 the new dormitory was filled. The unwholesome rivalry gradually gave way to a democratic school spirit which was to remain at Christian as a tribute to the man who patiently cultivated it.

Lee's democracy was quite sincere. To him the individual girl mattered. He appreciated her personality. Twenty years afterward, when he was far removed from the academic world, he could still recall her name. Often his duties seemed more those of dean of women than administrator as girls came to him with their troubles. His eagerness for every girl to have a chance was part of his downfall; for many who could not otherwise have had the education that Christian represented he secured scholarships, found little office jobs around the College.

With morale saved, he tackled the problem of scholarship. Raising the levels here would take longer, but he began to make the obvious changes in curriculum demanded by the accrediting agencies. The eight art courses beloved of Mrs. Moss but not all eligible for credit, were reduced to three. Music was de-emphasized somewhat, and required recitals became fortnightly rather than weekly events. Greek was dropped. Journalism disappeared, to be revived after 1928 as one section of English composition. German was offered, though few took it. Pageantry gave way to corrective gymnastics, "ornamental penmanship," to secretarial and bookkeeping courses. A two-year diploma in commerce required a shorthand speed of 120 and typing of sixty words per minute.

Mrs. Moss's progressive departments of home economics and physical education were retained. General psychology and more chemistry were added, but chiefly Lee followed the vocational trend which was coming into education. Most characteristic of Lee was his stress on teacher-training. During his years Christian offered more than twenty-four hours of professional education courses and graduates could receive a three year certificate to teach in Missouri public schools. During the twenties and early thirties half of the graduates of Christian were becoming teachers.

As rapidly as he could without upsetting equilibrium, Lee brought in better qualified teachers. The student assistants began to go. Instructors without higher degrees were retained only for such subjects as physical education, dancing, or music where a degree was not a traditional requirement. The exotic qualifications of study in Dijon for a French teacher or apprenticeship under a famous music master abroad—which Mrs. Moss and Mrs. Moore had so valued—Lee regarded as not a whit more important than a degree from the University of Missouri. Just as this self-made man with his homespun background broke the tradition of the southern gentleman-and-scholar president, so did the strongly local group of teachers he collected impart the rural, earnest flavor of the Missouri which was now the mid-west. When Miss Laws put her last copy of Thoreau on the library shelf and retired to Kentucky in 1923, she took back to her homeland almost the last link with its child, Christian College.

The new recruits who stayed long enough to leave their mark were good people, solid in the academic world. Perhaps the greatest contribution of Lee's administration was his roster of teachers.

There was Julia Spaulding, hired as principal of the academy in 1921 but who was to become first real dean of women in 1923 and eventually serve the school as dean of faculty. Miss Spaulding, fated to be remembered by the girls as guardian of the "date basket," was appreciated by all who worked with her for her sound judgment, loyalty, and scrupulous fairness.

Two outstanding young women were Esther Wagner Stearn and Stella Meyer. Mrs. Allen Stearn, through continued research and almost passionate devotion to her field—chemistry, bacteriology, hygiene—was to develop into one of Christian's most brilliant teachers. Mrs. Max Meyer, a Phi Beta Kappa, whose calm, shy exterior covered a strong vein of humor, taught Spanish and French, but was to serve later in administrative emergencies. These two women illustrated an advantage which Christian always had over other small private schools in rural communities. Both wives of University professors, and therefore barred from teaching at the University, they found an outlet for their ability in the junior college.

Three novices who justified Lee's faith in their potentials were Margaret McMillan, history, Ruth Graham, home economics, and Alma Gray Hill, English and speech. Carolyn Reed Drew, who "knew everything about horses and nothing about teaching," had to be convinced by Lee that she could set up the first horsemanship class at Christian, in 1927. He had the same faith in young teachers that he had in the girls, bolstering their youth with encouragement and generously pushing them into the limelight. He was not afraid of eccentricity if there was intelligence behind it. Unconventional Mary Paxton Keeley, first woman graduate of the University of Missouri school of journalism, was his choice to found the campus newspaper, the *Microphone*, and surely imparted a spark to Christian that brightened its next twenty-five years.

And young Franklin Launer, who arrived in Columbia to interview President Lee one hot July day with overcoat, mustache, and cane, all acquired in Paris—what would the future of the Conservatory have been without Franklin? He recalls having to play several hours not only for Lee but for his more critical wife, whose approval of a Percy Grainger arrangement of "The Londonderry Air" got him the job. So good a salesman was Lee that Launer was climbing back on the train before he discovered he had just signed a contract to teach in a *girls'* school!

Launer, hired simply as a piano teacher, illustrated Lee's shrewd judgment. The young musician and concertist was to grow in professional stature into an administrator who would develop a distinguished faculty. In the Moss era the Conservatory had existed as a unit almost detached from the rest of the College. One of Launer's first administrative acts would be to banish the undemocratic distinction of "Specials" which long had kept music students apart from the general

gar D. Lee, 1920–1935

the Twenties — Flappers

Missouri Hall

The Thirties brought variety — horseback riding and cheerleading

S. Briggs, 1935–1938

Frank Hughes Hall

crophone staff of 1936

TRADITIONS

Commencement Court

Going to church

"The Mail's Up"

Dr. Esther Stearn

Franklin Launer

Sue M. Gerard

Geneva Youngs

J. Harold Long and Sidney Larson

ting the Cannonball

CENTENNIAL

Student models historical bonnet

Tree-planting (Rose Banks and Mary P. Keel

Gov. Forrest Smith, Sen. James Fulbright, Dr. J. C. Miller, Dr. Frederick Middlebush

Above and below: A bittersweet ceremony — Ivy Chain

A picnic on the stairs of the 1851 building, "Look" photograph

Some things never change

student body. J. Harold Long, teacher of biological sciences, was another basic teacher and scholar Lee brought in. Others who were to stay more than a decade were Grace Rand Mitchell, instructor in physical education for seventeen years, Ruth Almstedt who headed the art department as long and was to become Mrs. Franklin Launer, Helen Myers Kellog, violin, Monia Cook Morris, American government.

Lee's additions to the staff were also likely to be "fixtures." Secretary Kathryn Douglass was to assume much of the business management of the College. Mrs. Agnes Funkhauser was to serve as dietitian for twenty years. Maurice Wightman, supervisor of buildings, had inherited his job from his father before him. "Maurice," who might be called on to do anything from posing in the art department to installing an organ was as much a part of the College as the foundation. And J. Kelly Wright, engaged in 1921 as the first fulltime recruiting agent, spread the gospel of Christian College with his projector and his slides, his enthusiastic promotion of horsemanship and music.

Among Lee's appointees was to be his own successor, but of course he did not know that as he went along, building up the faculty which was to stay on years after he had left Christian College.

The school year 1925-26 was, in many ways, a milestone in the history of Christian. It was the year school opened with 265 girls and applicants were turned away. It was the year which marked the beginning of large-scale promotional field work beyond neighboring states, notably into Texas. It was the Diamond Jubilee year, with a celebration scheduled for the Seventy-Fifth Commencement. Burris Jenkins, most talked-of preacher in the Disciples' ministry, was to give the Baccalaureate sermon; Governor of Missouri Sam A. Baker, the Commencement speech. The alumnae reunion was to center about Jennie Robards Rogers, now the oldest living alumna, and Miss Lucy Laws was to return for the occasion.

It was the year Christian put itself on the map by establishing Columbia's first radio broadcasting program. Since the town had no station President Lee had the ingenious idea of hooking Christian College on to WOS in Jefferson

City thirty-five miles away and broadcasting by remote control. The plan was backed by the Reverend Walter Haushalter, who pledged support from the Christian Church in exchange for a weekly broadcast of sermons. Christian's broadcast became a civic function, airing the state meeting of Kiwanis or the university Homecoming football game as well as its own bi-weekly programs produced by Mrs. Tyra Green, Mrs. Anna Froman and Franklin Launer, and announced by Alma Gray Hill from the control room at the east of the auditorium stage.

It was the year Christian loomed larger on the educational map because its executive was elected president of the American Association of Junior Colleges.[5] It was, to add a nostalgic footnote, the year the student body journeyed to St. Louis to see "The Miracle," and the Christian College Sunday School class got national publicity by announcing that no Christian girl would date a boy who drank.

All of these were outward, advertised events. But two underground forces were at work that school year of 1925-26 which were to have much more bearing on the future of Christian College. For it was the year of the Reeves survey. And it was the year, as Edgar Lee recalled later, "we almost did a flip-flop."

The Reeves survey was a complete stock-taking of Christian College, its assets and its liabilities.[6] Not since the fascinating inventory J. K. Rogers recorded in 1858 had the school been so thoroughly examined. Only this time the intellectual furnishings were brought into the light. The study was instigated by the Board of Education of the Disciples of Christ who were evaluating the work of their church-related colleges. It was conducted by a recognized expert in college administration, Floyd W. Reeves, Ph.D. It was typical of Lee—never afraid to take the lid off the box—that he welcomed it. It looked sharply into the administration, the finances, how well the plant was utilized, how efficient the teachers, how adequate the equipment, how truthful the catalog, and how good an education was received for the money expended.

It brought out many interesting facts about Christian College in 1926: that its student body was a well-to-do, non-local group from thirteen states, Oklahoma and Kansas leading. That only half were from Disciples' churches. That the plant was large per student enrolled but that "accessory" space somewhat overbalanced academic. It termed student government "wholesome," educational efficiency "excellent," and the financing "in many respects . . . remarkable." (It was the only school surveyed which lacking outside funds ran without a yearly deficit.) Also, like most honest appraisals, the survey packed a great deal of dynamite, so it is not surprising that it was never seen by most of the persons it concerned. Lee admitted that it had the situation summed up "to a gnat's heel." In fact, he could summarize the needs listed in its 122 type-written pages in one word: *endowment.*

If all the recommendations of the Reeves survey could have been put into effect immediately the last quarter-century of Christian's story would have been too dull for comment. But they were not ignored. Anyone reading the manuscript can see plainly in it the blueprint of every improvement made during the remainder of Lee's administration and, in fact, for the next twenty-five years.

The near "flip-flop" which upset the College in March, 1926, was really the crisis which had to come in the struggle between old ways and the new. For that reason it is recorded, and because it appeared in the journals of the day. Seemingly, the trustees had been satisfied with Lee's management of the College. In five years, the $135,000 debt had been reduced to $50,000. Underneath, they were not so pleased with his attempted management of themselves. Where Mrs. Moss had spared them financial details, Lee tried the same democratic policy he used with the students, constantly drawing their attention to the problems, asking them to help make the decisions, to share the responsibilities. It was his concept of how a college board should function. Apparently they preferred her version, for they required him to consult her on any large financial decision.

Mrs. Moss was not disposed to cooperate with Lee by now. His changes had alarmed her. His Lincolnesque qualities she saw as crude. Lately she had found on the Board itself a confidant as polished and cultured as Lee was plain. Trustee

Walter Haushalter was brilliantly educated, ambitious, handsome, a spell-binding speaker, novelist by avocation, sophisticate in tastes—the epitome of everything Mrs. Moss admired. He had a quality of daring she shared, and promotional ideas she thought perfect for Christian College. Whether or not he meant to become involved, she sought him out, conferred with him about her plans for the College, and drew him with her into the center of a whirlpool which sucked in most of the trustees and was about to descend on the unwitting head of Edgar Lee.

The secret session wherein her grievances were aired was arranged while Lee was in Chicago, attending a meeting of the American Association of Junior Colleges. In fact, he had just been elected vice-president. He had also learned that, because of a new ruling requiring junior colleges to have $10,000 income per year from endowment, Christian would be accredited only one more year. Coming home to find what had gone on behind his back, on March 22, 1926, he resigned.

A general shake-up followed, Dean Spaulding, J. K. Wright, and trustee A. G. Capps resigning also. Conservatory director Laudenbach had already accepted another position. Mrs. Hertig went busily among student body and faculty with a petition which was unanimously signed, urging Lee to remain.

After a great deal of publicly denying rumors of rift, it was announced in May just before the Diamond Jubilee, that President Lee had been retained. Miss Spaulding and Mr. Wright also consented to stay. Mr. Launer was persuaded to become director of the Conservatory. A male dean of faculty would replace Mrs. Lisenby. Her good friend, Mrs. Moss, looked around her sunny apartment and thought seriously for once of moving off the campus. "The great triumvirate" met for the last time at the Seventy-Fifth Commencement and separated in a whirl of petticoats.

There were two interesting conditions in Mr. Lee's new contract: (1) That his election be unanimous with the Board, and (2) that all authority as president be lodged in him alone. In addition, the Board voted him an increase in salary. Like the generous man he was, Lee forgot the incident and settled back to work. He had won the battle of the petticoats, but the bigger battle for accrediting loomed ahead.

It had threatened since 1922. In that year the accrediting association had first required a yearly income of $6000 from "stable sources other than fees." Christian College, which like most small schools operated chiefly on tuitions, barely was able to squeeze by this ruling. Annual gifts from individuals or the church were uncertain. The trustees still saw endowment as money for buildings and debts, to dip into in emergencies. Lee realized that educationally "endowment" spelled "accrediting" and that being accredited meant the future of the school. Now with the minimum yearly requirement raised to $10,000 Christian seemed lost. She was on probation, to be "surveyed" at the end of one year.

The dilemma that rose on Lee's horizon was a giant with two heads. How to secure an endowment in one year? How, even with endowment, to meet the increasingly detailed academic requirements—which also seemed to involve money?

These needed improvements were at least clearly outlined in the Reeves survey: more balanced teaching loads, higher salaries, more adequate library and laboratories. Lee scratched his head, turned the academic house-cleaning over to his new dean of faculty and went to wrestle with other chores.

The faculty dean himself had been a suggestion of the Reeves survey. Just as Lee was Christian's first professional educator, so was Louis A. Eubanks its first professionally trained dean. Like Lee, he was a Missourian bred, with rural school background, state teachers' college education, graduate degrees in education from the University of Missouri. Lee felt he was just the man to work out the maze of problems concerning efficient teaching, courses and use of classroom space which must be correct on the forthcoming accrediting blank. Unfortunately, before the year was out Eubanks was to become dean of the state teachers' college at Kirksville. However, the two men worked hard, that fall of 1926, with the result that the survey report of the North Central Association of Colleges and Secondary Schools on February 1927 found Christian College worthy of consideration for one more school year. During that time it would be inspected.

This reprieve was not so much occasion for rejoicing as despair. Whereas the survey was a preliminary test, formal inspection by a committee of the NCA was the end. On its findings a school stood or fell. To steer Christian through the straits of inspection would take all the hands Lee could muster.

Looking frantically for help, he thought of Reeves, the expert on higher education; Reeves who knew the needs of Christian College and was respected both by the church and by educators. The NCA survey had been throughout a repetition of the earlier Reeves report. In the fall of 1927 Lee hired Reeves as "educational counselor," according to the catalog "the greatest step forward the college has taken in years."

Actually, he was to visit only at intervals, to advise on educational and administrative moves, but mostly to help chart an endowment campaign. Other reinforcements were the new trustees. For recent vacancies, Lee had chosen school, not businessmen. A. G. Capps was a professor of education at the University. Claude A. Phillips had been one of the writers of accrediting specifications.

But the man who would face the giant must do battle on campus. The choice of a new dean was crucial at this time. In making it, Lee influenced the future of Christian College.

IX

THE LEAVEN IN THE LOAF

1927-1935

For if you bake bread with indifference, you bake a bitter bread that feeds but half man's hunger.

—KAHLIL GABRAN

THERE WAS A YOUNG MAN both Lee and Eubanks knew. Jim Miller had grown up with Eubanks. A farmer's son from a small Ozark community near Eugene, Missouri, Miller had worked his way through the state teachers' college at Warrensburg. He found time to sing tenor in the male quartet and act as president of the Athenaeum debating society. He had boarded at the Eubanks home when he became principal of the Otterville high school from 1913-1915. (The family remembered his jolly disposition and how he sang while shaving.)

At Otterville he had found a sweetheart, Ennell Harlan, daughter of a substantial farmer of distinguished Kentucky lineage. Her vow that she would never marry a teacher caused him to become cashier of the Fortuna, Missouri, bank nearby. His two years' experience with debits and credits was to stand him in good stead later.

When America entered World War I he had enlisted in the Naval Reserve. Then he and Nell were married in 1917. Nine months' service in the United States and another nine months overseas gave the lad who had never traveled beyond a sixty mile radius a broad view of continental Europe. He stored up everything he saw.

Coming back to a wife and baby, he had decided it was to be teaching, after all. He had entered the University of Missouri, studying under the same professors as Lee and Eubanks. Then he started up the professional ladder as assistant to Claude A. Phillips, director of the University's elementary education. Now, at thirty-six, he was principal of the University laboratory school. He had a charming wife and two small daughters. No more promising young man would have been found in the educational town of Columbia.

But the young man was not easy to convince. James Conelese Miller was purely a product of rural, middle-class, public schools. A private college for girls was entirely out of his realm of experience, and he was not at all sure that he approved such institutions.

If he had ever thought of them at all, he would have questioned the seriousness of the girls who were sent to them—the privileged few whose schooling was coming to them as lightly as his had heavily. He had always had to alternate semesters of school with work behind a team or on the railroad or in a bank. His dreams of the future had never once included a vista like this. Besides, his immediate goal was to secure his Ph.D.

In the end, this was perhaps what won him over. President Lee, the good salesman, convinced him that he could easily fill the position while finishing his degree. And, when the first fall crisis of registration arrived, Lee found the opportunity to sell him on the worth of girls in a girls' college.

Fall, 1927, was the largest registration in College history and it was the new Dean's first experience of what is—even to a seasoned hand—a week of strain. Too, he was attempting for the first time to include the modern tests which had been so stressed in his recent academic training. He pointed out to Lee that, with no registrar, he needed help and there was no one sufficiently trained to help him. It took all his urbanity not to show dismay when Lee brought to his office six girls. Lee was fond of boasting that at Christian College "most of our girls are hand-picked." These he had picked with especial care. Among them he would recall Mary Susan Moberly, Virginia Hulse, Margaret Cameron, and Alberta Davis.

"The girls will help you with registration," Lee told him. Miller looked at them with disbelief and scarcely heard their chorus of polite response as he dazedly seated them around his desk. All day long the girls followed his instructions efficiently, added knowledgeable touches of their own, and when it was all accomplished with success, he looked at the young faces around him with new respect. It was one of the real lessons Lee taught him.

Although he already had a reputation for scholarship, the new Dean had never lived in an ivory tower. Having had to push a plow with one hand while holding a book with the other, he had the rare ability to apply scholarly insight to practical problems. Now he sat down and studied the year's work before him.

He soon saw that it lay within the fourteen typed pages of the North Central Association survey report which had been placed on his desk. In simplest terms, it was: to right all the factors which the association found wrong with Christian College before the next accrediting meeting, in March 1928. He read it over and over, searching for a solution. The critical lack of endowment was beyond his province, he thought gratefully, admitting to himself that only a miracle could remedy that before March. So anything that would in six months save the school must lie elsewhere in that document. Studying it again, he found a loophole. "If any factor," it stated, "can be cited in lieu of endowment it probably should be found in a comprehensive program for the maintenance of effective teaching."

A program for effective teaching: that would be his goal.

Improvement of instruction. To take the material which was the faculty of Christian College and spark it into something so unique, so dynamic, so intellectually alert that it would make a blaze in the academic world—and in six months! That was a challenge which suited both his ability and his vision. Fortunately, he was young.

For the dozen-and-a-half full-time members of the college faculty were as diverse as could be and at least four had taught much longer than he had. Among them were those who knew their subject but could not teach, some who were popular teachers but not experts in their subject, some whose experience was their chief asset. Few had studied the theories of what makes a good teacher, or developed any philosophy of education. Only one had a Ph.D.

Some of them still remember the first faculty meeting at which he presided that fall. "Brilliant," they recall: "witty," "to the point." His outlined program for the year rather took their breath away: two faculty meetings a month, one devoted entirely to topics on the profession of teaching. The dozen best current books on the philosophy of teaching to be read and discussed. The results of student intelligence tests to be distributed and a unified system of grading planned. The aims of the school as a whole to be sought and an attempt made to state them. Sometime during the year each teacher would be called upon to educate the others on the content of his course and, in effect, to defend it. Meanwhile the Dean would start visiting classes and would talk over with each teacher the notes he took. They looked at the first mimeographed program they had ever received at a faculty meeting. It was the guide to a period of soul-searching. Like any catharsis, it promised to be exhausting. But because they were serious persons, teachers of integrity, and loyal members of the little college family, they caught the enthusiasm of their new leader and went up to the library after meeting to take out one of the new books.

Lee, meanwhile, with Reeves' help was working out details of an endowment drive.

The campaign was to be carried on by the Board of Education of the Disciples of Christ under the direction of their regional representative, Mrs. Dora Winter. Five hundred thousand dollars was the goal, and the trustees quickly pledged $5,000. A pamphlet, "Endowment Appeal for Christian College," stressing the seventy-seven years' service of the institution, pointed out that this was the first real endowment drive in its history.

Everyone in the college family was busy, that winter of 1927. Frances Heckman, first professional librarian, carefully pruned the dead wood from the library shelves and ordered the new reference books which made the most important enlargement to the library in years. New wiring and lights were installed in the science laboratories, where classes had been rearranged so that every student had full use of the equipment. In the office a new system of cost-accounting was being worked out which would take the finances of the College forever out of the shoe-box file days. As expenditures of the college were separated from those of the high school and all costs analyzed, it became more than ever apparent that the high school must go.[1]

With faculty enlisted under the banner of the new Dean, morale was high. Several had enrolled for advanced work in the University. The critical books were being read so avidly that extra copies had to be ordered. New methods of testing were being tried in the classroom and the first semester's grades showed less divergence as a result. At faculty meetings discussion was heated and even banquet conversations circled to academic questions.

Finally, with March 1, 1928, came the fateful week of inspection. George R. Moon of the University of Chicago visited the College and went home to write the official report which would mould the decision of the accrediting association. Dean Miller, receiving his copy, opened the document as one might a death notice.

The inspector had commented on the year's improvements one by one. He especially commended the home economics department and the new financial accounting scheme—"one of the best seen in any college which I have visited." Salaries were still low, but he attributed this partly to Christian's economic advantage in a town with a surplus of qualified teachers. He stated that the faculty of Christian College was its strongest asset, adding:

> I observed the classroom teaching of at least one instructor in each department. . . . I have never seen better teaching in Junior College work. The teachers are enthusiastic, alert, and are well versed both in their subject matter and in methods of putting it across. The students respond in an excellent manner.

He concluded:

> It is clear that at present Christian College does not meet the requirements of the North Central Association in regard to endowment . . . the educational work which the school is doing is easily better than that done in a great many schools about whose accreditment there is no question. The students are receiving an unusually high grade of training.

And—the sentence for which the Dean was looking: "On the basis of the unusual standing of Christian College in all of the requirements aside from endowment, I recommend that the school be accredited."

The President and Dean of Christian College may have disturbed the ghost of Dr. Moore with a victory dance on that gentleman's library carpet. . . .

It seemed the beginning of halcyon days for Christian, reminiscent of those after the turn of the century. Optimism pervaded the school, just as in 1928 it pervaded the whole country. A year before when young Charles Lindbergh had piloted the Spirit of St. Louis on the first non-stop flight across the Atlantic, America had gone mad, for in him it found a symbol of the times. Speed, daring, non-stop: the world was on a non-stop race to prosperity.

Certainly that was the spirit of Christian College. Enrollment overflowed. Teachers were moved off campus to make room for more students. Even with the endowment drive in full swing, trustees began to mention the possibility of a new dormitory. Contractor Berry McAlester was for building one at once, but the fact that the Christian Church and another college in town were both making city-wide building drives made the Board decide to wait a year.

In their discussion the old question of legal ownership

raised its ugly head—for Mrs. Moore was still collecting "rent" for her half-interest in the school. It was determined to see her and to revise the college charter so that in event of expansion there would be no doubt about clear property title. It was in this revision of December, 1929, that the word "Female" was forever dropped from the title "Christian College." Somehow, it had come to look obsolete.

Barriers were being expanded nowadays, for 1927 had seen the first annual educational tour, to Washington, D. C. 1929 marked the first school dance—with men! This momentous event, a Valentine formal at the Tiger Hotel, was scooped by the *Microphone,* which was also new that year.[2] Every detail, down to the last fringed skirt, was reported for posterity.

"Non-stop" might have been the slogan of Christian's Dean. He had dreamed up a continuous plan of faculty improvement.[3] The first year (1927-28) had been devoted to the study of professional literature on college teaching. The second year the faculty was stimulated to produce professional literature of its own through departmental research. Experimental studies were planned in frequent faculty meetings, and each teacher was urged to write his findings into articles. A creative wave swept over the College not to ebb for years.

The faculty created as the Dean created. He was the moon to their tide. He read, criticized, sometimes gave his own vivid touch to their articles, but always he was himself working—at nights, summers, going to school, writing on his dissertation.

Study after study appeared in professional publications: "Important Factors in Directing the Health of the College Woman," by Esther Stearn and Grace Mitchell; "Contributions of the Private Junior College," by Edgar D. Lee, "Musical Talent at the Junior College Level," by J. C. Miller and Stella Meyer, . . . "Success in Social Sciences," by Margaret McMillan and Stella Meyer. . . . The remarkable series went on, and with each addition the name of Christian College grew more respected in the tightly-locked academic world.[4]

The contagion even spread from the faculty to the students who, fired by Mary Paxton Keeley, wrote short stories, verse, plays that competed and often won in the dramatic arts contests at the University. Student creativeness culminated in two booklets published in 1934: "Christian College Prize Plays," and "Lyrics From a Linotype."

The third year, 1929-30, the searchlight of scrutiny was turned on each teacher's own course, and he was asked to prepare a syllabus of its content. What place did the course fill in the curriculum? How was it taught? Its objectives, bibliography? Such self-study led to changes and forced the growth of some philosophy in even the least imaginative instructor. The individual syllabi were bound into a 330-page volume to serve as a standard for incoming teachers.[5]

The topic of the fourth year (1930-31) was the Junior College curriculum in general. Catalogs from all the junior colleges in the United States were critically analyzed. For the first time since 1913 Christian College asked itself: What is a junior college? How is it different from the high school or the university? Why should it exist?

These were questions current in the world of education where the junior college was edging into the field of the four-year arts school in a way to arouse national controversy. Was it to be a sort of super-secondary school for retarded adolescents? Was it to serve as a refuge for non-academic types? Like Topsy, the junior college had just grown, its function never quite defined. As Dr. Robert L. Kelly, speaking to the Association of American Colleges on "The Future of the Liberal Arts College," declared: "The junior college needs philosophers more than promoters."

If, as this educator predicted, prophets were arising in the junior college, the earnest young Dean in central Missouri was certainly one of them. In James C. Miller, Christian had found its philosopher. With him the faculty was one of the first in the country to take apart its student body, to ask: What sort of students come here? What do they do after they leave? Is their training here relevant to their future?

They had embarked on their dissection agreed on two points: (1) that the junior college period was one for the completion of general education and academic repair; (2) that general survey courses were better adapted to its curriculum than traditional isolated sections of subject matter. They also took for granted the *preparatory* function of the junior college in offering the academic training which would enable transfer to the third year of a university.

Now they found that only half of the graduates of Christian went on to college. Forty-eight per cent married within five years, some of these of course being the university graduates. Those who did not marry immediately and those who did not go on to school usually worked. For either of these groups a *terminal* education was important, whether with emphasis on general culture for the homemakers to be, or on vocational training for the careerists. Finally, they added a third function which would serve all the students and which was peculiarly suited to the smallness of a junior college like Christian: *guidance.*

> Student guidance is recognized as one of the functions of Christian College. The real center of interest is not units of subject matter or credits, but the individual student. A study is made of each girl as an individual, and every effort is made to help her to realize all of her possibilities.

It was a reaffirming of the principle of the abundant life for all on which Christian was founded. This new statement of educational policy and the functions of Christian College in the eighty-third catalog is interesting in that it represents the voice of the entire faculty, not just the president or dean.

The direct outcome of the year's analysis was a system of freshman guidance with a week's program of orientation to bridge the gap from high school to college. This adjustment or "orientation" was a subject on which J. C. Miller was to become known as an authority. His doctor's dissertation, published that fateful summer of 1930, was entitled "The Induction and Adaptation of College Freshmen."

At Christian, freshman guidance became a counseling system whereby each new student was assigned a faculty advisor. This teacher studied her psychological and aptitude tests, discovered her interests and goals, saw that she chose the proper studies to achieve them, discussed her problems, wrote letters to her parents about her progress. Counseling, taken for granted now, was in September 1930 one of the prophetic contributions Miller made to Christian.[6]

The fifth and sixth years' faculty studies tried to measure the less tangible results of education at Christian. To what extent was Christian College affecting the social development, moral awareness, esthetic appreciation, vocational choice of its students? Any student who requested it was given a personal evaluation.

These years of studies, especially those last which explored beyond the usual academic boundaries, represented Miller's scientific, philosophical handling of what President Lee had, from the first, been trying to express in a less articulate way: the personal touch, the value of the individual, the fourfold life.

If Lee, with Mrs. Hertig, had seen the need of a "big sister" movement, Miller had broadened the concept into a complete system of counseling. If Lee felt that good education was "Mark Hopkins on one end of the log and the student on the other," it was Miller who furnished the modern synthetic log of "orientation." If Lee was something of a preacher, Miller was the prophet. It was an interesting fact that six years after Christian College had already been stressing the subjective values of education the North Central Association of Colleges and Secondary Schools should alter its complete accrediting standards along these very lines.

Lee and Miller supplemented each other, just as Lee had supplemented Mrs. Moss. Their achievements dove-tailed so perfectly that, in the after-light of analysis, it is difficult to say where the credit should go. To the man who instituted the soul-searching, or the man who carried it out? To the one who voiced the needs—or the one who knew how to meet them?

When, as Lee was able to report to his board, W. W. Carpenter, of the University's department of education, made the statement that "Christian College is doing the best work on the improvement of instruction of any Junior College in the United States," it was actually the triumph of Miller.

And when, at the time of Lee's contract renewal in 1929 an optimistic board of trustees had voted him president for life, it was partly owing to Miller's success in the background.

Previously, the businessmen who formed the bulwark of Lee's board of trustees had never quite been able to accept him as one of them. However, the initial success of the endowment drive had changed their opinion. Under such money-raising devices as "The thousand dollar club," a scheme of Mrs. Moss's, $50,000 of the goal had been pledged promptly, bringing the total endowment to $75,000. Though the more conservative trustees had overridden Berry McAlester's proposition to build a new dormitory in 1929, they all agreed that one should be ready by the fall of 1931.

When, one night at the beginning of 1930, the trustees gathered in the President's study for their regular monthly meeting, they listened to Lee's financial statement and nodded in approval as he proposed a $300,000 expansion campaign for a new residence hall. One of them even remarked that this was the best financial report he had heard in seven years. Not one saw, in the smoke from his after-dinner cigar that January night, that the vision was really a mirage, the non-stop flight was heading for a crash.

To the business world it had come in coded symbols, ticking relentlessly on lengths of white tape. Caught in this fatal confetti, men clutched their hats and jumped out of ten-story windows.

For Christian College it first appeared as an entry in the *Minutes* of May, 1930—only four short months after the cigar smoke had cleared away. "Unless the net income of the College justifies present salaries and operating expenses . . . at the end of the year, or any time in the future, the Board shall feel free to reduce salaries and expenses." Subsequent entries tell the story:

> June 17, 1930: "We hold in reserve sufficient cash to carry out our program through the summer without embarrassment. . . ."
>
> December 9, 1930: "In making up our budget we estimated that it would be necessary to decrease our expenditures at least $30,000 under last year, which would still leave us with a probable deficit."

January 13, 1931: "Reservations will be slower on account of unsettled financial conditions. . . ."

By May the President, without waiting for sanction of a board meeting, was forced to borrow to meet the faculty payroll and tide the College through the summer. This stopgap financing was to become a habit for the next three years, when each Commencement found Lee wondering where he would find the money to open the following September. By fall of 1931, instead of a new dormitory the College had a $70,000 debt. Across town at the University, President Walter Williams publicly denied rumors that that institution was about to close.

Lee was forced to cut all salaries one-third, dismiss some of the field staff, reduce the music faculty. Frantically, now, he tried to get his board to assume some of the responsibility. The primary function of a board of trustees, he told them, was to help raise funds.

If the Board did not seem to shoulder the worries of the College, there was one who did. James Miller was not included in their meetings, but he saw the annual reports, noted the dropping enrollment, heard about the mounting heap of bills. His practiced eye could interpret a bank statement. He did not have to hear the finance committee's report to know that "before the end of the year the situation will be desperate."

He said goodbye to faculty he had hired and wondered how they could possibly find other jobs. In St. Louis and Kansas City were bread-lines, soup-kitchens, men who had once owned businesses now standing on corners selling apples. On Eighth street in Columbia where farmers had always come to buy, the unemployed gathered by the courthouse columns or sat listlessly on the terrace by the jail. Sometimes, walking to town from Christian College, one would have to crowd past three hundred men standing in line all day for the prospect of one hour's work.

Even among one's friends the economy of family life was being upset. One could no longer be certain of the things formerly taken for granted: the decent clothes, the music lessons, the braces on the teeth. With this salary cut, Miller was glad now that he was under contract to teach at the University during the summer. His Ph.D. achieved, he had thought of resting. Actually, he could not remember when he had rested, when he had not driven himself. He recalled that the morning after he had received his Master's degree he had sat down to work on his Ph.D.

But he was tired. Sometimes his shoulders ached as if the burden could be measured in weight. Strange pains came in his limbs. At night there were bad dreams . . . dreams of frustration . . . of hurrying and hurrying, never to reach a destination. He began to feel as he had upon returning from the war—confused, persecuted. He wondered if he could be losing his mind?

Even then, it took a doctor to tell him that by Commencement, 1932, his non-stop flight had come to an end. "Nervous exhaustion" was the verdict.

He could not quite give up. He would rise in the morning, drag himself to school, accomplish two or three hours' work, and stumble back home. It was during these days that he formed the habit of his slow walk up to the College. Sometimes he would take ten minutes to follow the curved approach from Rogers' Gateway, past the hollow where the old elm once stood to the porch leading to his office. During this time he would collect his thoughts for the day; those thoughts which had always been so nimble and flashing and which now he had to lead patiently, like a toddler taking its first steps.

Once home he did not want to read the paper or eat the dinner which was waiting. He only wanted to lie down. There he would stay, hour after hour, drained and exhausted. Sometimes he would torture himself with questions: Should he have been a banker, as his wife would have preferred? Nowadays, bankers were no better off than teachers.

No, he had always wanted to teach, and before that, to learn. Memories would come back of the Flint Rock Schoolhouse and the little boy who went there with various of his seven brothers and sisters. School "kept," in its one room, only from September till Christmas, and extended only through the fifth grade. The one way to graduate from the fifth grade was to get married. He remembered how, when the older classes were reciting, he would listen, almost bursting to join in. Once the teacher asked a sluggish bumpkin, "Was Benedict Arnold a friend of the government?" "Yes," mumbled the youth, finally, and before he realized he had done it, little Jim Miller shouted, "NO!"

There was plenty of time to remember, during the year it would take to recover. All through this time Lee was kindness itself. He protected his Dean, shielded him from demands, insisted that he go home from work sooner, leave more undone.

The scheduled faculty studies went on. For fall, 1933, the new subjective accrediting standards proposed by the North Central Association were examined. Not again would the amount of money or equipment a college had be the deciding factor in its acceptance. For Miller, who had anticipated the trend, it was a sort of victory, but the victor was too burned out to appreciate it.

Faculty activity surged around him to culminate, his final year as dean, in a published summary of their six years' work. This forty-three page bulletin, printed first in May, 1934, as a catalog supplement under the simple title "Christian College," set forth the educational objectives of the College and of each specific course. Edited by Esther Stearn, it carried on the flyleaf a beautiful quotation from Kahlil Gabran. "The teacher . . . gives not of his wisdom but rather of his faith and his lovingness . . . does not bid you enter the house of his wisdom, but rather leads you to the threshold of your own self."[7] It reminded Miller of the way they had felt about teaching—those men he had looked on as giants, his first teachers at Warrensburg.

The pamphlet was an ambitious venture for a junior college. It appeared to answer a current demand for vocational guidance. So many copies were requested by educators and high schools that another printing was soon necessary. Through it Christian was gaining notice and its Dean being hailed in the educational world as an authority on guidance, matriculation, accrediting.

Thinking of this forced a smile. He remembered that gangling, earnest youth from the country who first faced the dean of the big normal college. He was asked how many credits he had. "Credits?" he repeated blankly, never having heard the word used that way. Since he obviously was not qualified for normal-school training, through pure kindness they had classified him as "probationary sub-normal." To him this sounded much more impressive than just plain "normal." Proudly he wrote the term back to his parents. It was only in the sophistication of later years—and a psychology course—that he was disillusioned, and the knowledge went to his heart.

And now he was an authority on accrediting! It seemed a long way to have come. And sometimes he wondered if he had reached the end of his journey. But the year was wearing on and he was growing stronger day by day.

As he regained his strength, the College skidded towards disaster. Tuition had been lowered and the Hop Alley wing of St. Clair modernized with baths in a last effort to fill empty rooms with girls. Many of those in school were on scholarships. Newly elected trustees declined the honor. Banks would no longer lend money. Creditors could not pay. Pledges were defaulting daily and sometimes before a check could be cashed, the bank it was written on would fail.

Mrs. Moss was out now desperately seeking funds to pay last year's debt, and "endowment" was almost a forgotten word. It blazed once more across the record of the *Minutes* as, in a valiant scene, she sang her swan song.

Again, she said, she would call attention of the trustees to the supreme need of a permanent endowment for the College.

> An income . . . from sources other than student fees would, in times of depression, spell the difference between deficit and a balanced budget. In years of normal financial conditions it would mean unrestricted funds for needed improvements, repairs, general expansion.
>
> There is perhaps not a member of this Board but who at some time could contact some person who could be interested in helping perpetuate the splendid work of this Missouri pioneer college. . . . After the manner of Cato who closed every speech with: "Carthage must be destroyed," I close my every report with, Christian College must be endowed![8]

It was the old refrain of the presidents of Christian College, uttered just before they stepped out of the picture.

That step came for Lee on the evening of December 18, 1934. The Board listened in silence as he gave his financial report for the fall semester. Both he and they knew it was the end. Another man might have gone into the next room and blown out his brains. Lee faced his trustees with courage.

"Gentlemen," he said, "I have done the best I could. I've worked hard. I've been honest. But in the face of times like these, my best has not been enough." So exit Edgar Desmond Lee, a victim of the depression and of his own generous nature; Lee, who had brought Christian College into modern times.

The Board accepted his resignation and called an emergency meeting for the following day. To their surprise their solution—that J. C. Miller take over the presidency—was politely shattered by the Dean. With his usual diffidence he gave as reasons his precarious health and the feeling that the qualities which had brought some success to the deanship would not necessarily make him a good president. Secretly he vowed that he would not under any conditions be the serpent his friend had nurtured in his bosom. He agreed to act as administrator during the emergency, however, and was thus plunged back into the tensions of life.

With his resignation, Lee accomplished what he had never been able to do as president, for there was no question about the trustees accepting responsibility now. As always in the dark days of the College's history it was the small local group who must rally to save it.

Next to Miller himself, Mrs. Moss led out. Her contribution was her supreme resolution in refusing to admit that the situation could be fatal. W. W. Payne, chairman of the finance committee, was perhaps next most effective. Payne, Columbia's wholesale grocer, was an able businessman, simple, wise in an unschooled way, and completely devoted to Christian. His wife, Effie Fine, and daughter Edith had both been educated there. Businessman Barton Robnett, one of the younger members of the Board, both understood finance and was willing to lead in giving money. He was of a family whose every generation had furnished trustees or students for Christian.

Another whose loyalty came down through his family tree was lawyer Frank G. Harris. President of the Board, his influence as Lieutenant-Governor of Missouri lent enormous prestige to the salvaging of the school. It was no accident that it was Lakenan Price, a lawyer in his firm, who patiently untangled the financial snarl.

Newton D. Evans, practical businessman, was an aggressive aid, as was Dr. E. E. Evans, retired director of the State Institution at Fulton, who gave generously of his wealth. Lumberman John M. Taylor, businessman E. C. Clinkscales, of the family so long connected with Christian, and Professor R. H. Emberson were faithful and active. Clarence E. Lemmon, appointed to the Board by courtesy of his pastorship at the Christian Church, now proved to be one of its more far-seeing members. It was he who called for a budget analysis, helped to enlist out-of-town trustees, and perhaps worked most closely with Miller in interpreting to the others the extent of their peril.

It was worse than they thought, although it was the standard picture of small schools throughout the country. Since 1929 the College had been operating under steadily increasing debt. Miller, toiling with lawyer Price over five years of audits, learned in those four months a lesson in finance which was to haunt him the remainder of his administrative career.

The crisis they faced was as absolute as in the days of J. K. Rogers and the Civil War. But the economy was different. No longer could the students be fed on slaw and beans raised in the College back yard. No more could a faculty be persuaded to teach for board alone. Moreover, the debt, increasing each semester, would have seemed astronomical even to Rogers' financial wizardry. The two men who met Christian's darkest days had characteristics in common. Where Rogers had stubborn determination, Miller had a driving conscientiousness. Where Rogers had faith, Miller had optimism. Both had penetrating minds, a genius for analysis, and a loyalty to the task in hand—which was Christian College.

In the clearest report which had reached the trustees in years, Miller surveyed the crevasse which gaped before them. Whatever could be done, must be done immediately, he emphasized. As for him, he would attempt to fill the College by fall.

Sometimes sleepless, confronted by the course he had to travel, he remembered those long nights spent as relief-navigator in the Navy during the war. As he took the wheel he would answer the calls of his aid whose duty was to report every obstacle in their course.

"Ahoy," he would call.

"Sighted, one bale of hay," the other would answer.

It had been an occasion for humor oftener than not. Never once in those submarine-infested waters had his destination seemed as obscure as it did in the weeks ahead.

While the finance committee nightly sweated out the details of refinancing, Miller hired seven field workers, the most the College had ever had, instructing each to bring in twenty-five girls before September 1. He laid down the law: promise no scholarships; accept none but full-paid tuitions; waste no recruiting effort on girls who could not afford to come. He was surprised that he could be ruthless. It was another quality he had in common with J. K. Rogers—engendered by confronting matters of life and death. He instructed the business secretary to push the collection of old accounts, withholding grades if necessary.

Among routine duties, he got the annual catalog to the printer, edited the best viewbook the College had ever had, attended the important accrediting association meetings, was elected president of the state Junior College Association, covered Missouri speaking to alumnae groups, and hired a full-time business-manager, Roscoe A. Miller.

By April, 1935, the College was again on a firm financial footing. All debts had been consolidated into two bond issues. Chief purchasers had been trustee William Dulany of St. Louis, the five banks of Columbia—and as in Civil War days—numerous other trustees and friends of the College. Even Mrs. Moore had agreed to a reduced annuity.

The new white sign swinging at the College entrance was security, as was the pump at the back door. All future profit was pledged to the quick liquidation of the bonds, which at all events, were due in ten years. But enrollment was up 21 per cent for the next school year. And, once again, the College was saved.

More than ever now, the trustees were sure of the man they wanted as president. Jim Miller had shown himself to be not only the scholar and educator they had expected, but an able administrator, a sound businessman, and, in the push of circumstance, a vigorous promoter.

It was a role he had never sought. Weary beyond rest and waiting for release which never came, in May, 1935, he wrote his friend, D. B. Robnett.

> Dear Barton:
>
> The time has come when I must give a definite and final decision relative to my future course. Barton, during the past few weeks I have repeatedly been reminded of my condition of three years ago. I am convinced that I cannot stand the wear and tear that it is going to take for the next three years here at Christian College. I hope the Board of Trustees will feel that I have given my best. . . .

He volunteered not to announce his move till August so as not to upset the "status quo" of the College. Unconsciously, he echoed the philosophy of Joseph K. Rogers who was determined in his time of trial, that life must go on.

THE HUB AND ITS UNIVERSE

1935-1940

Then here's to one who bosses us all,
If there's ever a parade, she's in it,
And any day in the week you may hear
Her command, "Come here this minute!"

—1920 COLLEGE WIDOW

LIFE DID GO ON, of course. While the depression surged like a flood through the land, while presidents and trustees struggled with finance, while deans had breakdowns and field agents tore their hair, in the little universe that was Christian College daily school life went on. And the hub of that universe was Mrs. Hertig. Ask any student of 1915 until 1945 what comes into her mind at the mention of "Christian College" and she will automatically reply, "Mrs. Hertig." Then she will deluge you with memories: the black-velvet neckband, the imperious air, the face of a cameo, strength of steel. The busy, nervous hands, the straight backbone, the strings of beads and baggy old skirts which somehow created the impression of court trains. Mrs. Hertig at the head of the dining room stairs collecting money for a dance. Mrs. Hertig inspecting the evening gowns for the first Open House and ordering girls back to fill in a décolleté. The next morning, Mrs. Hertig holding up the date book and announcing, "Girls, I'm proud of you."

There was Mrs. Hertig on the red love-seat, waiting for the dates to come in. With her quick, darting eyes and aristocratic, beakish nose, she looked like a wise little bird. Mrs. Hertig on stunt night pushing forward a reluctant member of her "Sniggles Family." (Would Christian girls ever again find anything as hilarious as this travesty on the arts, or Velma Tepe's rendition of "My Wild Irish Rose?") Mrs. Hertig soulfully directing "Follow the Gleam," then opening chapel with: "Now all of you know that your primary purpose in coming to college is to get a man." General Hertig snapping: "Hurry up, hurry up, girls. There's room at the front for you cow-tails."

She was so much more than could be explained by her evolving titles in the years of catalogs: 1911, Head of the Preparatory Department; 1911-19, Instructor in Physical Education; 1919-20, Field Representative; 1920-26, Assistant in English, History, Bible; 1924-46, Editor, *Christian College* (the Alumnae Bulletin);[1] 1928-46, Sponsor, *The College Widow,* 1933-48, Alumnae Secretary;[2] 1935, General Sponsor; 1946, Social Director. The 1920 annual's dedication titles her more accurately: "The college girl's friend, from Y. W. to vaudeville."

To some she was a tyrant. To most she was exactly what they had dreamed of in boarding school life—the "Mrs. Chips" of Christian College. It was she who greeted the girls at their first assembly. Fragile, erect, she made them think of their grandmothers—until she began to make announcements in the latest slang. It was she who saw that each new girl found her Big Sister and plunged into the immediate activity which would counteract homesickness: unpacking, shopping for bedspreads, locating the post office; a trip to Broadway and the picture show the first Saturday night; church, a recital, a letter home the first Sunday, until by Monday the routine of boarding school was safely established.

It was Mrs. Hertig who set the tone of the dining room—that center of college life. She believed in promptness and in conversation at table. There was no "Please pass the butter," or "Lovely weather we're having," when she was within earshot. She would have looked upon today's silent grace as the compromise of a bankrupt spirit. She knew by heart the poetry of the Bible and had Scripture to fit any occasion.

She helped plan the proms and saw that there were plenty of boys, marshalling them from the university fraternities or Kemper Military School in Boonville. At dances she was the favorite chaperon, becoming conveniently blind. She sponsored the Junior Class, and if its president could not write a suitable speech for the banquet, Mrs. Hertig would write it for her. She supervised the Annual, boasting that it always got "out" on time. Under her it had wit and sparkle. Some of its editions are perhaps her best memorial, for there exists no portrait of her as typical as the silhouette in the 1926 volume, while the "Letters from Minnie" in 1937 and 1938 are her characteristic satire.

It was Mrs. Hertig who initiated each generation into the traditions of the College. Many of these she created, to fill the gaps in the deadly confines of school routine. (One irreverent colleague remarked that "every time Mrs. Hertig sneezed it became a tradition.") However, Mrs. Hertig was wise rather than sophisticated, and she knew that the traditions so scorned by sophisticates are in after years the stuff that college memories are made of.

She founded the Lineage Club in 1930—that prestige group whose relatives had attended Christian, and whose president was appointed on the basis of the longest lineage. The May Queen and accompanying pageantry was her early creation[3] and was for many years a Columbia spring event, written up flatteringly in the papers. She loved to have the dancers outdoors and was never reconciled when the affair was moved into the auditorium. Although newcomers to the faculty deplored the childish ceremony and students groaned at having to sing "Gaily Now We Greet the Maytime"—on the fifth of June—the tradition became one of the firmest of Christian College. The artificial flowers which Mrs. Hertig considered sufficient to deck the throne were finally discarded for elaborate florists' arrangements. The old songs were forgotten, but the identity of the Queen is still one of the excitements of college life.

It was Mrs. Hertig who started the grand march at the Hallowe'en party and always managed to dig a costume from the inexhaustible trunk under her bed. (In fact, all the town's Thespians depended on her when in need of a feather boa, velvet cape, or beaded dress.) She blacked the minstrels for the vaudeville show, wrote the skits, and ordered the wigs for the chorus. She directed the YWCA bazaar at Christmas and planned booths for the Athletic Association carnival in the gym in spring. If money was needed for such projects as YWCA she invented ways to raise it, such as publishing and selling the first student directory in 1928.

She even bullied the faculty into performing, and the team of Jimmy Miller and Franklin Launer became famous for a Romeo and Juliet scene climaxed by Juliet's jump from the gym balcony. Dean Miller would, at her urging, do a rousing "On the Road to Mandalay," but Mrs. Hertig had her own Mandalay which was demanded by every year's class of girls as they left for Christmas vacation:

> In the old town of Columbia,
> In the Athens of Mizzou,
> There's an M. U. man a-waitin',
> And he's feelin' pretty blue. . . .

The version would change with the times, "beaux" becoming "dates," "spooning" changing to "necking," for Mrs. Hertig was nothing if not a realist. With the second World War the "M.U. man" became an "Air Corps man," but the popularity of the recitation lasted as long as Mrs. Hertig herself.

Doubtless it was her sense of mischief which endeared her most to these teen-age girls. Who else at a banquet would dare mimic President Lee's habit of scratching his leg, or satirize sober Dr. Long as always finding things "all wrong"? Like most genuises, she was prodigal of her talents and wrote her skits and rhymes on envelopes, backs of programs, pages of half-used chemistry notebooks. These scraps in Mrs. Hertig's scrawl were to turn up for years afterwards in drawers and boxes around the College, the observations on them still so pungent as to make a knowing reader chuckle.

Tourjours gai, Laugh, Clown, Laugh, the show must go on. . . . Everyone recognized these motifs in Mrs. Hertig, but none around her knew how authentically she came by her jester spirit. The facts, which would have fascinated the girls, were pieced together only after her death. There was the grandfather who had been a trouper with Van Amburgh's circus, the first of the great traveling animal shows. This strolling player, who traveled by stage-coach and wagon, fought flood and Indians to bring "Major Drumm's Band" to mud-mired mid-western villages. There was the father who owned the first Magic Lantern show in Union City, Michigan, and the mother who was noted for her readings at church programs. There was the child, herself, making her stage debut as Little Eva in *Uncle Tom's Cabin.* And there was the teenage Minnie Drumm with Shakespeare in her head, adventure in her veins, and an ambition which drove her out of high school to far-away Boston to study expression and become "Marion Willis, Dramatic Reader."[4]

There is a daguerreotype of this Marion Willis, a glamour girl of yesterday, with pompadour over a sweet young face and wide, soulful eyes. Perhaps it was thus that Roland Hertig first saw her on the stage, when this handsome, intellectual young ne'er-do-well cut short her career. The story is trite: impulsive marriage, poverty, babies, the disappearing husband, the struggle to pay the rent. Footlights gave way to study-lamps as her years alternated between going to school, teaching, supporting the two little boys who were her life. Still the talent welled up in her. She poured it out later, to the Christian girls, all the sublimated gusto, the originality, the insight into the never-never land of imagination to which grease paint is the passport.

She gave them something more. For if the clown wore a mask, the face behind it was of granite. In an era of disintegration, she had convictions. Where others would hesitate, she would decide, and act. Where others compromised, she stood firm. She combined a bitter, almost cynical realism with unfaltering ideals. In her, many youngsters caught in the whirlpool of adolescence touched for the first time the rock of real character. It was a contact they never forgot.

Few ever knew with what agony this character had been carved. The tell-tale chips, papers and letters, lay hidden in a tin box under her bed. There was a poignant valentine from the husband after years of separation. On it she had written: "A loyalty that forbids thinking is servitude." There was an obituary on the death of her eldest son after a high school tragedy. . . . A clipping about her youngest being valedictorian, predicting his brilliant future. . . . A penciled note, years later, from this same son—a runaway in a far-off town:

> If I were drowned in the deepest sea,
> I know whose prayers would follow me,
> Mother of Mine. . . .

Finally, the bill for the meager funeral of this young suicide.

She would not have wanted the girls to know these things. What they soon discovered was that, under her rigid exterior, was a perfect pumpkin shell of softness which gave at the first touch of the girl who was lonely or in trouble. This girl could always find solace in Mrs. Hertig's room.

"Mrs. Hertig's room" was a tradition in itself. Number 16, St. Clair, second door west from the dining room stairs, the nine by twelve oblong where she spent twenty-nine years of her life was an inexhaustible treasure house or junk box—as you chose to regard it. From the hall you saw the red bandanna which was always tied over the lampshade; the narrow iron bed with its head against the one window and at its foot an old wooden trunk. To the right of the door as you entered was a small washstand covered with various boxes and surmounted by bookshelves. (The books were usually poetry, annotated and underlined; devotions, and maybe a game or joke book.)

To the left, beyond the closet door, were two rickety green burlap screens behind which—where she could "jump right into them"—hung Mrs. Hertig's old sweaters and wear-sprung skirts. Along the same wall was a mirrored dresser and a plain little three-drawer desk. Under the dresser was a long tin box filled with formals and under the desk a matting hamper crowded with shoes. (It was one of Mrs. Hertig's tenets always to keep shoe-trees in her shoes.) Amidst the clutter on the desk was a dilapidated flat iron and an electric plate on which she heated it.

Here, or in the similar clutter of her office on the second floor of Dorsey Hall, she sat like a busy spider in her web, pasting the endless clippings into her scrapbooks, answering letters from old girls, scribbling items for the alumnae bulletin, or memoranda for the Commencement pageant.

Commencement. Who can think of Commencement without thinking of Mrs. Hertig and "Jerusalem the Golden?" It was she who marshalled the girls through rehearsal of the anthem, drilling them in the chapel for a week before Baccalaureate, until every girl knew every word and the rafters rang. There was no lackadaisical mouthing of words in her day and there were no uneven hemlines in the procession.

"I love the song so," she scribbled plaintively in one of her scrapbooks. "I want them always to sing it while I am here."

Even now as one stands in the crowded church on a hot Baccalaureate Sunday night and hears the marching strains: "Jerusalem the Gold-en with milk and hon-ey blest—;" as the white capped and gowned girls come into sight, and the song goes into the shrill sustained heights of the soprano voices, a chill goes up the spine and one can sense bugles blowing and banners waving. No, as long as they sing "Jerusalem the Golden" Mrs. Hertig will not be forgotten at Christian College. Perhaps she represented, as much as any one in its history, the value of a small college like Christian where the daily impact of personality teaches lessons not found in texts.

"She broadened my horizons," wrote one of her girls, Alma Gray Hill, years afterwards. What more can be got from a college education?

It was Mrs. Hertig, with her sense of tradition, who insisted that the tenth president of Christian College should have an impressive inauguration. For a president had been found. After Lee's resignation and Miller's refusal to accept the position, the disappointed trustees had finally made a contract with Eugene Stephen Briggs.

Dr. Briggs—he had the year before received his Ph.D. in Education from Columbia University—was at the moment the Board approached him, director of adult education for the Missouri State Department of Education. He was a prepossessing man of forty-five, with the hearty voice, ready handshake, and outgoing confidence of a professional public speaker. He was prominent in numerous civic and Christian Church organizations, having served on executive boards of Lions International, YMCA, and the Boy Scouts, among others.

A native Missourian educated at Central College, Fayette, and the University of Missouri, he had the typical school man's background: high school teacher, principal, superintendent of schools, president of a state teachers' college.[5] Most of his teaching experience had been in Oklahoma and he seemed to reflect the breeziness and optimism of the Southwest. To the line of Christian College presidents he brought a new type, frankly twentieth-century: the promoter whose job—it was not a "work" or "calling"—was to get around and establish contacts, to raise money, and to administrate its expenditure.

His educational specialties were also twentieth century: a "Finding and Broadening" course in public speaking for which he had written a text of that title; teacher-training in extra-curricular activities; adult education. He was a leader in this coming field. Characteristically, his additions to the staff were a publicity man, an alumnae secretary, a fencing teacher, and a hair-stylist. To the curriculum he added interior decoration, personal grooming, statistics, sculptoring, and changed dancing from a physical education course to one in fine arts. In fact, during his presidency seven courses were offered by the teacher of dance, Fern Morrison, so that Christian became the only junior college in the United States which offered a major in The Dance. (Shades of its founders!)

Doubtless some of President Briggs' very real interest in the fine arts was the influence of his wife, Mary. A gentle-faced, beautiful woman of southern background (she was a Gentry with Columbia connections) she had some reputation as a painter and was an ardent sponsor of the arts. To her goes credit for having Miss Elizabeth Potts restore all of the College oil portraits in 1936, for building a new interest in art with weekly exhibits, a live Art Club, and lectures by such notables as controversial Thomas Hart Benton.

Eugene Briggs became president in August, 1935, and was officially inaugurated February 19, 1936, in an elaborate ceremony wherein representatives of many colleges and universities participated. He came to Christian at a rather hopeful period in its history. It had just been successfully refinanced and, though the consequent indebtedness loomed ahead for years, the fall of 1935-36 for the first time since the depression found current income promising to meet expenditures. Improvement of the buildings and grounds as contracted for by Lee could progress: a three-year beautification program of planting trees and shrubs on the campus, routine refurbishing of almost all the buildings. There was no way for teachers' salaries to go but up, and the Board endorsed the raises the president recommended, also raising tuition. His promoting extended to teachers and students; he was generous with praise. When, under Mary Paxton Keeley, the *Microphone* won its usual award of being the best college newspaper in its class, he publicized the fact. When a student won a prize in debate, he reported this information to the trustees.

Enrollment had again commenced to climb, so that by the fall of 1936 he was able to claim "the largest junior class ever enrolled." He put field workers in new territories, Indiana, Southern Michigan, Eastern Ohio. He secured girls for the first time in many years from the Delta states. With typical twentieth-century reliance on statistics, he was the first president to set up enrollment quotas from each state, saying that from now on a certain percentage of the population of Christian College would come from Arkansas, or Nebraska, or Iowa.

Promotionally he emphasized what he called "choice" girls, and a select, small school with many extra-curricular activities. Not "the only such institution of its kind in the West," of D. P. Henderson's dreams or the transplanted Wellesley of Mrs. Moore and Mrs. Moss, but "the best small college . . . for young women in the mid-west."

Perhaps the wave of scholastic creation started by Dean Miller did not swell, but the publications flowed on. Booklets of a promotional nature: photographic brochures of "The Dance," "Horsemanship," "Betty Goes to Christian."

He made the first real attempt to organize the alumnae, hiring one of the most widely-known, Portia Penwell Stapel, as alumnae secretary. Ten-year class reunions were held at the Commencements of 1936, 1937, and 1938. By that year three-thousand alumnae addresses were on file, and there were clubs in Columbia, St. Louis, Kansas City, Jefferson City, Springfield, Mexico, and St. Joseph, Missouri; Denver, Colorado; Des Moines, Iowa; Wichita, Topeka, and Ft. Scott, Kansas; Springfield, Illinois; and Paducah, Kentucky.

Encouraged by the fact that after one year, twelve Juniors had come in through the efforts of alumnae clubs, Briggs averred: "It is my honest conviction that a small budget appropriated for the cultivation of the alumnae work will yield the largest returns of any single project to be undertaken."

All of these promotions President Briggs undertook. Unfortunately, they were ephemeral, and like wind over the prairie were to blow on, leaving little mark on Christian College. He did not remain long enough to accomplish the larger projects he advocated, but he must be given credit for seeing and stating their need. Consistently he urged a renewed drive for endowment and scholarship donations. From the first he appealed for a health unit housing an infirmary, botany and biology laboratories; a better-located library, with more books; a fine arts building. All these he thought could be added within five years.

Only the infirmary materialized, in less ambitious form, when in November, 1937, the Board arranged to purchase a two-story house across the street. This roomy building on the southeast corner of Rogers Street facing the campus released the "sick wing" of St. Clair for dormitory space, banishing the days of segregated corridors and covered trays.

Health care was a science now, with Columbia's leading physician, Dudley Robnett, making daily visits as college doctor, and a trained nurse in constant attendance. A physical examination had long been required of each girl and routine check-ups were made and reported to her parents.

But the laboratories stayed in Dorsey Hall basement. Although he secured a small Carnegie grant for books, the library remained in noisy proximity to the gym, and study continued to be punctuated by the dribbling of basketballs. As enrollment increased Briggs transferred his enthusiasm for a fine arts building into arguments for a dormitory.

Of this need the practical trustees were convinced. Encouraged by recent additions to endowment, notably gifts from Mrs. Moss's good friends, Frank and Ella Vaughn Hughes—they started a $400,000 building campaign and hired a professional promoter to raise money in the state. After a few months in 1937 they called it off, deciding the time was not propitious.

From experience the Board mistrusted promotions. Promotions were easy to launch, difficult to accomplish. And some of them had wondered, before the fanfare of his inaugural had quite died away, whether their new president would be long at Christian College. He was frankly committed to co-education. He was accustomed to a state institution where funds came, according to one's persuasive eloquence, more or less unlimited from the legislature. Back from his many speaking tours came rumors of positions offered.

The trustees were, on the whole, not surprised when Eugene Briggs, after a two-and-a-half year administration, announced in December, 1937, that he had accepted the presidency of Phillips University in Enid, Oklahoma. A co-educational, church-affiliated school in his chosen state, it was a position which suited him admirably and which he has filled with success to this day.

The embarrassment of being without a president in midyear was almost balanced by the Board's unanimity in knowing just what president they wanted. But it was a subtly different James Miller who returned to Christian College the first of February, 1938. Maturity had improved his natural good looks; deepened the resonant voice, assured the imposing stature, engaging manner, carefulness, even nattiness, in dress.

His diffidence was diminished. Two years as dean of a large state institution had made him confident that he could administer. Some disillusion in the job he was leaving—it had not held the future he anticipated—a knowledge of what he was returning to, good and bad, made him rather sure of what he intended to do at Christian.

He had left, a promising educator of forty-four whose name was becoming known wherever educational journals were read. He had gone to Maryville as somewhat of an authority on college matriculation, accrediting, student guidance. He came back to Christian in larger stature, as a figure in public education in Missouri. One incident among several illustrates how this happened.

He was serving on the Missouri Educational Conference established to set up a course of study for the elementary schools of the state. The results would be published as a textbook. As the conference went to work, the chairman remarked that the publication really should carry a statement of the philosophy of public school education in Missouri.

To Miller's analytical mind, planning a curriculum without defining its purpose was the cart before the horse. At Maryville, he was teaching a course in the philosophy of education. That semester he threw out the textbook. In its place, he and his students enthusiastically worked out one of their own. When the Missouri Educational Conference met to compile its findings, the dean from Maryville was the only member who had prepared the needed statement.

Thus, "A Philosophy of Education . . . for Elementary Courses of Study," by James Conelese Miller, was published as the foreword to 50,000 volumes which went out in 1936 to grade school principals all over Missouri. Later reprinted as a leaflet by the State Department of Education,[6] it helped to send him back to Christian with the reputation of being an educational philosopher.

There, he found little time to philosophize. With his dean, Robert Sala, he plunged the faculty into the project of revising the vocational guidance booklet, "What Shall I Do?" At first it seemed like old times, and faculty studies carrying the name of Christian College again appeared in print. But soon he found his talent for expression going almost entirely into alumnae speeches, promotional viewbooks, reports to the board of trustees.

"I thought I would spend 90 per cent of my time teaching and 10 per cent administering," he recalled wistfully. "Instead, I found it was 10 per cent educating and 90 per cent keeping up the enrollment." For an educational philosophy was desirable. A strong faculty was important. A balanced budget was imperative. But none of these, in a girls' college, can exist without girls.

Girls, girls. Enrollment, promotion. These were to become in Miller's subconscious the bugaboo which formerly the debt had been. The debt was still there, but he had helped refinance that and was confident that he could deal with it. Back in the old situation, it seemed for a brief while as if the old psychological reactions were setting in; the familiar tensions, the fear of crack-up. It took the childish query of his youngest, seven-year-old Barbara, to bring him to. "Daddy" she asked, puckering up an anxious forehead which was very like his own, "what's the matter? Did you lose another girl?"

He would grow accustomed to the fact that in February and March one scans the field agents' reports, rapidly deducts a percentage for cancellations, and predicts what next fall's enrollment will be. He learned to read financial columns with a broker's fear of inflation, weather reports with a farmer's dread of drought. The climax of Commencement was always spoiled by the knowledge that tomorrow morning, in the wreckage of abandoned halls, he must start to work in earnest to see that the rooms were filled again by September.

He thought out devices to handle the problems of promotion and put them into effect. He instituted a week of orientation, this time for the field representatives, bringing them back to campus in the fall to attend classes, talk with teachers, discuss the girls they had brought, and to be instructed by an outside expert in techniques of "selling" the College. He set up a quota for each, and published their competitive results in a weekly newsletter. Under him, they became not mere salesmen, but, increasingly, "educational counselors," prepared to advise on curriculum and credits as well as what sort of underwear to take to college. Although they no longer pinned long blue ribbons on their charges and herded them to the station, it was their job to see that each arrived safely in Columbia, to help locate her baggage, to stand on call any hour for a month afterwards to reassure pangs of homesickness or call on over-anxious parents. Such longtime counselors as J. Kelly Wright, Mary White, Betty Blake, Nell Fish, Lillian Pebworth, Helen Reifel, were fondly remembered by many girls as their first link with Christian.

The new President contracted for national magazine advertising. He issued promotional booklets.[7] He drove the Double Sextette all over Missouri and Iowa, a marimba strapped to his running board; spoke at teachers' meetings and church conventions. All of these efforts, plus good times, made a pleasant table of rising enrollment.

1937	246
1938	263
1939	284

While his right hand was steering promotion, his left hand was busy with all sorts of things. For the vicious part of the administrative circle is that, in order to attract the girls who pay the fees, you must already be able to offer what those fees pay for: a good residence hall being the most obvious asset.

It reflects the confidence of the trustees in Miller that by his second fall—September, 1939—he was able to open the doors of the long projected Hughes Hall. This $100,000 dormitory of brick and stone, to the west of the auditorium and facing Missouri Hall across the campus, resulted largely from the bequest of trustee Frank Hughes of Liberty, Missouri, who willed a total of $85,000 to Christian College.

Many a Christian College faculty member felt he owned a few bricks in that building, also, for soon after his return Miller had made a daring request. He suggested that each teacher pledge one month's salary towards completion of the new dormitory. Moreover, he did not recommend the salary raises his predecessor had led them to expect. Instead, after a firm look at budget figures versus enrollment, he had suggested that all the faculty be continued at their usual salaries *if* enrollment should reach 250.

This act illustrates the courageous realism which was to identify President Miller's administration. That his faculty accepted it, illustrates another of his distinctive administrative qualities: charm, and great personal powers of persuasion. Most of his success later would be traceable to one of these two qualities—realistic good judgment, and his personal relations with others.

His friendship with Mrs. Hertig, for example, was responsible for prompt payment of the debt on the new infirmary, when she furnished the money through a life-time annuity arrangement. For a while the house was called "Hertig Hall," but the name never stuck.

It was a disappointment that only two units of Hughes Hall had been built. The north wing of the "U" was still on the blueprint. However, sixty-six more girls could now be housed adequately on campus, and no tremendous new debt had been incurred. Miller was almost as conservative about incurring debt as were his trustees, for they had all been burnt together. His policy was, and continued to be, to keep up with the most needed repairs, constantly to reduce the debt, to expand when one could see where the money was coming from. This was not often, and his goals for expansion were to be repeated annually in the *Minutes* of the Board. They were: (1) the completion of Hughes Hall, (2) the building of a small library, (3) a fine arts building with provisions for visual education, (4) a suitable home for the president.

Since the days when students had practiced piano in J. K. Rogers' living room the presidents of Christian College had been shunted about campus with astonishing disregard for privacy. Even the Lees had spent their first years in a tiny suite off the administration corridor. Moving to the old Beta Sigma Omicron house had been an improvement but by now this cottage was less desirable. Dr. Miller justifiably felt that the home of the president of Christian College should compare favorably with those from which his students came.

Like Rogers before him he was motivated by the determination to "make things nice" for his family. He had three daughters who were constantly with girls from well-to-do homes. He had a serene and lovely wife whose interests were in the sphere of home-making; who never meddled with campus politics, but who supported him in the quiet, modest way of the southern lady. It was a firm support, nonetheless, and her strength stood behind many of his decisions. Her belief in his capability often had led him to achieve. Her encouragement during the low periods had pulled him through. For Nell, especially, perhaps to make up for their daily goldfish-bowl existence, he set the goal of a gracious home. But this expansion, like the others, was to come only as a result of exigency.

His concept of the library is interesting. It shows the visionary strain with which his realism had conflict.

> . . . It is my thought that if we could set it back just slightly, perhaps between Missouri Hall and the swimming pool, and connect it to the front with a corridor . . . the arrangement would be fine. I should like for this corridor to be wide enough and large enough so that it could be used as a kind of museum. We could collect therein Christian College treasures, things which the alumnae will cherish through the years. We could dedicate it to the memory of higher education of women, or perchance . . . to early womanhood in Missouri.
>
> . . . this entrance, which I believe is a better name than corridor, should lead into a small, but beautiful library, perhaps with a fireplace in either end, with arrangements made for study booths with a great deal of attention given to the appointments and accessories. I should like to make it a kind of dream place, a place that will linger in the minds of our girls long after they have gone from here.[8]

No one, reading his vigorous proposals made year after year to the trustees, could accuse him of lack of interest in physical expansion. But he kept his own counsel, and when he was forced to compromise, he compromised in favor of a balanced budget. The ideals and dreams were always seething underneath. The recognition—for he was a clear-seeing man—that ultimately it had to be his own decision which kept them underneath—cultivated a growing strain of irony in his character. It distilled out, occasionally, in prose, as in a later report describing the new incinerator:

> Although it seems a bit incongruous in college circles and among polite people to mention the word garbage, I cannot illustrate my point better than to introduce this somewhat unsavory word. For some time we have been warned . . . that our method of garbage disposal was far less efficient than the remainder of our food service. This summer, in order that we might dispose of the subject and conform to the recommendations of the State Board of Health, a small building has been constructed to the rear of the kitchen and if not with pride, at least with confidence, we can say . . . that no finer quarters are to be found on the campus than those occupied by the garbage.[9]

In the daily compromises between fine arts and garbage he kept a certain goal in mind. It began to loom ahead, as clear and lofty as the auditorium tower seen from Christian College Avenue. It would be the star to his wagon, the grail to his quest . . . what the Jubilee had been to Mrs. Moss. Thus, his proposals became part of a ten year plan whose climax was to occur January 18, 1951. For, he reminded the Board, on that date the College would be a hundred years old.

XI

THE TELESCOPED YEARS

1940-1949

It is possible that the future . . . will be shaped by men and women rather than by units of subject matter.

—JAMES C. MILLER

CENTENNIAL. As J. C. Miller first wrote the word, he savored its lyrical qualities. He was a man who appreciated words. It would be a summing up of all the history and tradition to which he was sensitive. It would justify those he had known, Mrs. Moss, Mrs. Hertig, and the incomparable Rogers who had been held up to him so often—people who had almost given their lives to the project of Christian College. At that moment he could see the campus ten years hence, debt-free agleam with new buildings.

The trustees made no comment on his plan. The public did not hear about it, for always Miller preferred a finished report to publicized air castles. What people could see in 1940 was that the school was filled, the plant looked prosperous, "good times" seemed on hand for Christian College. It was the best year financially since James Miller had been on the staff.

But to him "the most professionally satisfying year of my life" commenced in February, 1941, when he was elected president of the American Association of Junior Colleges.

It was not only that this was the highest honor in his own educational circle. It was not only the inclusion in various Who's Whos, the newspaper recognition, the interesting functions—such as the Centennial of the University of Chicago—which he was automatically delegated to attend. It was the stimulation of working with America's top educators, the challenge of expressing his opinion. For now he spoke as the voice of the 610 junior colleges of America.

His ascendancy in the educational world was not an accident. Though he had been forced to put promotion and finances first, he had managed to keep educational fences in repair. Christian had been represented, by president or dean, at all the important educational conferences each year. He and Dean Sala had been active in founding a Missouri Association of Junior College Administrators. Miller had kept his position as an educational leader in the Christian church, serving on the Missouri Educational Commission and the Board of Education of the Disciples of Christ. Now his election to office made Christian the only college in America which had furnished two presidents to the American Association of Junior Colleges. It was true that "for many years Christian College has exerted leadership in the American junior college field far beyond anything that its size would appear to suggest."

He had continued to stress the improvement of instruction. As a dean, he had done it from within, by influence and inspiration. Now he did it from above as an administrator. The policies of his first years as president were to be the policies of his entire administration. When a faculty member left, he tried to hire a better qualified one in his place. When he had to choose between quality and quantity, he would choose quality, tending to increase the responsibilities of one good teacher rather than add a doubtful one. His faculty showed not only a marked increase of M.A.'s and Ph.D.'s over the past, but high degrees from first class universities. There was real meat on the educational bones of Christian College.

He had instituted an opening week of faculty seminars—the old soul-searching. Each year saw a faculty project. (The 1940-41 study had been a survey of how alumnae of the last five years would evaluate their education at Christian College.)

Miller relied on strong deans. Precocious Robert Sala, competent Julia Spaulding, Stella Meyer, of penetrating mind. Margaret Habein, dean of students, was a young woman of intense personality, and a splendid public speaker. He hired the best people he could find, paid them as much as he could, raised their salaries when the College showed a good year and always was pricked by the knowledge that he could not pay them enough. He had a profound respect for both brains and versatility. Moreover he was a shrewd bargainer. It was one of his educational economies to search for the person with more than one talent. If the applicant for singing teacher happened to be a champion swimmer, so much the better. He admitted the advantage of being able to supplement one or two courses for which there was small demand with part-time instructors from the University of Missouri.

He expected loyalty. And when he had hired persons he thought competent for the jobs, he let them alone. It was a democratic principle with him. Hands off. Laissez-faire. As in a democracy, some were not equal to it. The unsure and incompetent might falter and look for more guidance. The creative, the competent, were free to go as far as they could in any direction, employing the methods they thought best. Sometimes there would be over-lappings, an unbalanced emphasis where some faculty member was outstanding in ideas and aggressiveness; but as in a democracy he would in time be balanced by someone else.

Mrs. Hertig's dominance was perhaps a result of the laissez-faire system. She served as the President's mentor in many little ways; wrote his publicity for the newspapers, jotted down anecdotes which she thought he might use in a speech, reminded him of a certain girl's alumnae connections or suggested that he write certain parents a note. She was the only person in the College who walked into his study unannounced, having been known to interrupt a conference with some idea that would not wait. He recognized her usefulness, was touched by her devotion, and kept a humorous detachment towards the inconveniences it might cause.

Along with these public relations functions she had reassumed the alumnae work, answering the voluminous correspondence, hoarding the wedding announcements, writing and editing the Bulletin, and recording name and address changes. All this she did in her own way, perhaps to the detriment of alumnae organization, for Mrs. Hertig was more interested in individuals than in clubs. Her tremendous personal influence must be balanced against her unorthodox methods; if she did not approve a certain girl's marriage she was likely to keep her on the rolls under her maiden name or throw out her card altogether.

If along with this faculty freedom of action went an amusing tendency for everyone to have his say on everything, it only emphasized the "college family" feeling which had always been so much a part of Christian. Altogether, it was a congenial atmosphere in which to work and it was to the administrator's credit that his faculty was to be the most stable in the history of the school.

The individual touch remained his criterion for good teaching. He admitted to a conservative view of the fads which were popping up in many colleges for women and hoped junior colleges would not go too far in the vocational direction. Christian had antedated many schools in foreseeing vocational courses. Every catalog since 1929 had carried a statement on the "terminal" as well as the "preparatory" curriculum available. Having recognized the need years ago, Miller saw no reason to raise the question again.

Most of the changes of his years reflected contemporary trends. Miller had immediately dropped Lee's education courses as no longer sensible in competition with the University's laboratory school. Stress on American government and political science mirrored his own interests as well as an enlarging world. To sociology he added Marriage and the Family; to home economics Home Management, Textiles, and Merchandising, where girls supplemented schoolroom periods by working in Columbia's dress shops. This represented a full circle from the days when young ladies were forbidden to open accounts with local merchants. Although sweaters, skirts and sox were the simple favorites of the forties, "dressing" the college girls was now Columbia's big business. Few cities had smarter specialty shops.

The secretarial department had expanded, for most career opportunities were in this field. All types of business courses were taught, and energetic Dorothy Shiley McArthur took her students on field trips to St. Louis or Kansas City industries. Since 1944 a system of on-the-job training had given Christian girls experience in local offices. Their Columbia "bosses" liked the social poise they brought to work along with knowledge of economics and business arithmetic.

In religion the formal courses were now taught by the student pastor of the Christian Church. On Sundays girls went to the church of their choice or one of the large student congregations in town. Other religious experiences were Thursday night vespers conducted by a student Vesper Board, and "Religion-In-Life Week." First held in 1943 as a period of spiritual emphasis on Columbia's three campuses, it became the annual high point of Christian's pre-Easter calendar. It brought to the students outstanding speakers of various denominations and possibly inspired as much spiritual inquiry in modern girls as the required year of studying the Pentateuch had in their predecessors. Miller felt it was one of the most vital additions in his time.

One of the President's concessions to demand (and, incidentally, publicity) was a Personal Presence program introduced by Josephine Dillon, first wife of Clark Gable. It was unimportant to the student body that she had the qualifications to coach girls in public speaking, manners, grooming, and dress which these lectures covered. Clark Gable was a magic name in 1939-40 when every college girl had sat through the four hours of *Gone With the Wind* and imagined herself a Scarlett O'Hara.

Student organizations under Miller reflected him more typically. The clubs Lee started, the extra-curricular activities promoted by Briggs, were retained and even multiplied. But during Miller's administration they became chapters of professional honor societies (Delta Eta Chi instead of "the Science Club"). On the whole he held to one philosophy: "As to our educational program," he wrote, "I propose to continue to add units that seem to be practical, but for the main part adhere to a substantial academic program which yields credit transferable to any reputable school."

No doubt the academic solidity of Christian College had helped to hoist the man most responsible for it to the top honor of his profession. He could not have become president of the American Association of Junior Colleges at a more significant time.

By spring of 1941 national defense was the hottest subject in America. By summer the educators of the country, like all other groups, had rallied to make their plans. President Miller, as representative of one of the eight large educational associations of America, was called to Washington to attend a conference sponsored by the Committee on Military Affairs. It was something he never forgot—dynamic little Mayor LaGuardia explaining plans for defending the largest city in the world, sessions with officials of the War and Navy Departments, the Federal Security Agency, the United States Office of Education. It gave a swift sense of being in the center of things. However, the school men were told to return home that fall and run their institutions without change "as long as circumstances would permit."

This was not long. On December 7, just as the girls at Christian were beginning to chant "ten more days till vacation," came Pearl Harbor—and war.

Immediately the key educators were called to Washington again. This time President Roosevelt asked them to prepare definite emergency plans to place before a conference of college and university presidents on January 3. It was a rich experience for Jimmy Miller, the Ozark farm boy who had trudged off to teachers' college not knowing what a credit was, to be conferring across a table in Washington with

President Conant of Harvard or Mildred McAfee Horton of Wellesley. When the subject arose whether students should receive credit hours for special war-time courses Miller spoke in favor of it, daring to disagree with some more rigid academicians. He was thinking of his own return from World War I, the sense of time irretrievably lost which might have kept him from finishing his education altogether had not a wise administrator observed that "a year tramping around Europe ought to count for some education," and waved him on with his class.

The conference of college and university presidents on January 3 and 4 in Baltimore was the largest such gathering of officials in the United States. J. C. Miller presided over the junior college section. One of the ten-man committee on recommendations, he helped formulate the policies adopted by United States colleges for the duration of the war: plans for the acceleration of learning, proper utilization of man power in schools, deferment of college students, safeguarding the teacher supply, sustaining proper morale, and the introduction of subjects more pertinent to the times.

This last was perhaps where Miller shone. He called together his faculty and set them their most vital project: to draft a plan of instruction which would enlist the students as active participants in the war effort. They responded with speed and imagination. By second semester, 1941-42, Christian College had in operation a War Service Program so outstanding as to attract imitators among many other schools.

Every girl was required to pass the standard Red Cross first aid course. Each student was required to take two hours per week in some war service course designed to ready her for defense work in her own community. These electives—typing, business machine operation, Red Cross sewing, nutrition, group feeding, home nursing, community recreation—were taught by staff members in addition to their regular work. Assemblies were devoted to a series of analytical talks on "America at War," and a weekly period was assigned to community singing. The girls gave dozens of programs for service organizations and traveled to nearby Fort Leonard Wood to stage variety shows for the soldiers.

The four years of World War II were a period of high excitement and low morale at Christian. It was not easy to be a schoolgirl when your brother or boy friend had suddenly become a hero. Less privileged daughters were rushing to work in factories or join the armed forces. Although few restrictions remained, boarding school life seemed more than ever a prison. Without dates to brighten the weekend the trivia that usually absorbed their day—the morning rush to the post-office, the concern over diets and laundry, the chatter about boys, bridge and clothes, the pajama stampede to the tea room after study hall—seemed tiresome and unreal.

Christian girls were not content to live out the times vicariously, as had their grandmothers who begged Professor Hurt to tell them about his experiences in the Mexican War. It was no longer possible to withhold the newspapers as Rogers had done during the Civil War, or build a higher fence around the campus. The student body of Christian College as it faced its fourth war was determined to enter into it—as far as women could. It might be with a dance for sailors passing through town, a mixer for six hundred university ROTC boys, a "Wing Swing" for the air force cadets, a "Thanks to Yanks" week of war stamp selling.

Inevitably the problems of adolescent emotions and morals were heightened. Disciplinary infractions were likely to be serious ones. Discussions on war marriages were held in an effort to forestall sudden elopements. Many a sober session took place in "Hobbie's" room or potential tragedy was untangled across the President's desk. Although he thought that by now nothing could surprise him, he was sometimes shocked in his dealings with parents. How much more concerned some were with their own pride than their daughters' problems! How eager to blame him for their own delinquencies. He could be scathing, but his usual method of dealing with criticism was to deflect it. "You are quite right—" he would commence; and before he finished the critic was wondering what he would have done in the same situation.

The girls' problems came very close to Miller, for his own eldest, Jean, was at home with her baby while her husband served abroad, and his second daughter, Carol, was in college. Although, as he became increasingly preoccupied, his door might be closed to many, it was always open to the girls. He never ceased to marvel at the underlying seriousness of these adolescents, whether bubbling or blasé. Sometimes they would make him feel again as president the humility of his first week as dean, when he found himself the teacher taught. One such World War II incident stands out as an example of the spirit of Christian College girls.

It was almost impossible to get help in the dining room or kitchen by 1942. Dietician Louise Yeager who had recently replaced Mrs. Funkhauser, even utilized some of the office staff to try to serve meals as efficiently as ever. The girls sat patiently through the delays, outwardly concerned that the point of their pie was turned towards them so their lovers would be true, or listening for that moment of silence at twenty past six when the ghost of "the gray lady" walked. But as they sat, they wondered: Why couldn't they wait tables as a war service? Their brothers were doing more menial tasks in army camps. When three girls approached the President with the idea, he thought it a mistake. He felt it might detract from the atmosphere of the dining room, be undemocratic to lower some girls to the rank of serving others. However, when he agreed to let the student body vote on it they showed him how truly democratic they were. Overwhelmingly they rushed to serve.

Louise Yeager's system of captains and teams was an education in itself and serving in the dining room continued as a popular feature of the school. Even a wealthy girl felt the thrill of earning her first dollar this way. The traditional refinement of Christian College dining—candlelight, goblets, real linen and silver—did not alter. At formal dinners the uniformed girls with trays felt no envy of the seated girls in evening dress, especially since they could keep on their bobby-sox and saddle-oxfords!

If it was not easy to be a girl in war-time, neither was it simple to be an administrator. Christian lost faculty as young men left for the service, women followed their husbands. Miller was grateful for those who remained to carry a heavier load: R. A. Miller, who handled the irritations of rationing and war-time travel; Stella Meyer, who acted as dean when Sala joined the Air Force. All the pressure was against keeping education normal. Schools were operating the year around, night and day. Educators predicted that soon 60 per cent of students would be in industry. President Miller added such timely courses as ground school training in aviation. But the chaos only convinced him that Christian should remain academically sound. He philosophized that the women's college in prolonged wartime might even become what the church had been through the upheaval of the Middle Ages—a citadel for culture.

Unlike former presidents, he had no problem keeping the school open. With more than half the nation's colleges closed to civilian students it was a field day for women's colleges. There were long waiting lists by each February of the war.

The question of building was taken out of his hands. There was no civilian construction now. But the enrollment boom accomplished some of the expansion his previous arguments had not. In 1944 the College purchased the two-story frame home of Mrs. Moss across the street opposite the infirmary. "The White House" became a Senior annex, housing twelve girls. An excellent brick building two doors down Christian College Avenue was bought as a home for the President, and ten girls moved into his cottage on campus. St. Clair basement was entirely rebuilt to enlarge the dining room, create a Town Girls' suite, and add new classrooms for the commercial department. In 1945 Eagle Rock Farm on Highway 63, which the College had been leasing, was purchased as the Christian College Riding Farm to be operated by Mrs. Claud Drew.

"We are riding the crest of the wave," Miller warned the Board. But he was human. Where, five years before he had felt 300 was the ideal enrollment, in 1944 with an all-time high registration of 363 he was saying . . . "we should never plan to go beyond an enrollment of 400. . . ."

The boom brought money to make improvements, to increase salaries, to set up a faculty retirement plan. The old need to borrow in summer to tide over until fall disappeared during Miller's administration. Just as his personal goal of a home was achieved almost overnight so, with the end of the war, came the administrative triumph of his ten years' struggle with college finances. In 1945—"it was the happiest day of my life"—he was able to sign and hand to the equally jubilant "R. A." the check which meant that Christian College was out of debt.

It brought a feeling of relief he never wanted to lose. It was to affect his decisions always and make him cautious. Of late, the decisions, like the struggles, had been largely his. The trustees would have been the first to credit him with the fact that, after steering them through the depression, he had now brought them through the war. They recognized his leadership with a vote of thanks and a generous bonus. He hoped, a little wearily, that they would remember it later if the tide began to turn. "The post-war years will be different," he prophesied. "I think we should not be tempted to veer too far from our course . . . to disturb too much the century-old continuity of Christian College."

Century . . . centennial. . . . The word was sliding back into his consciousness. Only now the ten-year plan of preparation would have to be a five-year plan. Should the College plunge and build? Some schools were already contracting for dormitories, libraries, reckless of unknown cost and dubious materials. He got out the blueprint for Hughes Hall and mailed it to St. Louis architects for completion.

Then suddenly the war was over. The restlessness, the black headlines, the blare of radio, the abnormal social problems. At Commencement, 1945, one looked immediately backwards to the death of President Roosevelt, the chartering of the United Nations, the hysteria of V-E Day. Just ahead, if one dared look, was Hiroshima and the start of an atomic age.

A footnote to the past was the death of Mrs. W. T. Moore, ending a thirty-six year hold over the fortunes of Christian College. During that time the school had paid her more than $90,000 in annuities. And the end of an era for Christian College girls was the fact that Mrs. Hertig was dying. In 1947 she was moved to a convalescent home and the real Mrs. Hertig after thirty-six years had left Christian. It fell to her friend, St. Clair house-mother Maud McConnell, to clean out her room so that a new girl might have the space. The costumes, the clipping books, the endless scribble-scrabbles of correspondence and memoranda, were consigned to attic or basement, the moths and the whitefish. As she shut the door on the bare room, "Mrs. Mac" remembered how Mrs. Hertig herself had often closed it after a good evening of talk, with her favorite farewell: "Goodnight, sweet prince. . . ." She hid away the portrait of "Marion Willis, dramatic reader," and the photograph of two little boys.

President Miller went to see Mrs. Hertig when he could. Sometimes she amused him with a lucid return to dominance and bossy bits of advice. Once she made him promise that when she died he alone would take her back to Union City.

December 1, 1949, he kept the promise. He accompanied her coffin to the dingy station platform of the town she had left years before as Minnie Drumm; shook hands with the little party of strangers—a brother, a childhood friend. He looked once more at the figure so quiet in her favorite red evening dress. ("I like any color just so it's red.") He watched the last spadeful of earth scatter on her grave. Then he took the train home.

It had not been easy to take time for this trip. He was a very busy man now. New honors and responsibilities had given him constant appointments to keep, meetings to attend. In 1946 he had been elected vice-president of the North Central Association of Colleges and Secondary Schools. As one of fourteen men who set accrediting standards for twenty north central states he further assured Christian's academic respectability. He had been active in the Disciples of Christ Crusade for a Christian World, a fund drive for church institutions which ultimately was to net Christian College some $70,000.

Wartime turnover in deans had left more work for him. For the last ten years he had directed college promotion almost entirely. Always he had to struggle with poor health. Now, for the first time, enrollment was slipping. It was well that his faculty was self-functioning. If the President was busy, if the President was sometimes away when a problem arose, only a few did not appreciate that he was cementing the foundation under their ivory tower. Sometimes he felt remote, remembering what an old administrator had told him: "A college president has no time for friends."

But he had long ago pushed to the back of his mind the conflict between administrator and educator. It was only rarely it stirred, as when his remarks at faculty meeting brought one of his teachers impulsively to his side.

"Oh, Dr. Miller," she said. "That was like old times when you were dean! Why did you ever let yourself be president?"

"I had a family to support," he answered dryly. . . .

He remembered this, and other incidents, on the dreary trip home, in the retrospect that funerals bring. He thought of the changes in his back-ground . . . of Eugene, Missouri, the home-town his father had named, with its red and white barber pole and the chickens crossing the road . . . of little Jimmy Miller whose job it was so long ago to keep the sorghum running. Now he had a tow-headed grandson who probably had never tasted sorghum.

He thought of the things he had not accomplished since those far-off days, and for comfort, totted up the compensations. Some of the best were small things: the upturned faces of the girls by candlelight as he quoted from "Locksley Hall" at the Christmas banquet; the sweet sad sound of their voices as they sang in the dining room. "For all we know we may never meet again. . . ." His daughter Barbara had written one of the songs: "When you're just around the corner from life's wide-open door." He thought of the eternal youth that flowed around him renewed each fall, that kept him young and made him feel old.

He thought of what he had accomplished in his job—which was the College. Academic soundness, a fixed enrollment, a balanced budget, a good name in school and church circles—these he could admit with modest pride. If he had compared himself, in the past, to the man who had buried his one talent, it was going to be increasingly pleasant in the future to be able to dig it up! But he sighed for the unbuilt buildings.

The Board might have followed his authority, but always after looking at the budget he had put the blueprints back into a drawer. Prices were rising too fast. Schools that had plunged were closing their doors. The crest had passed, there was every chance of recession ahead. The peace, the security, that the world had looked for had not come.

Publicly he expressed optimism, the conviction that the atom would be harnessed for human welfare. Privately, he thought often of a news story which had made a great impression on him—of a pilotless rocket plane which had attained a speed of 1,500 miles per hour. Was it a symbol of life in the post-war world?

Yes, stability was important. Even if a black-lettered budget sheet was to be his chief memorial, he would continue to follow the middle ground of common sense. He would not gamble with all he had earned. Surely, in these chaotic times, if he could bring the old College safely to its hundredth year, he would have accomplished enough.

Before he got off the train he thought of what he must write for the alumnae bulletin about Mrs. Hertig's death. "The Last Journey," he might call it. He walked the half block downhill from the Wabash station to the big brick house on Christian College Avenue feeling suddenly very tired.

XII

OF FAITH AND IVY
1949-1951

We gather now about this scene
With hearts all full of love;
We plant below the ivy green,
We plant our faith above.
—CLASS DAY SONG, W. T. MOORE, 1901

THE CENTENNIAL LOOMED too close now. Like most birthdays as one grows older, it brought into focus all the discrepancies, the projects uncompleted, the sense of time running out.

To James C. Miller it began to bring the old tension. True, he had strong new help on the administrative staff. Thomas T. Blewett, dean of faculty, was personable, a good public speaker, full of progressive ideas. The new dean of women, Mrs. Dora Johnson, who succeeded youthful Jean Sloan, was gracious, able, a woman of firm character. Neil Freeland, a former state supervisor of secondary education who had also had experience in promotion, was hired as director of admissions as Miller for the first time turned over the chief responsibility of filling the College to other hands.

Promotion was a prime necessity in 1950. Prices were still rocketing, expenses and tuitions must go up, the situation in Korea was heading for war, and cautious parents were not committing their pocketbooks. Small colleges were caught in the squeeze between rising operational costs and decreased revenue.

It had been agreed to celebrate the Centennial with two distinct episodes—Charter Day on January 18, 1951, when the founding would be emphasized, and Centennial Commencement Week, which would be a giant homecoming for the alumnae. Miller himself was chiefly concerned with finding two top flight speakers for these occasions. During the lean years when he became president he had rejected the idea of a ceremonial inauguration for himself. But for the College—if pomp and ceremony were to be appropriate he wanted them achieved with distinction.

Instantly the details arose: the hundreds of invitations to go out, the involved correspondence, the time and transportation schedules, the housing, the entertainment, the radio coverage, the information for newspapers. Anticipating these, he had hired Raymond Derr, a former newspaper man, as director of public relations. Derr was to answer the who, what, when, and why that arose daily, to be in charge of what was euphemistically called "arrangements." The task of notifying alumnae and planning their homecoming was assigned to a regular staff member whose versatility Miller admired, William Bedford. Teacher of organ and music appreciation since 1938, he had also edited the alumnae bulletin since Mrs. Hertig's illness. But copies of the Bulletin, almost the last link now with out-of-town alumnae, were returning from the post office at an alarming rate. War years had brought constant address and name changes, dissolution of most of the alumnae clubs. Bedford pointed out that in order to notify old girls of the Centennial he would have to correct five thousand names on the files. Thus one big project of the Centennial year—the Alumnae Directory—was started, the only such publication since 1911. A Centennial history was under way, too; the history Mrs. Hertig had refused to write. This also had ramifications, for a plea to Bulletin readers to help fill gaps in college information brought in such a wealth of records and souvenirs that it became necessary to set up a museum to house them. Another project was a fund drive launched by local alumnae for a chapel organ as a memorial to Luella St. Clair-Moss.

Aside from this low-pressure drive, carried on entirely through the Bulletin, Dr. Miller was determined to ask for no money. He held fast to this against the opposition of some around him who felt that a large gathering of alumnae was the supreme opportunity to solicit financial support. Like a parent whose children are coming home, he wanted to give them the best of everything. He would, to use an expression from his childhood, "put the big pot in the little one." Also, he was determined that everything about the College should look prosperous for their visit. New paint was needed here, new slipcovers there. A new stair carpet must be laid, a floor retiled.

R. A. Miller bore the brunt of most of these activities, aided by the dormitory hostesses, Mrs. McConnell, Mrs. Hitz, and Mrs. Jay—and, of course, Maurice. (Efficient, ubiquitous Maurice.) The Centennial had a special significance for Maurice, who knew every brick and shrub on the campus, and had survived a succession of students, faculty, and presidents. His wife, Louise Yeager Wightman, also had large responsibilities, for if the President was determined to kill the fatted calf, it was left to Louise to cook it. Months ahead she was ordering supplies, filling scratchpads with higher mathematics on pounds and servings, instructing her staff in the mysteries of Angel Pie.

Even in these domestic details there were consultations and decisions for the President, who would sometimes pause to scan a menu or point out a corner that needed tidying. At the office, each mail brought a flood of questions to be settled, each opening of the door revealed a line of persons seeking his opinion. The pressure was so unrelenting and his own physical powers fell so far from meeting it! For some time he had tried to disregard a numbing in his side.

Usually he was philosophical about making decisions, figuring that he had to be right at least half the time. Now, he often felt like a rat in a maze. Or rather—for he always kept his humor—like the hired man in one of his favorite stories; it wasn't sorting the apples that slowed him down; it was the decisions!

It was all quite different from the Centennial Miller had imagined years ago as a climax of dreams come true. All the plans he had set in motion had snowballed so amazingly. As the celebration approached, it was growing into a sort of Frankenstein monster which threatened to destroy its creator. Looking ahead to January 18 he began to think: "If I can just live through the day."

As January neared, another founders' celebration had been added to the agenda. "Recognition Day," a service at the Christian Church, Sunday, January 14, was to honor the trustees and friends who had helped to found and maintain the College. Their descendants were traced enthusiastically by a local committee of alumnae, and sent invitations. This genealogical project undoubtedly heightened interest in the College, while the information which poured back from all over the country disclosed a continuity in Christian's background which in some cases extended to the fifth and sixth generations of a family.

Ethel Robnett Estes '02, of Columbia found that sixty relatives of her own and forty-eight by marriage had been students or trustees of Christian. The Hon. W. Ed Jameson of Fulton could stand for both his grandfather, an original incorporator, and his mother, one of those 1856 students to return to Kentucky with President Williams. Edmund Wilkes, of Kansas City, would represent his grandfather, President L. B. Wilkes. Honorees were to be recognized under the Christian College window; the choral club was to sing, minister-trustee C. E. Lemmon would preach on "The Past Serves the Present," the service would close with the stirring "Faith Of Our Fathers."

Charter Day, the following Thursday, was set up with delegates from more than 120 American colleges, universities, and professional societies scheduled to attend. Formal responses, impressive scrolls with ribbons and seals, were arriving daily. (Few of the faculty and none of the office force could read one from Princeton which was in Latin. So had education changed in a hundred years!)

United States Senator Fulbright was to make the keynote speech. Radio coverage had been arranged on Kansas City's WDAF, on KGRH, Fayetteville, Arkansas, on Columbia's KFRU. Who could tell, this speech on "The United States in World Affairs" might become a political event, for some had mentioned the young Senator as a possible future candidate for the Presidency. Publicity had been good—especially a full-page illustrated article on Christian College in the St. Louis *Globe-Democrat;* a feature by Mary Paxton Keeley in the *Kansas City Star,* a twelve-page section of the *Columbia Missourian.*[1]

All the wheels were in motion, and J. C. Miller was trying to concentrate on his speech of introduction. It was unfortunate that this was the time of year one always examined the enrollment for next fall. It was still going down. Not only that. Would he, this time, have to strike the words, "the College is in the best financial condition in its history" out of his annual report?

On the morning of December 27, just two weeks before the first Centennial event, President Miller suffered a heart attack.

Consternation spread through the little college family. Whispers traveled the red corridors. College physician, James Allee, who was a family friend as well, Haden Bright, Hartley Banks, L. A. Nickell, C. E. Lemmon—those trustees closest to the President—urged him to drop everything at once and take a complete rest. But J. C. Miller knew what he must do.

In three days he was back in his office. He walked laboriously, feeling in his coat pocket the pills which, at any moment, might mean the difference between life and death. There were a great many important letters still to write. But first, one to an old friend who had just resigned from a neighboring—and to that extent, rival—women's college. As he picked up the dictaphone, the words came with effort. But they were characteristic:

"Dear ———," he said. "Are you gone from ——— ———? Sorry, we hadn't missed you. . . . You got out of the frying pan when the heat was pretty well turned up." Humor was always to be a stronger support than pills.

The dignitaries assembled at 9:30. Charter Day was one of those balmy mornings in January which would surprise anyone but a Missourian. The crowds came early and greeters, standing in the auditorium lobby, saw many out-of-town visitors. The Vice-President of the University arrived; Deans Elmer Ellis, Francis English, Frank F. Stephens, the three interested equally in education and history. Floyd Shoemaker, secretary of the State Historical Society of Missouri, and Claude Spencer, curator of the Disciples' Historical Society, appeared. On hand were trustees Louis Blosser of Marshall, Mrs. Vivian Dulany Murphy of St. Louis (who had succeeded her brother, Will Dulany, on the Board), J. C. Mundy of Mexico.

Frail little Mrs. Julia Ewalt of St. Louis, whose mother at the age of three had been carried up to the College on D. Pat Henderson's shoulder to be enrolled, took her place in the section reserved for those connected with Christian's founding. All the audience was in good spirits, greetings hummed across the auditorium, as visitors sank into the luxurious new red velvet seats. Many more were planning to listen over the radio to the Senator's broadcast.

The academic procession was colorful and imposing as it lined up in the gymnasium and spilled onto the campus. The black gowns and mortarboards of the Masters, distinguished by the gold, purple, or red tassels of their profession; the rich hoods of the Doctors, lined with crimson or claret velvet or slashed with gold. An exotic cape edged with ermine worn by Christian's French teacher, Madame Olga Bak. Familiar faces looked mystical, medieval, everyone seemed taller and more dignified than usual. As cameras clicked and ground, teachers and trustees commenced the march from Dorsey Hall to the auditorium with a briskness which would have pleased even Mrs. Hertig.

Everything had been timed, and now moved to perfection. At the precise moment, Dr. Miller and his party, who had come through the building, met the processional and led it on stage. The invocation was given, the speaking began, each speech going almost faster than had been anticipated.

President of the Board of Trustees Hartley G. Banks welcomed the audience with a dignity that would have pleased his great-uncle, J. K. Rogers. Mrs. John Stapel, president of the local Christian College Club, spoke for all the alumnae, and Suzanne Ziegler added a student welcome. Mayor Roy Sappington voiced the congratulations of the city of Columbia. Governor of Missouri Forrest Smith brought the greetings of the State. He reaffirmed the founding of Christian as the first institution of higher education for women to be chartered by a state legislature west of the Mississippi, and said that "small, select, serious in purpose" characterized its hundred years.

President Frederick A. Middlebush of the University of Missouri brought greetings from sister institutions of higher learning. He spoke of the quality of education for which Christian was known and which had brought it "to the very forefront of colleges of its type in America." Recalling that two other presidents of Missouri University, James Shannon and William Hudson, had also been instrumental in founding the girls' school, he remarked that the State University had, in early days, always considered Christian College as "its distaff side." He spoke of the enlightened leadership of J. K. Rogers and Luella St. Clair-Moss. But he saved his greatest tribute for James Conelese Miller, calling his administration "distinguished," "sound," and "inspiring."[2]

Miller, tense on the crowded platform under his heavy robes, was torn between natural pride and the feeling that this might be a good obituary. Then it was time for him to stand. Thanking the others, he remarked that he had never intended this as an occasion for building up his own self-esteem. He mentioned wryly that the honors of being a college president were well-balanced by its tendency to be fatal. Former President Briggs had accepted the invitation to come to to-day's function, but had become too ill to do so; former President Lee had arrived this morning and had been stricken by a heart attack.

He then started to introduce the speaker, Senator from

Arkansas, James William Fulbright, a former president of the University of Arkansas, and a Rhodes scholar.

Miller had been warned that Fulbright was to go on the air at eleven. Perhaps all the greetings had clicked along too smoothly. Perhaps people had said less than was expected. As Miller neared the end of his introduction, it became apparent to him that the radio man working with the microphone was making frantic gestures. He realized with horror that it was still almost fifteen minutes until eleven. It was imperative that Fulbright's address be delayed until the moment of broadcast. There was nothing to do but continue the introduction.

He mentioned that public attention had focused on the Senator from Arkansas with the introduction and passage of the Fulbright Peace Resolution in 1943, that Fulbright was now a member of the Senate Foreign Relations Committee. . . . He glanced again towards the operator and cleared his throat. (The situation would have been an amusing challenge for the old Jimmy Miller.) He commenced to review, one by one, the Senator's record on peace bills in the legislature. . . .

At first only a handful in the auditorium knew what was happening. Those most familiar with Miller recognized the fluttering of papers in his hands as a characteristic nonplussed gesture. As he went on stalling for time, those who knew agonized in empathy.

He mentioned that the Senator was born a Missourian . . . recalled facts of his biography . . . that one sister and an aunt had attended Christian College. . . .

He spoke of the Fulbright Scholarship Plan, the program enabling hundreds of American students and professors to work in European universities. Christian's own drama teacher, William West, had just returned from a Fulbright scholarship. . . .

By now, people were aware of the radio operator's gestures and were glancing at their watches. A whisper went through the audience. Amusement . . . apprehension, depending on how intimately one knew the speaker. Good friends and faculty sat tight in their chairs. A man downed by a heart

and Mrs. Kenneth Freeman (1957–1965) and Artie Mason Carter

ıng hod-carriers help with the construction of Miller Hall

William H. Dulany Hall

Pleasant dining facil

ns for the Fine Arts Center

Inauguration (Hartley G. Banks, Sr. and Dr. W. Merle Hill)

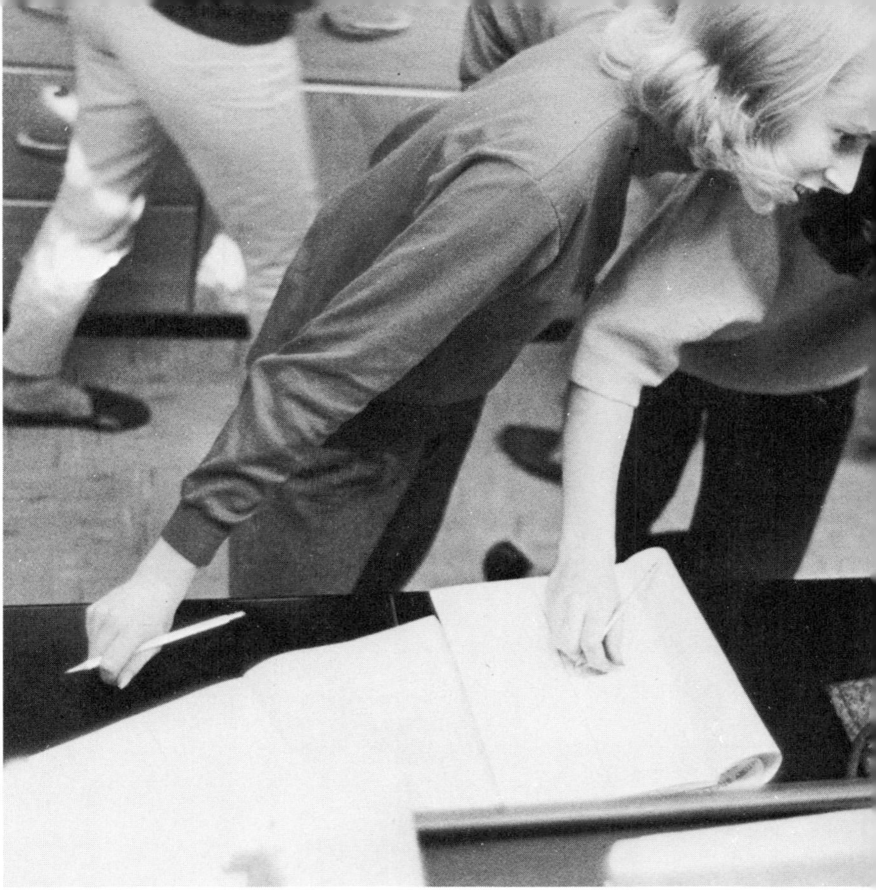

A search for knowledge

Biology class

Mrs. W. P. Kirkman, Dean of Women

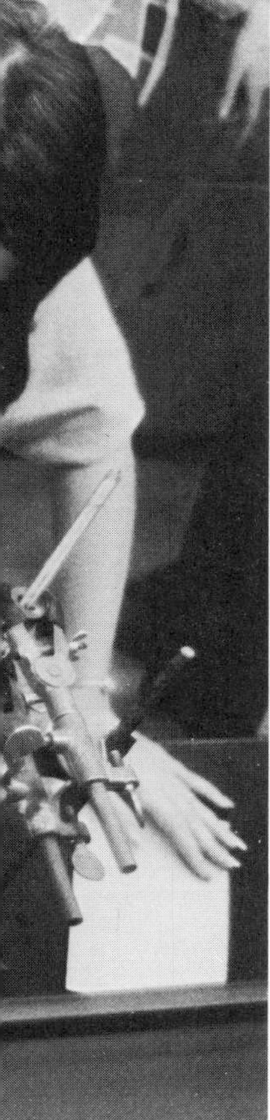

Dan Hoagland

Jack L. Batterson, Dean of the College

Inauguration processional

North Hall

me. Hortense Davison meets with students

. . . in the French House

Helen Hayes and Jane Froman

Miss America, Debbie Bryant

A look to the future — service projects

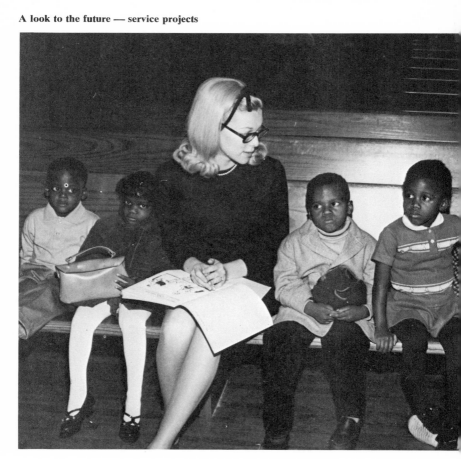

attack two weeks earlier should not be put under such a strain. Suspense became electric, admiration filled the onlookers as the President continued to introduce Senator Fulbright.

Finally it became necessary to tell the audience what was happening. He told it with humor and the crowd laughed. As he talked on for the final seven minutes they entered into the spirit of the situation, wondering what on earth he would find to say next. When the signal finally came, the President abruptly cut off his sentence. "And now, United States Senator J. William Fulbright." A spontaneous roar of applause went on the air.

"I haven't had so many nice things said about me since I entered politics," were the distinguished speaker's first words.

The remainder of Charter Day went smoothly. The luncheon for delegates and guests was perhaps the most important meal ever served in the Christian College dining room. Some saw a happy portent in the menu, which featured steak. The atmosphere was jovial rather than stuffy, as the toastmaster managed to hold nine talks to a total of thirty-five minutes.

Bringing greetings were Dr. Lowell C. Bryant, representing the International Convention of the Disciples of Christ; Harlie L. Smith, president of the Board of Higher Education, Disciples of Christ; Dean Frederick J. Marston, representing the American Association of Junior Colleges; Dr. John Rufi, representing the North Central Association of Colleges and Secondary Schools; Hubert Wheeler, State Commissioner of Education; Homer P. Rainey, President of Stephens College, Columbia; President Wilber Cramblet of Bethany College, West Virginia; Neil Aslin, Superintendent of Schools, Columbia; and Margaret Habein, now dean of women at the University of Kansas.

Miss Habein, the only woman speaker, was perhaps the most effective, as she recalled an incident illustrating education at Christian. Late one night, seeing a suspicious light, she had crept up to investigate. When she opened the door, there was the culprit, lying on her stomach on the floor—writing a sonnet!

Charter Day afternoon was "open house" on campus with

Lineage Club members as guides. Their authentic costumes were planned by Mrs. J. C. Miller, who sponsored the club in its hostess duties this year. It was interesting to find on the guest book such signatures as J. S. Rollins and to reflect that this same college on this same spot one hundred years ago had been purchased from his grandfather. Even those hardened to such ceremonials declared that Christian's Charter Day Centennial was the most pleasant they had ever attended.

But this was only the half-way mark of the year. In the two months that President Miller went away, under doctor's orders, to regain his health, Centennial Commencement plans rolled on to a frenzied climax. As in most families when disaster threatens, the individualistic faculty members of Christian College united to meet the emergency. Almost every teacher had some special project he was fostering. (This Commencement would highlight the fact that eight of the forty had spent more than twenty years at Christian College.) Mary Paxton Keeley, of the short haircut and explosive personality, was promoting the *Microphone* gift, a painting of Vinnie Ream to hang in St. Clair parlors. The Centennial history was being written by one of her former students. The two of them were collaborating on an historical skit, which Mrs. Hazel Perryman was already rehearsing, instead of the time-worn pageant.

The "Mike" staff was planning a special Centennial edition to "hit the stands" the minute the crowd rolled out of the auditorium after Commencement. (This Commencement issue was a tradition. It meant that the staff and Brooks Bradley, the printer, must stay up the night before—only the paper being "put to bed"). Colorful "Mary Pax," who had launched so many journalists on their careers! Next year—the twenty-third—was to be her last of teaching and when she flung bookbag over bicycle and rode away one of the unforgettable characters of Christian would be gone.

Esther Stearn and Harold Long were trying to contact former science students by questionnaire. Old girls would find them surprisingly unchanged, Dr. Long with his quiet, dry humor; Mrs. Stearn with her zest and uncompromising standards after twenty-four years. Reports from former students showed a succession of laboratory technicians, nurses, young doctors, who gave Dr. Stearn credit for their choice of career.

"Mom" Drew, another pace-setter, was working up a super edition of the annual Commencement horse show. Calm, handsome, almost worshiped by her students, in the twenty-four years since Edgar Lee and J. K. Wright had assured her she could teach she had managed to set the standards for college equitation courses in the United States. With her at Christian and daughter Shirley (C. C. '35) following in her boots across town at Stephens College, Columbia was a recognized leader in the horsemanship-teaching world.[3]

Ellen Dahl, clothing instructor, and Margaret McMillan, teacher of history, were aiding alumnae on the Museum committee, for by now hundreds of interesting objects had come to the College and room 18, St. Clair Hall, was being furnished as a Centennial museum. It was the first attempt since Mrs. Hertig's day to bring together all the significant archives relating the old school's history.[4]

Popular Mabel Buckner, as sponsor of the Junior Class had extra duties this Centennial year. Ruth Graham, who had seen home economics at Christian evolve from baking twenty-egg angel foods to testing cake mixes, was working with Christian College Club members on a series of "Generation Teas." Geneva Youngs, who could look back on fifteen years of success brought about by quietly expecting perfection, was drilling her double sextette to a peak of performance. She and Margaret Tello were senior members of the second complete Conservatory staff Franklin Launer had directed in twenty-seven years at Christian. William Bedford besides putting out a monthly edition of the Bulletin this year, was scheduling the class reunions. Raymond Derr had prepared a Centennial booklet[5] and coined a motto: "One hundred years of uninterrupted education for women."

R. A. Miller preserved stoic calm in the flood of room reservations. Maurice, Mrs. "Mac," and Rowena scurried from attic to basement in response to such queries as: "Where is Mrs. Moss's silver vase that always stood on the mantel?"

"Whatever happened to the class-day staff?" Manuel, of the stockingcap and jingling keys, stalked the halls on endless errands. It was exactly like having all one's distant relatives arriving for the weekend.

By the time J. C. Miller returned he found the Centennial well organized, a higher enrollment in prospect, morale good.

In every way, the sun shone on the Centennial. By nine o'clock Friday morning, June 1, the parlors of St. Clair seemed to bulge as "girls" of all ages came back. They came from Washington, Florida, Massachusetts; from twenty-six states and Canada. Soon more than eight hundred had registered and there were probably two hundred who failed to do so.

Random glimpses must describe it: the meetings in the halls, the squeals of recognition. . . . "You haven't changed! I'd know you anywhere!" "Do you remember?" Mrs. Mollie Dorsey Hill, erect at ninety, marching out to practice hall to look for her old room; the four Wells sisters, in school together in 1927, arriving simultaneously from Chicago, New York, and points west. . . . Mrs. Hertig's beloved cut-ups, the Tepes from Texas. . . . Room-mates of 1886, Virginia Moore Wingate and Lucy Duncan Wright recognizing each other after sixty-five years.

Somewhat sheepish among the women were two dozen fathers and grandfathers who had once been the "small boys" enrolled at Christian: R. B. Price, Haden Bright, Jim Lipscomb, Will Garth, Jesse Bateman, Joe Estes, Sidney Rollins, Frank St. Clair, Arch Prather, Clyde Shepard were some who were back to enjoy a barbecue near where the schoolhouse once stood. The most distinguished of their number had sent regrets: Dr. Isadore Loeb, founder of the business and public administration schools of both the University of Missouri and Washington University in St. Louis.

Forty women of the first half-century met for luncheon in the College dining room. Two of Columbia's senior alumnae were hostesses: Mrs. H. H. Banks (Rose Allison) and Mrs. F. G. Nifong (Lavinia Lenoir). A poem written expressly for the Centennial by the oldest living alumna was read, since the author, "Minnie" Winans Horner '76 could not come in person. Then a flood of reminiscence started, as each woman told some escapade of her school days. The 1951 Seniors who were waiting tables heard about feather-pillows being emptied on incoming guests by girls on the landing above, of students eating the ice-cream reserved for President Oldham's reception, of girls swiping boys' clothes to hold a surreptitious dance in the parlor.

After luncheon all went outdoors to plant a sapling near where the Old Elm had stood. Mrs. Keeley presented the tree in memory of her three Gentry aunts who were early students at the College. Mrs. Banks, who had become engaged under the old tree's branches, gave the dedication, hoping that in the next fifty years this elm might become a landmark to future Christian girls.

The alumnae banquet Friday night had outgrown the dining room and turned into a fried chicken buffet on the back lawn. Afterwards the 550 guests moved into the auditorium where Mrs. Thomas N. Coppedge (Elizabeth Davis '14) was toastmistress for the program. Mrs. J. B. Skinner (Julia Lenoir), the earliest student present, showed some of the starch the first half-century put into college girls as she spoke wittily of "The Bonnet Girl." Who better could represent fifty years of life at Christian, for she had entered the grades there in 1870, been graduated in '81, and returned to live there with her instructor-husband in the nineties. She was linked to its beginnings through her father, Dr. Walter Lenoir, her mother, one of the earliest students, and her mother's father, James Shannon, founder. "The Emancipated Woman," was an able characterization of Mrs. Moss and her times by Maud Franklin Allee '03. Attractive Elizabeth Toomey '42, United Press correspondent and syndicated columnist, spoke on "Today's Woman."

Lumps came into many throats as Mary Lynn McCormick Sutherland '46 repeated a farewell conversation with Mrs. Hertig and Dr. Miller told of taking her on her last trip. Many of the audience thought, "How she would have loved being here to run the Centennial!" Then her portrait—gift of Indiana alumnae—was unveiled and there sat Mrs. Hertig herself, on the old red sofa, the only untrue thing about her being the silent hands.

Alumnae recognitions were fun—those who had come the greatest distance, that class which had the largest representation. (There were a surprising number of "girls" from the '80's.) Edith Hulett Simon '09 of Columbia won a prize for having the most children (eight) and Marjorie Dysart '50 for being a fourth-generation graduate. Her mother, Mary King 1908, grandmother, Madge Robnett 1888, and great-grandmother, Sallie Mosely 1860, had all attended Christian.

Saturday was a hub-bub of class reunions, snapshot passing, talk-fests. The class of '26 had their picture made with classmate Jane Froman. The thirties met for lunch. Sixty alumnae of 1922-25 had a gay meal at the Daniel Boone. Beta Sigs and Eta Upsilon Gammas buried the hatchet over a supper. Phi Mu Gamma, the other disbanded sorority, had a breakfast. Old girls, strolling down Columbia streets, were pleased to see Miller's Shoe Store still doing business after seventy-one years, as well as Harris' Café—that jelly-joint of the twenties. Phi Theta Kappa kept open house in its chapter room; former "Mike" staffers chatted with Elizabeth Toomey over the tea cups at Mrs. Keeley's. Visitors thronged to "Mrs. Hertig's room," attractively furnished by the St. Louis alumnae but, alas, unrecognizable without its bandanna-lampshade. In a service in the chapel she so loved the Luella St. Clair-Moss memorial organ was presented to the College by Jacqueline Chrane Bihr '35 and received by trustee W. F. St. Clair, Mrs. Moss's nephew.

Saturday afternoon a spirited business meeting took place as alumnae asked questions about Christian. They were grateful for the Centennial and amazed that everything should be offered to them free. They wanted more and thicker alumnae bulletins. They wanted an alumnae secretary. ("We don't know where to write since Mrs. Hertig left.") They would like to join alumnae clubs. Most of all they wanted Christian to contact their daughters. They vowed to go home and send back students.

Although the group was small, its influence motivated President Miller to revitalize alumnae work. The next two years were to see twelve to sixteen active Christian College clubs,[6] a part-time alumnae secretary on campus, a transformed twenty-four page Bulletin with newspictures, a Bulletin fund-drive topping $1,700 and—not altogether incidentally—a climbing enrollment.

Saturday night was the dream come true. In perfect weather some four thousand persons gathered on the front campus before a flood-lighted stage—St. Clair entrance converted with palms, awning, spotlights, a concert grand piano. It brought memories of the Jubilee, of May pageants on the front lawn, or of older days when the town turned out for strawberry sociables at Christian College. The artist who was to perform that night had made one of her earliest appearances in a scarf dance before these steps.

Franklin Launer, in white, was a beaming master of ceremonies. The crowd applauded each pronouncement he made, for everyone liked Franklin. And Jane Froman, star of stage, screen, and television, whose courage had pulled her from near-death in a ship-wrecked plane through countless hospitals to be lauded as an example to America by the President of the United States; Jane stood now in the spotlight, the unseen braces on her limbs, the enchantment in her voice. The audience could not get enough. They cheered when she called to the stage "my first and best accompanist—my mother," and Anna Froman Hetzler joined her daughter to sing "I Love You Truly."

Jane was one of many who stayed after the reunion for the three days of Commencement events.[7] Every program this Commencement had standing room only from the graduation concert to the crowning of 1951 Commencement Queen, Barbara Bolanz. The historical sketch, "Under the Ivy," which replaced the traditional pageant had a nice touch: the Sextette singing the dedicatory ode of the College written in 1852 by John A. Williams and set to music by Franklin Launer.

The old excitement of "Jerusalem the Golden" on Sunday night merged into admiration as Mr. Abram repeated the original 1853 Baccalaureate address of Christian College. Dear old Mr. Abram, who had said the vows for so many Christian College brides, whose voice had given new meaning to the Christmas story year after year for forty-three years! As he poured out from memory the eloquent message of Augustus Williams, written for girls like these a century ago when the College—and female education—was young, the words had a surprisingly current ring. Usefulness was the theme; to find real meaning in life a woman must be useful. Perhaps this speech, more than any other feature of the Centennial, brought back the beginnings—those first six graduates also seated in church, those dedicated men who set out to prove that they were not building castles in air.

The Commencement speech on Tuesday morning was delivered by one of the outstanding woman educators of America. Mildred McAfee Horton, former president of Wellesley, wartime commander of the WAVES, spoke on "Predictions for the Unpredictable Future." She recalled that it was a small group which founded Christian College. She suggested that none of these founders could have predicted a future which included television and the atom bomb. Yet, standing almost alone in the face of the unpredictable, they had the courage to act upon one of the problems of their day—the lack of equal education for women. This was their message for today's college graduate. (It was a speech the twenty founders would have admired, though delivered by a woman!)

President Miller heard it with the satisfaction of one who watches a long-laid plan succeed. The Centennial was over; he had seen it through. For him it was the climax of all his years at Christian. In a way he felt as if his work was done; it would have been the dramatic time to stop—to rest. But college presidents were not replaced overnight, he reflected without egotism. He had a few things left to do before he retired.

He wanted to secure a capacity enrollment that would continue until the population "boom" of babies born after Pearl Harbor should reach college age: 1959, 1960. But top enrollment meant more dormitory space. He had a plan for moving the Conservatory to a building of its own, releasing the ground floor of Missouri Hall for dormitory space.[8] "Practice Hall" should be emptied and practice rooms put with the Conservatory. This would free the original college mansion, still sturdy with its graceful staircase. (He remembered his dream of a small but beautiful library.) Besides, his plan would not place the College in debt. He was determined to leave the balance sheet, if possible, still in the black.

But how? St. Clair Hall was venerable now. Hughes still called for another wing. The amazing growth of the art and commerce departments demanded larger housing. A new science laboratory, a library, a fine arts addition, were needed. The curriculum must constantly be enriched, this one small school must have something special to offer, if it were to keep its reason for being. What was it the old catalogs had said? "Christian College has taken high ground upon the subject of Female Education. . . ."

Unconsciously he had lapsed into the old habit of scarcely being able to concentrate on giving out diplomas for thinking of what must be done next.

And what of the Centennial graduates marching up for those diplomas? Had these college girls of 1951 lived up to the daring of their bonneted forebears, the grandiloquent prophecies of Wilkes and Rogers? Today's Cathy Christian[9] who would remember putting on the costume of great-grandmother's day to greet her "little sister" at the Wabash station had, under her bonnet, quite different thoughts from Grandma's.

Never again would the needle be her symbol or the Bible her only textbook. Where members of that first graduating class had married or taught school, three-fourths of today's class would go on to senior college. Gone with the corset and mortar board were the stiff restraints of yesterday. Today's girls would face more moral dilemmas before twenty than Grandma met in a lifetime.

The hats and gloves of Mother's day were gone, too, but so was the bitterness of her "lost generation." The present generation's earnestness, their convictions, their trend to return to religion, sometimes made their teachers feel inadequate. James C. Miller felt a little humble himself, in the midst of this finest hour. A letter had come to his desk—one of those rich rewards in casual white envelope which quite often brightened his day:

Dear Dr. Miller:

It's 12:15 in the morning; I just got the diapers all in; and I just had to write. . . .

Doing so much so late could have been very dull except for my two years at Christian. The reason—Mrs. Moffett said in class one day that as much as she would like to think she was facing twelve potential English scholars, she realized that instead she was facing twelve future wives and mothers. And it was so nice to have something to think about while washing dishes!

One reason for this letter is to thank C. C. for guiding me to a richer life, but another is to apologize. I didn't realize what a truly wonderful opportunity was before me. . . .

Christian did me one ill; I was so accustomed to challenge, inspiration, and a mentally stimulating atmosphere that at the university I attended I did just enough work to get by. But Hepples, Dahls, Moffetts, and Stearns don't grow on trees. . . .[10]

No, he thought, looking at his faculty about him on the stage. Those who had walked the whole way with him, those who before long would be replaced by others. Each in his individual way had helped set the quality and tone of the College. Each had put dedication to work before pay. . . .

The girls were singing now, tears running down their cheeks, the lovely solemn words of the Alma Mater. "Alway—alway." How easily they spoke of "always." Would it be here always for their daughters; the Ivy Chain and the tears, the classes on the lawn, the serenades in the night air? Part of the answer depended on these girls who were graduating.

As for him, he would remember that Christian had always had students who sent back their daughters. He would regard the stability of its hundred years as a sort of insurance; the fifth generation already on its rolls as proof of eternal rebirth.

Like the Commencement speaker, he would reaffirm the conviction of the founders—that young women are worth the best education possible, that the best education must include values of the spirit, that a woman's education should be designed for the differences that make a woman. He would have faith that always there would be those willing to invest in such values to see that they endure.

XIII

EPILOG: A TIME TO BUILD

For everything there is a season . . . a time to plant, and a time to pluck up what is planted; . . . a time to break down, and a time to build up. — ECCLES. 3.

BEFORE PRESIDENT MILLER died of a heart attack in November, 1956, he had helped to name as his successor a man whose background strongly resembled his own. Kenneth Freeman had even been dean of faculty at Christian College from 1946 to 1948.

Born in a small Missouri town, graduated from Northeast Missouri State Teachers College, with a doctorate in education from the University of Missouri, he, too, had started his career in professional education as an elementary school principal in Columbia. He had also published articles on administration and on teaching science. He had served in the Navy, like Miller, and he, too, had a gay and gracious wife and three adolescent daughters. At forty-one, he was acting president of the State University Teachers College, Geneseo, New York.

Freeman returned to Christian at a time when unprecedented growth was projected for United States colleges following World War II. A Harvard professor was publishing a book that would characterize America for the next decade as "The Affluent Society." Soviet scientists were completing an object called "Sputnik," the first man-made satellite, that would be launched into outer space at exactly the same time Kenneth Freeman would launch his plan for a new Christian College. For if Miller had imagined his own career reincarnated in his successor's, he had been mistaken.

Freeman found a small, stable school with a balanced budget but no funds for expansion, a physical plant almost unchanged since his days as dean. A third of the faculty had been there for twenty to forty years. Most of those who set the tone of the institution — Abram, Launer, Youngs, Stearn, Long, Drew, McMillan, Buckner, McHarg, Tello, Perryman, Graham, Dahl — would soon retire. All were operating in a *status quo* of salary, equipment, method which appalled the ambitious new President.

"A college cannot coast on past performance," he wrote in the *Bulletin*. "It is bound to move, either upward or downward."

Christian in the past had been "a church-related school with objectives inherent in that definition . . . character building, home building, stress on teaching excellence, on solicitation of students who have apparent intellectual superiority." Its two-fold program of "Living and Learning" offered transfer, terminal, and pre-professional curricula and degrees of Associate in Fine Arts and in Commerce as well as the traditional Associate in Arts. These Freeman deplored as "spreading thin," but two-thirds of the students took the A. A. and transferred to senior institutions.

He inherited a student body of well-reared girls with well-rounded personalities, more extroverts than scholars. Perhaps two-thirds came from small cities and rural areas, almost half from the Midwest and half from the South, with a handful from the West and none from the East. Perhaps sixteen out of the 344 had names that were non-Anglo-Saxon-Protestant;

in church affiliation one-third were Methodists, with Disciples of Christ, Presbyterians, and Baptists following. They were daughters of small businessmen, doctors, lawyers, farmers, teachers, and preachers who often were making some sacrifice to give them the advantage of this school. Four-fifths of the students waited tables several hours each week. A third were preparing to be teachers, another third were in the fine arts, particularly music.

The school of music, with its junior conservatory, was a separate entity and Director Launer was one of the administrators of the College. Administration was a pyramid: the president at the peak, the business manager and the director of admissions at the corners, the director of the conservatory and the dean of faculty along the base. Beyond these, Christian depended on a few persons wearing many hats. The registrar was also administrative secretary to the president and the dean. One public relations person sent out all news releases, wrote promotional brochures, edited the alumnae magazine, supervised the yearbook and *Microphone*, and sometimes taught journalism. A staff of seven, aided by student typists, functioned informally from six small offices without an electric typewriter or photo-copier in the place. It was a school which to a large extent had operated on tuitions; tightening the belt in lean years, expanding in good, having to think small and make do.

President Freeman saw progress immediately as physical expansion — a new Christian College. He would have moved it bodily to the college farm on the highway and changed its name if he could have. He was not sentimental; he noticed that under St. Clair's ivy the mortar was crumbling. The quaint tile fireplaces were anachronisms in offices, the high ceilings took space.

Physical expansion meant fund-raising, with its contemporary syndrome of development, public relations and promotion. He said "we should not be afraid" of six million dollars. For if J. C. Miller's caution was a product of his War-and-Depression generation Kenneth Freeman's daring belonged to a day which saw no limits in space. Using the methods of modern business, he had a professional survey made of the school's fund-raising potential; this assessed affirmatively, he engaged the architectural firm of Hellmuth, Obata, and Kassabaum in St. Louis to prepare a blueprint for a twenty-five year plan for Christian's campus to be achieved in six phases by 1984.[1]

A master plan was imperative for a college now that federal loans, foundation grants, and gifts from industry were new sources of income for schools. But these sources required specific details about the function and plans of the institution and so set in motion the same sort of academic analysis that the accrediting associations had instigated in the twenties.

Freeman appointed Christian's first professional director of public relations and development, Mrs. Peggy Phillips, in 1959. The College publications were redesigned: a larger, glossier alumnae magazine by October, 1959; a more professional yearbook in 1961; the attractive catalog of 1960–62 bearing Christian's new hallmark of entwined C's, one facing backward to tradition, the other forward; a new, more feminine College seal in 1962. In the next five years Christian would receive more national publicity than ever before through articles in *Mademoiselle, Glamour, Seventeen, Look, Junior College Journal,* the *New York Times.*[2]

Development was made a separate function in 1961 with William Winstead in charge as Freeman's administration of the College began to shape around this more contemporary triangle. The staff tripled; professionals replaced amateurs, secretaries replaced students. St. Clair's first floor was remodeled into offices; fireplaces, guestrooms, even Mrs. Hertig's room, replaced by equipment automatic, electronic, fluorescent. If some staff intimacy was lost behind doors closed for air-conditioning, faculty rapport improved as for the first time they had offices of their own on St. Clair's second floor. In turn, providing faculty offices greatly improved student counseling by making teachers more easily available.

The food service was professionalized – an efficiency measure – the dietician and student waitresses replaced by an institutional catering service, with University boys as waiters. (This led to a new rule: "Girls must not carry dishes to the kitchen.") And in the tearoom Mrs. Ashlock – the last of a series of cheerful women who produced hamburgers in closet-sized quarters—was replaced by a vending machine. She became operator of Christian's first telephone switchboard as, finally, girls could phone from every floor!

The admissions staff was professionalized. The lady counselors as they left were replaced by young men with M.A.'s in education. "Educational counseling" was emphasized as Christian adopted the standardized entrance examinations now used nationally.

One small act early in Freeman's administration was symbolic: Rogers Gates, at the entrance to the campus, were sandblasted and straightened. "An old landmark," said the *Bulletin*, "got a new look." Restoration and a new look would characterize his era and if some upheaval ensued it was congenial to him as the natural atmosphere of creation.

Freeman had immediately involved the faculty in his blueprints for the future, calling for a total evaluation of the school. Christian's master plan must be an expression of the elements that made up the institution—people, courses, buildings, programs—put together in a logical way to show where it had been, where it now stood, where it should go, and what it would take to get it there.

A "Plans and Projects" committee studied the building needs in each department and worked out specifications that formed the basis for architects' plans. A second committee was to define "Philosophical Position and Goals" and a subsequent group would evaluate the curriculum so that it might be tailored toward these goals. Finally, the faculty was to prepare a "Profile and Purpose" statement in conjunction with the Board of Trustees.

As the faculty surveyed and analyzed, the President probed the campus on his own. He turned over every stone of usage to ask, Why is it *here*? He asked each teacher to justify his course content. As he went about "sticking pins in the *status quo*," recalled Sidney Larson, "it tested our thickness of skin. . . . This man, trained in science, questioning how I taught painting!" The confrontation led to strong friendship, however.

William Winstead, sociology instructor and a relative newcomer, led Freeman's innovations, acting as dean while Dean William Bedford was on educational leave and as Assistant to the President from 1961. Sidney Larson, as chairman of the original planning committee of 1957 helped shape the renascence of Christian College. This was fitting, for since 1951 Larson, painter-sculptor-teacher-advisor-writer-lecturer-art historian, had been its own Renaissance Man. Newcomer Dan Hoagland was correspondingly versatile: teacher of math and astronomy, violinist, composer, and photographer, he was to write the final statement of Christian's purpose. Jack L. Batterson, who joined the faculty as teacher of history in 1959, would exert the most consistent, long-term influence of Freeman's appointees. As chairman of the Honors program and the committee on curriculum, he was charged with designing the studies that would carry out Christian's newly-crystallized philosophical goals.

Hazel Kennedy, sponsor of Phi Theta Kappa and teacher of English literature; Hortense Davison, teacher of French; Sue Meyers Gerard, physical educator, all women of judgment and imagination, were stable figures among the newcomers. William Bedford, faculty member since 1937, as *ex officio* coordinator of all committees brought perhaps the most experience and devotion to the early planning; Christian's first chaplain, Jack Scott – these and others would define the aims of Christian College for the next twenty-five years. But Freeman's one faculty appointment which would most affect the future was that of W. Merle Hill as academic dean following Bedford in June, 1963.

The twenty-five year plan for new building at Christian College was designed to express its unique qualities: intimacy (low structures), smallness (one central academic-fine arts building to serve the entire student body), traditions (open space in front for Ivy Chain), femininity (fountain courts and extra closets).[3] The central building which would supplant St. Clair and Dorsey Halls would suggest the central academic interest of the College. A chapel and bell tower, adjacent, would be the dominant visual symbol, approached past a reflecting pool aligned with Rogers Gateway. The west side of the campus would form the living area – a dining-social center, next to Hughes Hall, and three new residence halls; the east side would emphasize physical activities – a new gymnasium with dance studios adjoining the present pool; a modern infirmary.

Buildings would be connected by courts and terraces; driveways would be replaced by lawn, with parking built into a green belt surrounding the campus; the miscellaneous buildings on Christian College avenue, except for the President's house, would be replaced by a landscaped approach.

With the same logic he had applied to structuring the master plan Freeman went about implementing it. In his nine years he reached out towards every individual or group who could conceivably be interested in supporting the school.

He challenged the trustees to analyze their function, as he had the faculty, and to publish their definition in the booklet, "Trusteeship." He had in mind a series of publications on the creation of a modern college for women, like those faculty studies that had made Christian well known in the thirties. He threw out questions: "What kind of college do you want?" – a school that exists in "an aura of genteel poverty" or one that can "compare favorably with the best?" [4] Naturally, they voted for the latter, although some felt that these were not realistic alternatives. They appointed a development committee, headed by J. M. Allton, and hired the firm of Gonser, Gerber in Chicago as development consultants. Thus they were committed to the salary raises, the tuition raises, the money-raising that would launch Christian College towards 1984.

Next Freeman engaged the alumnae in a way that no one had done since Mrs. Moss. The valuable work William Bedford had accomplished in the Centennial directory of bringing alumnae records up to date was resumed until 7,500 alumnae names were on the mailing list. The first full-time alumnae secretary was hired in 1958 and by 1961 her functions were divided between a professional director and an editor for the magazine. The "first annual Homecoming" was held in May, 1958; the "first" annual fund drive in 1959. (Luella St. Clair had tried both in the 1900's.) A source that recent presidents had felt could not be tapped by a two-year college began to yield a consistent stream and there were even "Challengers" who pledged $1,000 or more a year.

Although appreciative parents had often given gifts ranging from organ chimes to rose plantings, Freeman's administration was the first to enlist them in systematic giving by initiating annual Parents' Weekends. These occasions came to serve an important counseling function as parents and teachers conferred.

Freeman — again like Mrs. Moss — involved the town of Columbia in the life of Christian College, inviting individuals and groups to College plays, concerts, dinners. She would have admired the ice swan sculpted by the new foods service director for such occasions. Since the College spent most of its capital in Columbia, where students and parents contributed several hundred thousands to the economy each year, and since nearly one-fourth of the graduates transferred to the University of Missouri, it was surprising that local businessmen had been solicited so seldom. A Columbia Capital Gifts campaign in 1959 quickly raised $100,000 towards the new dormitory, which was completed through a federal loan, another source Freeman hoped increasingly to tap.

Among the traditional friends of the College Freeman sought to involve was the national body of the Christian Church. Although Christian's past large donors, like its administrators and trustees, had usually been Disciples of Christ, it derived less than one per cent of its income from that body by the mid-sixties. Its appeal might as well be addressed to the Methodist Church, which for twenty years had sent the most students, or to the Presbyterians or Episcopalians who now numbered more than Disciples. The "non-sectarian" clause in Christian's charter had been a prophecy; in the future, protestant churches might be sources for an ecumenical appeal, as most were now engaged in reorganization and merger.

Freeman's administration secured the first corporation grants; one typical of the times, for an Aerospace Careers Assembly. But the large foundations tended not to include two-year or women's colleges in their giving and usually demanded some experimental program that a small school was not equipped to try. Indeed, Freeman realized that the women's college was becoming a rare breed in the educational world. Some had become co-ed or, like the famous "seven sisters" in the East, were affiliating with neighboring men's schools. Other two-year schools were shifting to four years as the term "junior college" began to change in connotation along with the fantastic increase of public junior colleges.

The junior college, William Rainey Harper's radical idea which Mrs. Moss adopted in 1910 had become, a half-century later, an educational revolution. It was a revolution whose history Christian had helped to write. When she became an officially standardized junior college in 1913, there were perhaps eleven such in the United States. When James C. Miller initiated studies defining the function of the American junior college in 1930–31 there were about four hundred, half of them private. In 1941, as president of the American Association of Junior Colleges, he still had to explain the institution, and its "leap from invisibility to the limelight" occurred in the decade 1956–66, immediately after his death.[5]

Ironically, the tremendous success of the junior college movement, which proved Mrs. Moss a prophet and justified J. C. Miller's life-work, would be seen by President Freeman as a threat. For "junior college" in the sixties was fast coming to mean something that Christian was not: a large-enrollment, non-residential community school supported by public funds and having a strong vocational and adult-educational function. This insight formed part of Freeman's compulsion to move Christian away from the vocational associations of a public school and to define its identity and future.

Thus, early in his administration he worked with old neighbors, Stephens, William Woods and Monticello, to form a Council of Midwestern Women's Colleges for mutual promotion and later joined with twenty-three leading private two-year residential colleges for women to publish an exposition of their function as a magazine feature in the *New York Times*.[6]

By his second summer, ground was broken for the new $720,000 dormitory, first major construction on the campus in twenty years. In the fall of 1960, students moved into James

C. Miller Hall. The low-rise brick building, surrounded by a veranda with access from each double bedroom and reached by "bridges" over a sunken garden, won national design awards.[7] While some critics shook their heads at the many outside doors, the girls sunbathed happily in their private "moat." In fact, the building represented something of the concrete practicality, the new freedoms, and the break from convention in the administration.

By 1964 the second phase of the twenty-five year plan took shape: William H. Dulany Hall, a striking $780,000 dining facility, seating five hundred persons. The free-form arrangement with its expanse of glass and skylights, outdoor terrace, fireplace foyer, controlled lighting and burnt-orange carpeting featured tables for six "where students learn courtesy . . . in a cordial atmosphere." "The building will be one of the finest of its kind on any college campus," announced the alumnae magazine.[8]

As the buildings of the master plan appeared, the academic blueprint for the future also took shape. But here changes would not be so drastic, for the foundations were extraordinarily firm. The work of the blueprint committees resulted in a statement of "Convictions," carried in the catalogs after 1960, which amplified the "small, select, serious in purpose" of the Centennial slogan; also in the official "Profile and Purpose" statement printed in the catalog of 1963–64. These statements committed Christian College to liberal arts studies, excluding transient trends and special interests. Her primary educational tool would be a faculty of significant individuals: her educational environment would remain intimate for faculty-student dialog and individual opportunity for in-and-out of class learning.

On the whole, the philosophical conclusions of the faculty studies were a redefining of Christian's century-old standards. They did provide valuable guidelines during the swiftest period of change in the school's history. In twenty-five years "small" might mean a college of seven hundred but student-faculty ratio should remain at fifteen to one; "select" would mean recruiting only students who could profit by Christian's type of education, and "serious" would mean not being sidetracked into emphasizing vocational preparation, "gracious living," or extra-curricular activities whose goal was the well-rounded personality.

These by-passed goals, in a way, indicated viewpoints of women that had become outmoded. In 1870 when President Rogers advised his students that they might become telegraph operators, or in 1890 when President Oldham grew eloquent over stenography, these vocations represented great progress for women. "Gracious living" represented women's added leisure in Luella St. Clair's new century and "personality" the freedom of expression of President Lee's 1920's. The combination of all of these with the academic might reflect the complexity of educational aims for women since the 1930's.

Christian also by-passed a trend in women's education that had been growing since about 1945, to emphasize woman's function rather than her brain and aim at "life-adjustment" rather than intellectual achievement. This sex-directed education seemed directly correlated with the rise of young marriages and the steady decline of the percentage of women attending college and of women Ph.D.'s. By 1958 more girls were marrying from fifteen to nineteen years than from any other age group and the average age of marriage had dropped from 21.5 (in 1940) to 20.3. The proportion of women among college students had declined from 47 per cent in the twenties to 35.2. In effect America was sending women "back to the cave." Wrote Betty Friedan, in her best-selling exposé of 1963, *The Feminine Mystique*:

> The one lesson a girl could hardly avoid learning, if she went to college between 1945 and 1960, was *not* to get interested . . . in anything besides getting married and having children . . .
>
> As psychology and anthropology and sociology permeated the total scholarly atmosphere, education for femininity also spread from Mills, Stephens and the finishing schools . . . to the proudest bastions of the women's Ivy League . . .[9]

Sputnik helped to start a reversal of this trend, as the race for the exploration of space brought comparisons between the Soviet Union's more content-centered, scientific education and ours, its use of woman's intellect in contrast to America's shocking waste.[10] (In the U.S.S.R. 70 per cent of doctors were women; in the U.S.A. only 5 per cent.) Recognition of this reversal doubtless motivated Freeman and his faculty to stiffen the curriculum but Christian, not having swung as far with the tide as others, had less to reconstruct.

Some items disappeared. The Conservatory ceased to function as a separate entity and in 1959 moved from the Willett building Miller had purchased for it back to old "practice hall" behind St. Clair. The Junior Conservatory for teacher training and the orchestra were eliminated. (Geneva Youngs had said, "What future is there for a girl in violin nowadays? They all want to sing on television.") Music scholarships were discontinued, and in 1962 the Fine Arts degrees were discarded for the single Associate in Arts. As music decreased in course-hours offered, art increased almost 60 per cent. Christian's famed Horsemanship was dropped soon after Mrs. Drew left. Whereas wealthy girls had sometimes brought their own horses to Columbia at least one student arrived in her own plane by 1963.

The Space Age demanded more science courses; by 1960 enrollment in mathematics had increased 140 per cent at Christian. Credits offered rose from nine to twenty-four; calculus was added and — for the first time since 1889 — astronomy. Social studies increased, adding anthropology and more psychology. Languages were strengthened.

The most significant change brought about by the curriculum committee was the overall upgrading of academic requirements. In 1961 the College initiated an Honors degree program. Beginning with the graduating class of 1962, all candidates for graduation must have a C average or better. By 1964 the faculty voted to raise requirements in core subjects from twenty to thirty-three hours. These tightening standards also reflected the growing stringency of universities as they burst at the seams. Christian's scholarship program was expanded greatly. Here, too, Freeman professionalized, discontinuing the courtesy scholarships granted to daughters of ministers and teachers, increasing the funds that had been called "William Dulany Scholarships" since 1914 from under

$1,000 to $13,000 annually. In 1963 fifteen Trustees Scholarships were established.

Freeman apparently hoped to recruit only students from the upper third of their high school classes. In 1958, 60 per cent were such and 75 per cent of graduates were requesting transcripts to senior colleges. His redesigned catalog of 1960 took an austere tone, repeating the 1851 injunction that "no young lady seek admission who is not determined to devote her whole energy to her improvement."

Freeman might hope to make Christian "a place of the mind," but the tuition raises he found necessary drew wealthier students who took college for granted. And as recruiting was extended to the Chicago-Great Lakes area, California, and the East, the composition of the student body subtly shifted: more daughters of upper-middle class business executives, urban girls whose names implied a variety of national origins, girls from eighteen religious backgrounds, including Catholic, Jewish, and Latter Day Saints. (There were fewer daughters of alumnae, so that increasingly the name of the College had to be explained, as the first president had predicted.) Most of these changes represented trends in the U. S. population, even the affluence; apparently the student handbook regulation against bringing one's own television set was needed.

Being affluent, more girls were politically conservative. In a campus election of 1961 they voted for Nixon against Kennedy; but on that Black Friday, November 22, 1963, when President Kennedy was assassinated they moved as one to the chapel to bow their heads under the stained glass window. Theirs was the first memorial service held in Columbia. President Freeman declared a three-day period of mourning and — because Christian's southern aura had not changed completely — he urged compassion for the residents of Dallas and of Texas.

If the quality of a student body related to financing, even more did the excellence of faculty. Since the late 1950's the world of the teacher had changed from the ivory tower to the market-place, as he became an increasingly-sought-after commodity. Aware of this, Freeman from the first had moved to increase faculty salaries, to recognize merit by educational leaves, to provide modern teaching equipment, to promote teachers and teaching through a series of brochures issued from 1959–1963.

The annual fund drive was originally publicized as "Christian's Continuing Challenge" to provide the best in instruction, and it was announced that the bulk of funds raised each year would go towards distinguished teaching. While it was not always possible so to restrict it, results soon were visible in the form of several educational experiments.

During the summer of 1962, two-thirds of the full-time faculty participated with pay in a six-week in-service training program on the improvement of teaching. Guided by educational experts they investigated new developments in teaching materials and devices, evaluation of instruction, independent study programs, and counseling procedures.

From the first, Freeman had foreseen "new dimensions of teaching and learning . . . extended to residence halls." This idea materialized specifically in "La Maison Française," a living-language laboratory unique in Columbia and rare among two-year colleges anywhere. Starting in 1961 as a French table in the dining room, it opened in September, 1964, in Hertig Hall on Christian College Avenue as a residence for sixteen seniors majoring in French. Here, under the perceptive guidance of Resident-Directrice Mme. Hortense Davison and a native "assistante" their own age, students translate their daily living into another culture, from cooking to parliamentary procedure.[11]

Another innovation was the Campus Community Program, directed by psychologist Robert Montaba.[12] It was an attempt to organize the guidance and counseling for which Christian was known, in a more professional and sophisticated way. Young women personnel assistants, recent university graduates, would live in the dormitories to provide intellectual stimulation and be the first link in communicating between the student and the official counselors: the Deans, chaplain, or psychologist. Teachers would be academic advisors only, and the former house-mothers would become "head residents."

This experiment was typical of the administration in its imagination, its flight from the traditional, its emphasis on the catchwords of life in 1962 — "self direction," "the search for identity," "freedom and responsibility." It was short-lived and somewhat unrealistic, for a House-Tutor system which created intellectual sparks at Harvard did not work on a junior-college level. And the psychologists found that, though a program can be structured, students and personal relationships cannot. The individual girl continued to take her troubles to whichever adult met her needs — "Uncle Sid" or Mrs. Kennedy or Dean Kirkman — whoever would give her that "dose of sympathy or small spank" that she needed, as the faculty at Christian had done for more than a hundred years.

Out of the experiment did come a complete reorganization of the student government in 1962. Now called the Campus Community Government, it was patterned after the federal system, providing useful experience in campaigning, voting, and democratic process. It also gave students more responsibility in planning college functions, less in monitoring trivial rules.

Unquestionably, the disciplinary problems of the sixties were more complicated than in previous eras. "The New Morality" in America might remain mostly discussion in the insulated Midwest but the collegiate issues of the East and West sifted back in some form. The question on eastern campuses was "parietal hours":[13] when, under what conditions might a girl visit a man student's dormitory room? Harvard College conceded that she might visit in the afternoon, providing the door remained open "the width of a book." (This was interpreted by some students as a book of matches.) At Christian, where girls still shouted "man on second" when one climbed the stairs of St. Clair, the hours question was translated into "apartment rulings," when the University began to allow underclassmen to live in private apartments.

In the East, Vassar College, pulled into a discussion of what went on behind those dormitory doors, gained fame for President Blanding's pronouncement that girls who did not wish to observe Vassar's rules need not come to that college and her intimation that Vassar girls were expected to be virgins.[14]

(This incident brought into controversy a value not openly discussed before in normal conversation.)

Drinking, a related campus problem, was a fairly theoretical one at Christian. Missouri law forbade liquor to any under twenty-one. The *Mike* discussed it as a moral issue and in 1966 the student handbook admonished: "Liquor bottles are not acceptable as room decorations." By then the handbook carried only four major rule infractions leading to a "campus." From drinking to car-riding, these related in some way to what President Oldham had so quaintly called "the mingling of the sexes." (How innocent his worries seemed to an administrator of the sixties, facing the product of a sexual revolution that extended from the Kinsey Report on *Sexual Behavior in the Human Female* to the first oral contraceptive, "the pill.")[15]

Characteristically, the professionalizing of student government during Freeman's tenure did away with anachronistic rules to improve the basic structure, as pulling away St. Clair's ivy was imperative to preserve the brick.

"The impact of the Campus Community Program was strongly felt as soon as it got off the launching pad and promises to increase its orbit of influence in ever widening circles," said the alumnae magazine of October, 1962. This might describe that halcyon year itself for it would seem to Kenneth Freeman, in looking back, a high point of excitement and achievement.

The blast-off had been successful, the ship was in orbit. Ideas, like a shower of stars, exploded everywhere. In 1960 the Board of Trustees had gone on record, in a statement surely worded by the President, in support of

> . . . a college whose faculty, students, plant and program compare favorably with the best, having a program based on solid and continuing research, a challenging curriculum constantly updated to meet current needs and attracting national prestige and recognition, with no need for apology for any phase of its program or for any part of its physical plant – all of this undergirded with a stable income that will permit the realization of "the bright promise of the future."[16]

"The Bright Promise of the Future" – his synonym for outer space – that was the title of President Freeman's remarks to his faculty at the first fall meeting of 1961.

In June, 1962, the College was completing its most successful year. The operational budget showed a surplus. St. Clair Hall was rehabilitated, Miller Hall, the first phase of the twenty-five year plan was completed, a projected enrollment of 425 seemed conservative and the College was already staffed to serve a school of eight hundred.

In May, 1963, the Board voted for a Ten Year Plan in which Freeman had engaged them since his arrival. As the twenty-five year master plan was a physical projection into the future, this was a statistical-financial projection of enrollment, faculty, salaries, and budget over a decade ending in 1973. By that year it anticipated a college of eight hundred students, 51 faculty, salaries averaging $12,549, tuition-room-and-board charges of $3,250, a total budget of $3,452,000, capital expenditures of $5,000,000.[17] To Christian's credit, this Ten Year Plan was chosen as the case study in a planning conference sponsored by the American Association of Junior Colleges and the Ford Foundation. It was a good example of Freeman's professional expertise. It was also, as he told the Board, "bold and visionary."

By the fall of 1963 the College faced a deficit and the spaceship was aground. The President reported the chronology of flight to his trustees somewhat plaintively:

> The dilemma of the private junior college for women, attempting to maintain stability and quality in its staff, student body, and educational program and remain financially solvent, with little gift endowment income, has been vividly demonstrated in the history of Christian College during the last fifteen months. . . .[18]

He urged them to "a massive effort." His words had a familiar ring. Perhaps more than any other character in Christian's history Kenneth Freeman resembled that original plunger into space, D. Pat Henderson: the founder whose outer space was the undeveloped West and whose plan was to launch from Christian College a cluster of satellites projecting a new type of education for women. One hundred years before, Henderson had made his farewell address to the trustees with similar lines:

> That we are surrounded by difficulties . . . is too plainly seen. . . . I am cheered by the hope that we shall, by a united effort, succeed in demonstrating that we have not been pursuing "phantoms," erecting "airy castles" or building up "visionary schemes."

"Bold and visionary" – words that describe Kenneth Freeman: a description he would have liked. It puzzled him somewhat that he had been accused of having scant respect for the past. Actually, he had taken the trouble to acquaint himself with the history of Christian College and to learn from its examples. With logic and imagination he had abstracted the most successful ideas of his predecessors: Williams' philosophy, Rogers' directness in financing, Oldham's materialism, Mrs. Moss' fund-raising and expansion, Lee's alumnae appeal, Briggs' promoting, Miller's improvement of instruction. He adapted a phrase here, an idea there – Mrs. Moss' "Thousand-Dollar-Club," her campaign for each girl to furnish a brick for the new building. He attempted to synthesize all the good, if contradictory, ideas from 115 years in his own administration and he added his own master plan.

Perhaps Freeman, like his decade, projected into outer space at an expensive cost, yet the plans made during his years would become the realities of the future. Most of all he labored to make Christian College contemporary, to bring the methods of his electronic age to one small, individualistic school which to some extent resisted his effort. He modernized, publicized, mechanized, masculinized, synthesized and – above all – professionalized.

Freeman himself was a "pro." If the first five years of his administration were a period of promise and achievement for Christian College, the last four were a record of personal fulfillment in his profession. In 1962 he was cited for distinguished service to education by the University of Missouri; in 1963 he became vice-president of the American Association of Junior Colleges. In 1964, like Lee and Miller before him, he became its president.

One of Freeman's last formal acts at Christian was to dedicate Dulany Hall, the second phase of his twenty-five year plan and the second beautiful building within three years. (The last meal in St. Clair dining room was the Christmas banquet of 1964.) Phase three, the Fine Arts Building, was already on the drawing board, the planning enabled by a gift of $15,000 from Artie Mason Carter '00 of Los Angeles.

He resigned in March, 1965, to become president of the Kansas City Metropolitan Junior College and Dean W. Merle Hill was unanimously elected his successor. For some time their efforts had overlapped, for as the professional consultants had observed, whoever might set the goals of Christian College, the academic dean would be responsible for carrying them out.

In the Larson portrait of Kenneth Freeman, dedicated at the inaugural of President Hill, Freeman is aptly pictured, something of the rugged quality of brick and concrete in his face, holding the blueprints for the new Christian College. In the background are the towers of the 1911 Dorsey Hall, last building of the last great builder, Luella St. Clair Moss.

St. Clair remained, her pride and his despair, with its transoms and drafts, its bescrolled cast-iron radiators so modern in 1899. One of the features of Inaugural Day, October 19, 1966, was the historical recreation in St. Clair parlors of a drawing-room, student room, and president's office of sixty years before. Some visitors felt that the parlors looked better than usual. One was heard to say: "Where did they find those radiators? How perfectly they fit in the room!" The new president heard of the remark and laughed. "They *are* in the room," he said.

A sense of humor was characteristic of Merle Hill. It was also characteristic that he had preferred to serve his first year as president before being officially inaugurated. In that year he had shown himself to be intelligent, analytical, and energetic. He had a rather unorthodox background for his new position. A graduate in languages of Oberlin College, with a Ph.D. in education and psychology from Purdue, he had taught German at that university for twelve years before coming to Christian. He had produced the first German language course used on commercial television and had designed a Russian course for the Fifth Army Reserve Corps. Extremely articulate, he had been a professional radio sportscaster and had worked some hundred games a year as an athletic official while earning his doctoral degree. Indeed, his first year's function as president of Christian had been to serve as a sort of umpire: in a critical moment to call together the faculty teams and see that the action progressed toward the goal.

Two new touches were introduced at the inaugural of this thirteenth president, held outdoors on St. Clair porch: the ceremonial mace carried by Mrs. Kennedy, senior faculty member who marshalled the procession, and the Presidential Seal of Office. President Hill noted that there was "plenty of chain on this medallion for me to hang myself."

> Even if I do, I shall still feel a sense of accomplishment at having finally reached the entrance to St. Clair Hall in 1966. In 1946 . . . when I hitchhiked from Oberlin College to visit a Christian College student, Dotty Rowe, now Dotty Rowe Hill, and arrived about 8:00 a.m., I was thrown off the campus by the janitor of Missouri Hall. In those Dark Ages young men were not permitted on campus until late afternoon.

The inaugural speaker, Donald A. Eldridge, vice-president of the American Association of Junior Colleges, defined "The College Woman: 1966" in contrast to those original seven students at Christian who wrung from the males in their community the grudging admission that they were "human beings . . . possessing a nature in common with our own sex." After a century they have won their equality but are required to be superwomen.

In the second half of the 20th century college women, like men, are expected to prepare themselves for work of consequence in the increasingly complicated worlds of commerce, industry, and the professions. They are also expected to marry, rear children, transmit to them the spiritual-cultural values, serve their communities, and understand their husband's profession. A woman's education must train her for all these needs, said Eldridge, foreseeing that more women would complete two years of general education, work briefly, marry, rear a family, then at age thirty-five resume their formal education with a specific vocation in mind.[19]

The speaker did not cite his young listeners the statistics that would prove how drastic, indeed, were the changes for women in America, where one out of three workers now is a woman, six out of ten women work and most of these are married. If American women were finally guaranteed equal vocational opportunities under law by the Civil Rights Act and the Equal Opportunity Act of 1964, there was a formidable implication in Bureau of Labor predictions that by 1970 women might be expected to divert twenty-five years after childbearing to the labor force. For, whereas a woman in 1900 had a life expectancy of forty-two, the woman of 1966 could expect to live eighty years and have a period of twenty to forty years – almost a whole new life – after her children were grown.

Eldridge saw in the new pattern of woman's future a special place for the two-year college and described a small, selective college like Christian as privileged in having the time to work out problems that giant institutions could not consider. He described the phenomenal development of the junior college in the United States as another drastic change and the new community colleges as "the most dramatic educational movement of the past quarter century . . . the most significant . . . development since the free American high school."

Today, as President Hill took office, there were almost one thousand junior colleges in America. By 1967 there would be a new community college each week and by the year 2000 the first two years of college would come almost wholly within the province of the junior college.

Merle Hill, listening to the speaker, was aware that the American Association of Junior Colleges would represent less and less the voice of schools like Christian. Even as he spoke in response, of Christian's having been "a viable force in American higher education" he knew that its place in the history of the junior college movement would now be with the minority. He might have said that Christian had gone against the majority when that first girl stepped over the doorstep, that in 115 years it had often seen its experiments become the accepted fact. "We shall not be afraid of change and experiment," the new President promised,

> . . . we shall reject the parochial and that which is consistent only with a culture that was. We shall work, instead, for a program that will create an educated mind capable of coping with the polycultured world of today.

But the catalog of 1965–66 for the first time in fifty-two years did not carry the words "junior college" on its frontispage, but defined Christian as "a non-sectarian two-year liberal arts college for women."

At thirty-nine, President Hill resembled the earlier presidents of Christian College who were gifted in teaching and personal relationships, men like John Augustus Williams and George Bryant. His empathies lay with faculty and students: with practice, over theory. Not since the earliest days when the College family lived in one small building had the President's household been so open to students. When Dorotha Rowe Hill returned to Christian as the Dean's wife, she had commenced to act out the school's personal approach to education in her own quiet way; now she announced she would revive a custom of the original president, "drawing room privileges," the students' use of the presidential parlor. Hers was a close-knit family, with one son, Lee, but soon there were a handful of girls who were "like daughters to us."

"Daughters" was a word Williams had used, and indeed there were other parallels between the first president and the thirteenth. Hill was popular, like Williams, and for some of the same reasons: his youth, handsomeness, informality. Again a president might come into the hall singing. Hill had studied music at Oberlin conservatory and played trumpet with the faculty combo. Williams was a composer and conducted student choirs. Both had unusual self-discipline. Hill's years of sports were effective training for the sixteen-hour day of a college president. Now that administrative duties had him desk-bound, he began to rise at five-thirty and run around the Hickman High School track. As teachers both Williams and Hill tended to be iconoclasts, one in the days when Christian College was new, the other, facing the problems of the new Christian College. Hill himself had noticed the similarities of the times, at least. When an elderly alumna sent him a photograph of J. A. Williams, he kept it on his desk, wondering briefly how he would look in a beard.

Hill's first concern as president was to define personnel practices and expectations. The Faculty Handbook issued in October, 1965, greatly boosted morale.[20] It involved committees of both faculty and trustees for the first time in committing onto paper official policies regarding tenure, employment qualifications, and fringe benefits. By setting up a system of grants for professional conferences and sabbatical leaves it encouraged better teaching and research and helped to attract that "faculty of significant individuals" which was the goal of Christian's master plan.

Jack L. Batterson, who followed Hill as dean of faculty, fit this description himself; the sort of able, enthusiastic teacher and scholar any institution would seek, he frankly enjoyed the teaching life at Christian and was one of its best exponents. With him teaching history and his wife, Paulina, teaching government, the appeal for social studies increased. They were one of several husband-wife teams (the Ellises, the Johnsons, the McIlvains) that furthered Christian's family feeling. A leader in academic policy since 1959, Batterson as dean was now immediately involved in building up the library and in seeking educational grants.

Hill's first business with trustees was to secure salary raises for all faculty and staff. He vowed that whatever else in Christian's master plan might not progress on schedule, faculty salary increases would. He pointed out that the real threat of the public junior colleges would be in the competition for teachers. By 1970, there would simply not be sufficient to go around.

In 1960, Kenneth Freeman had predicted that "the next ten years will truly be a fight for survival as a first-rate college." In 1965, at midway, and drafted into the presidency at a moment when future promise had become potential crisis, Merle Hill led out his campaign with vigor. For national population projections had not materialized on schedule, women's colleges had not automatically been filled; instead, a "tight money" era that had not been projected, coinciding with drastic tuition increases, had left Christian in 1964–65 with its smallest student body in a decade.

He collected the most effective administrative team that has ever run Christian College: Jack Batterson, Dean of the College; Howard Kelley, Dean of Admissions and Assistant to the President; Charles Mai, Director of Development; Don Landers, Business Manager; Robert Craig, Associate Dean and Registrar; and two who had already proven their abilities, Elizabeth Kirkman, Dean of Women; and Jane Canedy Crow '57, Director of Alumnae Activities. Where staff could reasonably be cut, he cut; where expenses could be pruned, he pruned. There were fewer glossy publications; the Faculty Handbook was mimeographed.

Within three years, 1965–66 through 1967–68, enrollment climbed from the low of 306 to the highest on record, 566. In less than a year, North Hall was built to house the additional students. (The name was temporary so that some future donor could make a naming gift.) This three-story, 108-bed residence hall, completed in the fall of 1966 at a cost around $450,000, was the third structure built under Christian's master plan. It contained 54 double rooms arranged around a center core of stairways, baths, and study lounges, and its view windows and air-conditioning particularly attracted the girls.

In these same two years, with judicious management and the direction of able trustees led by Hartley Banks, one-fourth of a million dollars indebtedness was cleared.

Physical expansion continued through 1966–67 in less flamboyant but equally significant ways. The size of the library was quadrupled, by moving it to the former dining room in St. Clair Hall, reconstructed at a cost of $60,000. Here in carpeted, air-conditioned quiet are study areas for one hundred girls, private carrels, administrative offices, and a listening room also used for seminars. An attractive art gallery was created as an approach to the library, and a new dance studio was constructed in the former library area of Dorsey Hall.

Space for art was doubled by converting the former kitchens, with their ground-floor light and sinks, into design studios. St. Clair recreation room was remodeled to contain a large self-service bookstore. A coffee house for serious student discussions was set up in a corner of Hughes recreation room. The biological laboratories were newly equipped. (The physical science labs had been renovated in 1964–65 by chemistry teacher Dennis Grev with grants from the Parents' Fund and the A. B. Chance Foundation.)

The major project of the Fine Arts-Academic Building would have to be funded gradually, but its fountain court was partially paid for by the Class of 1967. It would include a 200-seat open-stage theatre, an exhibition area, ten practice rooms, a classroom and several art studios. The President saw it realistically as costing a million dollars. Meanwhile, he announced in 1967 a Robnett-Spence Student Health Center, the gift of Mrs. E. L. Spence (Mittie V. Robnett '04). This would be Christian's first building to be given by one family and would commemorate a long lineage of students and benefactors associated with the history of the College. It would stand between Hughes and Dulany and would replace the isolated old infirmary.

With the library investment, St. Clair would remain for a decade or two. Dorsey, consuming repairs, must be replaced before long. "Practice Hall," (now the Conservatory) the original main building, should be conserved as the oldest women's college building west of the Mississippi. Restored into period rooms and museum exhibits, it could become a more meaningful focal point than the architect's proposed bell tower: a monument to 117 years of continuous college education for women.[21] But unless some donor intervened, sentiment might have to be sacrificed to the real needs of the future.

The Ten Year Financial Plan, at mid-point, was also being revised in practice, for it had projected a student body of eight hundred by 1972. The new administrative team was convinced that Christian, after five years of analysis and upheaval, needed a period of stabilization to assimilate its rapid growth. The student body should be held to around 550 residents for the next few years; building plans should progress on a sound level, fund-raising according to schedule. By 1972, the next predicted peak of college-age population growth, the school might again expand.

If the expansion set in motion less than a decade ago by

Christian's master plan was revolutionary, the accomplishments of the last few years have been truly a success story. Before 1958, Christian College had no organized channels for fund raising; by the year ending June, 1967, it was raising more than $100,000 annually for development. Until 1958, alumnae had never been asked to support the College consistently; by 1967 they raised $38,000 with 17 per cent participation in giving to the Annual Fund and in 1968 alumnae gifts from all sources exceeded $100,000. The first Parents' Weekend was in 1960. Now more than seven hundred parents come to campus from thirty-two states and parents give upwards of $27,000 a year. A Medallion Club of individuals pledging $1,000 or more in a fiscal year, added nineteen members who gave more than $40,000 in 1967. Columbia friends and firms support an annual campaign that has grown from $26,500 in 1965 to $51,600 in 1968.[22] The College is starting a deferred-giving program and has already received several annuity gifts and designations in wills. Deferred gifts appear to be the large untapped potential in individual philanthropy, offering the donor benefits along with the gift, such as tax reductions, lifetime income, or special consideration for heirs. These results should be visible in another decade and may be the principal means of building an endowment.

President Hill would be the first to insist that the financial vitality peaking in his administration represents the work of many individuals acting in efficient teams. The imagination and scope of the development plans directed by Charles Mai; the competent and devoted organizing of alumnae by Jane Crow; the successful piloting of Columbia campaigns by trustees Tom Allton, B. D. Simon, Jr., Sidney Neate, Andrew Bass, Jr., and such Columbians as Raymond A. Young, and of parents' drives by E. C. Adams, Warren Norton, Darrell Eichhoff, and others; the personal contributions of the one trustee who has influenced Christian's direction more than any other in the last decade, Hartley G. Banks, for nineteen years president of the Board; the influence of the alumnae board of directors; all have made possible Christian's vigorous entry into its second century.

Alumnae themselves have produced perhaps the most dramatic achievements in the shortest time. Since the Christian College National Alumnae Association was organized in 1962 its fund raising has won the American Alumni Council's $1,000 first prize for sustained performance among junior colleges in annual alumni giving. Organized alumnae groups currently exist in St. Louis, Columbia, Springfield, and Kansas City, Missouri, Indianapolis, Tucson, Louisville, Dallas, and Denver; alumnae meet occasionally in Phoenix, Oklahoma City, and Houston, and are organizing in Memphis, Tulsa, the Los Angeles and Washington, D. C., areas.

In five years the alumni organization has sent the College more than five hundred prospective students' names, has sponsored annual Homecoming reunions in May, assisted with a Charter Day event in January, a yearly Distinguished Alumna Award and a Distinguished Women of America Award which has brought to the campus such notables as Dr. Frances Kelsey and Helen Hayes.[23] An alumna representative now serves on the Board of Trustees each year.

Outstanding in alumnae work and its contribution towards the new Christian College are the first three presidents of the Association: Elizabeth Estes Gentry '20 of St. Louis, Leta Jones Spencer '28 of Columbia – both College trustees – and Evelyn Schrom Estes '34 of Columbia. Their enthusiasm is sifting through the general body of alumnae in significant ways. At the 1967 Homecoming, Elizabeth Toomey Seabrook presented a twenty-five-year-reunion gift of $1,500 from her class of 1942 with the suggestion that each twenty-five-year class follow suit. The next year's class gave more than $1,000 for the Fine Arts Center, and former members of the Double Sextette established a memorial there to Geneva Youngs. Restoration of the Memory Garden in the name of Ethel Robnett Estes '03 and furnishing the foyer of the new Health Center to commemorate Mary Robnett Bradford are among recent family memorials; the C. E. Lemmon library collection and the James C. Miller scholarship fund established by Mrs. Miller and her daughters are others. The Deborah Bryant $1,000 Phi Theta Kappa award for scholarships represents the youngest individual alumna to be a large donor. Mrs. C. B. Miller (Helen Singleton Conley '98) and Mrs. Albert M.

Johnson (Harriet Johnson '01) have made the initial annuity gifts under the new deferred-giving plans available from the College. In the last few years the ranks of Medallion Club givers have grown so that no printed list would be inclusive for the life of this book.[24]

Usually, a small two-year college for women has not been eligible to compete with large institutions for federal funds and foundation grants. However, since Sputnik the American public has awakened to responsibility for higher education in general. Also, the Berkeley student revolt of 1964 first demonstrated that the multiversity is not the simple answer to an expanding college population. At the White House Conference on Education in 1966, solutions were explored and innovative ideas emerged about the importance of supporting diversity in education, one possibility being to encourage existing small colleges to educate a share of the population rather than to enlarge already monolithic plants.[25] As the Conference underscored the value of an individual approach, a relevant liberal arts education, good teaching by teachers who can develop student potential, Merle Hill could reflect that all of these were available at Christian College.

President Hill's administration has been characterized by financial stability, a remarkable record of development, an 80 per cent growth in enrollment, and high faculty and administrative morale. At the same time, the educational program of Christian College has been consistently strengthened.[26]

Despite its lack of endowment, Christian College spends $63,900 yearly in scholarship assistance. The Trustees Scholarship program, based on leadership as well as academic superiority, has steadily expanded and attracts to Christian each year those girls who tend to become the College pacemakers. In January, 1967, the annual Charter Day Scholarship Banquet was initiated, the $1,600 proceeds to add scholarship in art, music, and drama.

Under President Hill, Christian is becoming international-minded. Beginning in 1968–69, scholarships will be given students from ten foreign countries. Two native foreign-language instructors are now on campus; the President has a German exchange student in his home, and is teaching speed-reading in German. The success of La Maison Française encourages a German and a Spanish house, as soon as proper directors and financing can be found. The European tours have focused more seriously on art, musical, and political science experiences as they are conducted by teachers in these fields.

Curricular trends reflect the increased arts-and-science core requirements: a climbing enrollment in social studies, English, science, and art, with a stable demand for languages and mathematics and a marked decline in home economics and secretarial studies. The term 1966–67 marked the first course in research; the first student literary magazine, *Opus I*; the forming of a concert choir; and the first summer school term. Innovations in class-sectioning according to ability, independent studies, student evaluation of teaching, and out-of-class learning experiences designed to make the subject relevant to the student's world are being tried. A 1968–69 experiment will change the school calendar to start classes September 1 and complete final examinations before the Christmas break.

The tremendous improvement of the library in size and quality, implemented by Dean Batterson and Mr. McIlvain, the librarian, is a measure of Christian's academic progress. This administration has consistently increased the amount of the budget spent on the educational program, has increased the size, salaries, and retention of the faculty, even as it aims at smaller classes and a still lower faculty-student ratio than the present one-to-fifteen.[27] A new stability is reflected in the increased rate of student retention: today 66 per cent of first-year students return for the second year in contrast to 55 per cent a decade ago.

President Hill has challenged his faculty to question the sacred traditions of the fifty-minute class, the standard text, the rigidly factual lecture that tries to cover all the content. He points out that no longer can a teacher hope to cover the knowledge in his field.

> The knowledge of the world doubled from 1900 to 1950, doubled again from 1950 to 1960, again from 1960–1967, and will double within the next five years. More important than trying to teach the facts is teaching our students how to analyze and find the facts. I don't care whether a student knows that the first Negroes were

> brought to this country by a Dutch slaver in 1619 if she understands some of the problems of civil rights. . . .
>
> Each of us has, I am certain, some untried experiments with teaching our subject-matter. Why don't we try them? . . . Let's ask ourselves how our courses differ from their counterparts at the University of Missouri or at any other college in the United States. . . .
>
> Two years ago, when I was a younger and more naive president, I asked for support to make Christian the best two-year college anywhere . . . Now I would make a plea simply for daring to be ourselves and doing well what we know how to do best.

As the new dean, Merle Hill had once told an alumnae workshop that "the small, independent college, to survive in today's world, must have something different to offer." As president, aware of the vast resources of the multiversities, the easy financing of the community colleges, opening *Time* magazine to read that "the woman's college is an anachronism,"[28] he reflected on Christian's justification for existing. As he traveled from Oregon to Florida and was asked daily, "What is *different* about Christian College?" he felt compelled to define that difference. By doing so, he succeeded where presidents and public relations persons before him had so often failed.

> I have concluded that outstanding teaching is our main reason for being . . . The best thing we have to offer is the faculty, the teaching they do, the attention they give to individuals. We cannot hope to compete with more affluent schools in buildings and setting . . . but on faculty we can compare with the best. I want you [he said to his teachers] to make the name Christian College synonymous with outstanding teaching at whatever intellectual level we find our students.

What makes an outstanding teacher? If the teachers at Christian College account for its "difference," in what way are they different?

In 1967–68 Christian College had a full-time faculty of thirty-nine. Half are men – a change from the fifties, more like the original school. The average age is thirty-eight, younger than in previous decades. The average teaching experience is ten years – in contrast to the inexperience of the graduate assistants who teach freshmen and sophomores at large institutions; the average tenure at Christian College is six years, although one-third of the faculty have taught there longer.

The faculty remains, more truly than the student body "small, select, serious in purpose." "Enthusiasm," "versatility," "talent," and "integrity" are other words that apply. Not primarily interested in money or material advantages, these teachers have a vested interest in a college which in turn recognizes them as its most valuable asset and whose renascence they themselves have planned.

Dean Batterson says of his colleagues:

> They have several characteristics in common which bring real strength to the Christian College program: they are dedicated to Christian's philosophy that the most meaningful education for young women during the first two years of college is one in the liberal arts. They believe that of all the scholarly pursuits, teaching is the most important in accomplishing the stated goals of the College. Finally, they are convinced that effective teaching must not and cannot be confined to the classroom.

William Arrowsmith, a critic of American higher education, defines a good teacher as one who is involved in the same struggles as his students. He declares that a student can go through the average college or university today without meeting a teacher who is a really worth-while person.[29] This is not possible at Christian.

Sidney Larson, a teacher for seventeen years, explains: "For us in the arts, there is an all-pervading need to stay involved in the production of our specialties. You may know institutions where students are exposed to teachers who teach about a subject without knowing themselves *how* to do it. Everyone here also knows how to do it." Probing why anyone "of sound mind, with ambition, education, and a desire for the good things in life" would select a career as faculty member at Christian, he decided:

> Christian College provides unique satisfactions. Unique because they have persisted for 117 years, because they can be believed in and lived by . . . Somehow, in spite of human fallibility there is distilled here a delicate es-

sence of meaning and purpose which permeates all of us, which is caught and funnelled into the air your daughter breathes on this campus . . . the uniqueness I refer to is the *degree of total involvement* which our faculty assumes as its role.[30]

Dan Hoagland explores the same questions from his viewpoint as a scientist.

Those of us who have served on multiversity campuses have seen a conflict between scientific and literary culture. A chemist may have no significant outside contact; a musician is similarly isolated. Partly, this is a consequence of sheer size . . . The occasional student who insists upon pursuing several different interests may have to battle for his right to do so. This situation does not exist at Christian College.

Its academic community is a close-knit entity. Each student is in daily contact with others whose interests in part overlap, in part diverge from, her own. Each teacher is necessarily a specialist in some field. But, either because of a subtle selection process which operates before the teacher comes to Christian or more explicit influences on campus, no one on the faculty is only a specialist.

I share a suite of offices with four other teachers; three are linguists, one teaches swimming. Across the hall are a historian, an economist, and a geologist. In the faculty lounge, a typical conversation may involve a chemist, a musician, and a specialist in English literature. Under these circumstances it is difficult to avoid a growing sense of the essential unity of our purpose — and that of human knowledge itself.[31]

We might seek a woman's opinion, from that swimming teacher Hoagland mentioned. Although her appearance belies the years, Sue Meyers Gerard has taught physical education at Christian since 1935. She is as articulate and versatile as the two men; she has a degree in journalism as well as one in education and has published more than one hundred articles. Mrs. Gerard illustrates Arrowsmith's definition of a good teacher in a way especially pertinent to a woman's college, for she is one of a dozen career teachers at Christian who are also mothers and homemakers. She is in the faculty lounge, a modest room whose windows overlook the original building of 1851. Two coffeepots simmer as teachers enter with sack lunch or sandwich.

"I'll show you the most important thing that has happened at Christian College since I've been here," says Sue. She sets up a slide viewer — she is also a photographer — while the others groan. ("What now, Sue? Ten new ways to save a drowning man?") Mrs. Gerard has been recognized as a national expert in water safety for her development of the safety post "rescue station" publicized by the Red Cross and of a mouth-to-mouth resuscitation technique that can be used while the drowning victim is still in the water.[32] She estimates that she has trained 1,100 senior lifesavers and produced 95 swimming instructors.

Her slides are of a group of teachers standing around a ramp that reaches from the second-story window of the old library in Dorsey Hall to the window of the new library in St. Clair's basement. The ramp is Bill McIlvain's solution for moving twenty thousand books. He starts the cardboard boxes, Dean Batterson, in shirt sleeves, directs them down the chute, and others, Bill Brown, David O'Hagan, Merle Hill, jump to catch them. The women are serving coffee. Polly Batterson, "Petie" Davison, hold up their cups in jubilation. "September 15, 1966" records Sue, "the day we moved the library."

"The new library is the most important thing that has happened at Christian since *1914*," — when the last was built — President Hill would correct, and others would agree.

The recorded moment of family rejoicing recalls others on this spot — J. K. Rogers surveying the new brick wings, Oldham exulting over the first plumbing, Mrs. St. Clair displaying "the finest natatorium connected with an institution in the Middle West." Perhaps the special ambiance that people notice about Christian College lies in its ghosts — the memories of those past devoted, even fanatical teachers and presidents that haunt the corridors, all saying with their different voices, the same thing: "Let all else go, but educate your daughters."

Dr. Blanche Dow, president of the American Association of University Women, speaking at Christian, declared that any college that has survived in excellence for 117 years is "its own excuse for being." According to Marshall McLuhan, self-styled prophet of our electronic age, "the medium is the message." Perhaps it is true that Christian, through the medium of contemporary brick and glass rising behind antique gates among century-old trees on its original campus is communicating the message of survival and renewal: that there is still a small, selective place for living and learning in the world that moves towards 1984.

But "Why a Two-Year College for Women?" Is it an anachronism in higher education today? Dr. Pauline Tompkins, a distinguished educator, has another answer:

> . . . the strongest justification for the private junior college is that it does not march exclusively to the prevailing tune of higher education but that it hears a different drummer. . . . our institutions of higher learning are more and more involved in servicing the sophisticated technology they have created . . . preoccupied with "how" to make the thing go, rather than "why." Ultimately, however, the character of a society is shaped by its response to "why" . . .
>
> The two-year college for women is uniquely qualified . . . because it has greater independence . . . to address itself to this dimension of higher education . . . the junior college provides a residential setting where, for two years, the student can pause from life's occupation, not to escape or seek refuge, but to take stock of herself in the universe.[33]

What is her universe, Christian's college girl of the sixties, and who is she?

A child of today's "nuclear family," she has lived in an atomic age, a space age, an electronic age; in a transient Pop-Age of paper dresses, cardboard furniture, and self-destroying sculpture – and always in an age of anxiety. Auschwitz, Pearl Harbor, Korea, are her ancient history; Selma, Watts, Memphis are milestones in her present memory. "The Death of God," "Berkeley," "LSD" – these bombs have burst on her horizon and left their fallout.

She is surrounded by revolution, the revolt against authority, the individual against the machine, poverty versus affluence, black against white, the sexual revolution, the youth revolution. Of these two she is inevitably a part, being a woman and under twenty-five – the age group that by 1970 will make up half of American society.[34] It tends to question the other half as The Establishment and its traditional values as "phony." The target is the discrepancy between values as professed and practiced by one's elders; the motto, "Don't trust anyone over thirty," and the watchword, "Keep your cool."

If she reads at all, she has read the campus classics that indict her society: Salinger's *Catcher in the Rye*, Golding's *Lord of the Flies*, perhaps Camus' *The Stranger* or Huxley's *Brave New World*. At Christian she has seen "No Exit," along with "Blithe Spirit." Film is her medium, and her day's films are strange and violent: "Georgie Girl," "The Graduate," "Bonnie and Clyde"; her day's songs are wistful, "The Times They are a-Changing," "We Shall Overcome." She has grown up with the Beatles and has danced the Twist, the Jerk, the Bugaloo – the other swiftly-changing contemporary dances of alienation.

It takes detachment to confront a world where war can be watched daily on television as entertainment, where school children can be stoned on American sidewalks, where three of the nation's leading young idealists – a President, a Nobel Peace Prize winner, and a U. S. Senator – can be assassinated within five years; an absurd world where religion is debated in the pages of *Playboy* magazine and the Playboy concept of woman as a plaything – object – Bunny, is promoted as part of the American dream.

Whatever their teachers' aspirations for them, small wonder that the dozen Christian College students polled for *Seventeen* magazine all mentioned "poise" and "maturity" as among their educational aims. Actually, poise – or seeming to be mature – was a characteristic that visitors often remarked in Christian girls.[35]

For the most part they stayed sheltered by their youth, the school's size and its location from the storms that shook students on either coast, almost as in Civil War days when President Rogers had called his eighteen-acre campus a "citadel." While East-West coast students marched with placards and held sit-ins in the halls, Christian girls sought the freedom to stay out till 1:00 a.m. on Friday and Saturday nights. When the alarms about drugs on campuses reached Columbia by 1966, Cathies were collecting psychedelic posters, not psychedelic drugs. Their secret rituals were not Zen, but the ancient schoolgirl mysticism of Candlelights: the anticipation – where would the candle stop? – one for luck, two for "lavaliered," three for "pinned," four for engaged; then the squeals, the kisses, the dunking in the shower.

Their yearly calendar moved on, partly updated, partly unchanged. Although they could ride freely around Boone County now, their daily world remained bounded largely by Zero House or Ernie's for food, the Strollway for shopping, the University columns, stadium, library, Union, and fraternity rows. Big Sisters no longer met the train: the "Wabash Cannonball" was no more, having merged with the Norfolk and Western Railroad. Girls arrived at college by plane, car, or chartered bus. But each new student was still introduced to the gray lady legend, sunbathing on back campus, and botany excursions along Hinkson Creek.

Mrs. Hertig's Hallowe'en party persisted, although she would have censored its skits in 1965. "Personal Presence" had become the Modeling Club, but its stated aim still was "to bridge the gap between the girl and the mature woman." The May Queen had in the fifties changed to Commencement Queen; her court pageant with page-boys and faking trumpeters had come to seem humorous and after 1965 faded away as Commencement was condensed into two days. By 1968 her successor, the Ivy Chain Queen, was celebrated only in the yearbook, along with a "Rose Queen" from the junior class.

"Religion-in-Life Week" in 1965 was contracted into three discussions on "The Deputy" by a protestant minister, a rabbi, and a priest. A film series, with sessions afterwards in "The Hungry Ear," campus coffee house, is the current vehicle for ethical discussions.

In 1964 the *College Widow* became the *Ivy Chain*. The long-stemmed American Beauty rose is now as much a symbol of Christian as the ivy, from the custom of the seniors carrying an armful of roses on Class Day, writing "rose notes" to favorite juniors, and the final Rose Vespers. A set of new traditions has grown up around Christmas: the Phi Theta Kappa tree-lighting ceremony followed by the party for faculty children, the inter-dormitory carol-singing contests since 1959, the Big Sister-Little Sister banquet (1966), a living nativity scene in Rogers Gateway since 1964, and in 1967 – an interesting milestone for a college named "Christian" – the celebration of Hannukuh along with Christmas vespers. The 1967–68 school year, celebrated at the University of Missouri as "the year of the Tigress" marking its one hundredth anniversary of admitting women, marked the admission of a fifth-generation student at Christian: Barbara DuBois.

Perhaps student affluence was the most conspicuous change from other days, reflecting the change in America itself. Still noteworthy was the mother snapping pictures at Ivy Chain who wore a charm bracelet of solid gold commemorative oil wells – and the student on last year's European tour who purchased as souvenir a London double-decker bus! It was more characteristic that her classmates never realized she had wealth.

On the whole, the changes in student life were serious-minded. Often the teachers might wish girls were more concerned with the major issues of their day – civil rights, social justice, student-teacher dialog, peace. The Battersons might appropriately title an article: "Women and Politics: the Failure to Think and Act."[36] And it was probably true, as the yearbook said, that "Ten years from now you are not going to remember 1965 as the year of great challenge to modern youth, tremendous strides in the space program, or the accelerated war in Vietnam. You will remember that was the year you spent at Christian College . . ."

Although many more girls assembled for a discussion of "Sex and the College Student" than for one on Vietnam, a crowd of 250 participated in debate on fair housing in Columbia with the mayor present. In 1968, teachers Polly Batterson, Eldon Drennan, and Chaplain Jack Scott, three who greatly influenced student thinking, initiated a series of panel programs on "Today's Issues." And the *Micophone*, while decrying "apathy," also records earnest concerns: joining the Peace Corps, supporting a foreign foster child. In 1967, Christian, still one-third southern in enrollment, had a Negro student.

In 1968 a Service Project Board sponsored by the student Religious Life Committee involved 150 volunteers in weekly service to such local agencies as the community nursery, the Woodhaven Home for Exceptional Children, the St. Paul's A.M.E. Sunday School, the University Medical Center, and the Fulton State Hospital and School for the Deaf.

It may seem ironical that the serious approach was demonstrated nationally by a beauty queen, Deborah Bryant '65, Christian's straight-A graduate who became Miss America of 1966. Hers is a parable of how much America's viewpoint toward women has changed in a century.

In 1851 no decent young woman would have stood on a platform before a crowd except for some serious occasion like a Commencement exercise. In 1900 a progressive like Luella St. Clair might have mounted a box for woman's suffrage—but would risk being jailed, or labeled "monster." In 1921, when the Miss America Pageant originated as a bathing beauty contest few of the sort of girls who attended Christian College would have paraded publicly in a bathing suit. In 1933 when Sally Rand gained world fame for her fan dance at Chicago's Century of Progress, no one mentioned that for a few months she had attended the Christian College academy; but by 1966 her dance had become an art form and the staid Chicago Historical Society accepted her fan as an exhibit. And by 1966 both the pageant and nice girls had changed. The contest, now a talent competition, had become "the largest scholarship opportunity for women in the United States"; the contestants seeking its $10,000 to $100,000 benefits were usually bright, ambitious college girls.[37]

More ironically, the contest had also become a last stronghold of traditional feminine virtue in a hedonistic age. At the same time that an American society girl posed nude for *Harper's Bazaar* and *Esquire* printed photo-interviews of Ivy League couples who had set up housekeeping unmarried, Miss America contestants could not smoke, drink, had little time for dating, and were accompanied everywhere by chaperone.

If Miss America is usually written off as a symbol of a synthetic, mass-produced American girl-product, *Time* magazine noted that in Deborah Bryant "somebody changed the stereotype."[39] And New York art critic John Canady, a skeptical judge, wrote of Debbie:

> . . . if she ends up all sleek and stylized after the year that is ahead of her, I am going to give up. I didn't know they were still making girls like her, and if they spoil her, I will know there is no defense against the forces that have made girls like her so rare.[40]

When she returned to campus for "Miss America Day," former classmates asked how it felt to come back. "It's not like any other place under the sun," said Debbie, who should know after her year's travels of 200,000 miles; "Christian will never change."

That night at the formal banquet the goblets held mock champagne and Deborah was honored by an official representative of Phi Theta Kappa, national junior college scholastic society, of which she had been Christian's president. She presented the College with a thousand-dollar scholarship for textbooks for honor students. And when she left, her schoolmates, remembering the dozens of red roses left behind in hotel rooms, gave her a book. It was one that Grandma had enjoyed: *The Rubáiyát of Omar Khayyám.*

Photographer Dan Hoagland, starting out with his camera to find the one picture that might symbolize Christian College, ended by taking a simple photograph of a girl sitting in a tree with a book. So he recorded that pause in youth when one has time to sit alone above the world and "take stock." A parent, wanting to give his daughter the best, might think: what greater gift in today's existential world than a moment of time itself?

A student might describe what she found at Christian more simply . . . "A warm, personal place," said Nancy Stuver '66. "Christian is the involvement you have with other people. And through that involvement you come to know yourself."

Involvement is at the heart of what draws people to Christian — presidents, faculty, students, donors — not the ego-satisfaction of being a large frog in a small puddle but the excitement of helping to mold a living institution. Christian has always been responsive to creative people. Christian's limitations have never been lack of imagination or lack of freedom, but only lack of money. Perhaps because there is never enough to work with in a small college there is, conversely, a tremendous opportunity to make one's effort count. And in the depersonalization of the late twentieth century, Hiroshima at our back, a computer-age ahead, men and women are looking more anxiously for assurance that their lives have purpose and meaning.

"Can Christian College continue?" asked Kenneth Freeman at the start of his administration. "What kind of school shall Christian College be?" Past the tenth anniversary of the space age, the astronaut's questions remain: questions that will be answered according to the unpredictable future, the generosity of benefactors, the commitment of faculty and friends, the quality of students. Hopefully, they are questions that will never be answered but will be revised and re-asked by each generation.

The appropriate date for assessment would be 1984 — the target date for completion of Christian's twenty-five year plan. But already television is projecting the twenty-first century, if man avoids the hurdles of domestic and atomic war. The optimistic fact is that a college well over a hundred years old is again being forced to define its educational purpose and make plans.

Since its Centennial, Christian College has weathered a period much like the years of its origin — of great flux and uncertainty, large visionary projections which seemed wildly impractical at the time. Its history has been the story of tremendous changes for women, a true sexual revolution, and it has been a factor in the rise of this once-minority group, the end of its segregation, its struggle for civil rights. If before 1851 higher education for women was itself an out-space concept, now women's colleges are challenged as "obsolete" and the pioneer has come to be called an anachronism. The school that once claimed to be the "first in the West" to offer a college education to women is now oldest in the West.[41] And since that April day when its first class assembled, its doors have never closed.

In reality, Christian College is only shedding skins, facing the unknowable as it did in 1851, again under the leadership of a youthful, dynamic president and a group of devoted individuals who are determined that it shall succeed. In its second hundred years Christian College is breaking new ground. If those involved in its future are as resolute and daring as its founders, it will always stand on high ground as well.

ABOUT THE AUTHOR:

Allean Lemmon Hale had her first writings published at Christian College in "Lyrics for a Lineotype" and "Christian College Prize Plays." While she was a student of Mary Paxton Keeley her play, "The Hero," took first place in both the University of Missouri Dramatic Arts Contest and the Zeta Phi Eta national playwriting competition. She was graduated from the University of Missouri, where she earned Mahan short story and essay prizes and placed first in the 1935 Midwestern Intercollegiate Playwriting Contest.

She combines free-lance writing with marriage and a family and has published a number of plays, articles and some verse. Daughter of a long-time Christian College trustee, the Rev. C. E. Lemmon, and mother of a Christian College graduate, Susanna Hale Wolf, she wrote the school's centennial history in 1951 out of close acquaintance with its recent presidents and personages. She continued her education by taking an M.A. degree in Humanities at the University of Iowa in 1963 and by studying at the Writers' Workshop there. She is married to Mark Hale, director of the Jane Addams School of Social Work of the University of Illinois at Chicago and Urbana. The Hales live in Urbana. Their daughter is also a social worker, and their son, Mark Jr., is a research mathematician.

She received alumni honors from two of her Alma Maters, being elected to Phi Beta Kappa in 1960 by the University of Missouri chapter and receiving Christian's Distinguished Alumna Award in 1964 for her service in collecting the college archives and in writing this history.

Chapter Notes

CHAPTER I

[1] Letter from T. M. Allen to John Gano, June 25, 1839, in *Letters to John Allen Gano,* John Allen Gano Family Papers (Letters from Thomas M. Allen to Gano), Western Historical Manuscripts Collection, University of Missouri Library. The letters covering 35 years from Thomas Allen to Gano which are preserved in this collection were the source of most of the author's quotes from Allen and much of her interpretation of his character.

[2] Allen to Gano, Sept. 29, 1844.

[3] The government census of 1850 does not divide colleges in the U. S. into "male" or "female." The term "college" was used more freely in the south but some southern "colleges" did not equal some contemporary eastern "seminaries." Some of the oldest schools which in their day seem to have approached collegiate level and which still exist as four-year colleges are:

1836—Wesleyan College, Macon, Ga.
1837—Mt. Holyoke College, Mass. (Called a Seminary until 1893.)
1838—Judson College, Marion, Ala.
1842—Mary Baldwin College, Staunton, Va.
1846—MacMurray College for Women, Jacksonville, Ill.

Of these, Wesleyan College claims to be "the oldest regularly chartered institution for conferring degrees upon women in America . . ." and Mary Baldwin is listed in the World Book Encyclopedia as "the second oldest college for women in the U. S." Loss of records to compare and the fact that such other early schools as the Wesleyan Female College of Cincinnati (1842)—important in their day—are now defunct make it almost impossible to prove any claim. Actually, the best collegiate education a woman could obtain before 1850 was probably at Oberlin, which admitted women to the same courses as candidates for the same degrees as men students by 1837.

Many schools with early claims, such as Mary Hardin-Baylor of Texas or Rockford College in Illinois, are found upon examination to have been chartered years before they actually functioned as a women's college. Further confusion is caused by such schools as Missouri's Lindenwood, chartered as a college in 1853 but citing 1827 as its founding date; or Stephens, chartered in 1857 but claiming 1833. Such remote antecedents as an early grade school for girls existing on the same site form no true basis for inclusion in a date line of early *higher* education for women.

[4] Columbia Missouri *Herald,* Oct. 12, 1871. (Obituary)

[5] The author's facts on Henderson are correct but not necessarily chronological at this point. The statement that Lincoln practiced law in Henderson's court is in a letter from D. Pat Henderson to James Lamar, written just after Lincoln's election and quoted in full in Edward Moseley, *Disciples of Christ in Georgia* (St. Louis: Bethany Press, 1954.) Here Henderson gives his views of Lincoln based on a 25 year acquaintance.

[6] T. M. Allen was a trustee of Columbia Female Academy in 1848. In August, 1848, the papers announced that the school would reopen under J. D. Perryman as principal. He apparently served that fall, but by

May, 1849, the superintendent was "Miss McGee, an experienced teacher." (Columbia *Missouri Statesman,* June 1, 1849.) By October 22, 1849, the trustees "secured Miss Child to take charge . . . for the ensuing Session. . . ." *(Ibid.,* Nov. 9, 1849.) Miss Child completed the spring term after which the school seems to have had only temporary supervisors until Tyre Harris came in as president the fall following its reorganization in 1851.

7 Local historian William Switzler says that Caleb Stone chose Shannon as president of the University of Missouri, the two having been old friends. The curators' Minutes of the University record that Shannon was nominated by Addison M. Lewis, a Baptist minister and that other Baptists on the board voted for him.

8 James Shannon, "A Brief Narrative of Facts Pertaining to the Origin and Establishment of Christian Female College," Christian College Board of Trustees, *Minutes of Meetings,* June 19, 1856, p. 98, State Historical Society of Missouri, Columbia.

9 Part of the untrue gossip directed against Shannon even before he reached Columbia was that he had 16 children of his own and 7 step-children. A legend has persisted that "Shannon founded Christian College so his daughters would have a place to go to school."

The facts are that in 1849 when Shannon accepted the presidency of the University of Missouri he had 8 living children and one dead. Only one, Frances Caroline, 14, was nearing college age. The eldest, Ann Maria, 20, soon married. The others ranged from 11 to one year.

In Missouri four more were born, including one girl: a total of 13 children—6 daughters. He had no step-children but educated his dead brother's daughters Rebecca and Emma. They did not come to Columbia until 1851, however. This information is based on Shannon family Bible entries, court birth records, and correspondence with James Shannon's descendants as well as standard biographical references.

10 In regard to the word "conspiracy:" The Whig-Presbyterian clique in Columbia accused Shannon of trying to convert the University of Missouri to "a training school for Christian Ministers" as Bacon College had been. Shannon always denied this. However, there are certain interesting connections between the two schools going back to the date when the University was founded in 1839 and curator T. M. Allen wrote his Kentucky friend, John Allen Gano, asking: "Who will make a good President. . . . Any of our Brethren? . . . Send me the by-laws of Bacon College."

Shannon's inaugural address as president of the University of Missouri was essentially the same speech delivered at his inaugural at Bacon College. *(Millennial Harbinger,* 1850, pp. 690-695. Bible College of Missouri Library, Columbia.) Whether he attempted to bring other colleagues than Hatch and White with him, might be explored. He actually did bring Prof. George H. Matthews from Bacon. (Relative to "conspiracy" one might also ask whether there may have been a connection between the fact that T. M. Allen was a trustee of Columbia Female Academy in 1848 when J. D. Perryman became president of that school. This same Perryman was helping Hatch run Bacon College in 1850.)

It would not have been surprising in that era for the Christians to have been attempting to dominate the University with their own principles of non-sectarianism and unity. (They did not consider themselves a sect.) In Missouri in 1850 almost every other important church had a school which was an actual rival to the state University: the Methodist Central College, the Baptist William Jewell, the Presbyterian Westminster, the Masonic College at Lexington. However, there seems to be no evidence to support the accusation that Shannon and his friends were trying to make the University into a training-school for Christian ministers.

11 The plans for the proposed Female Collegiate Institute are described in the *Statesman,* Nov. 23 and Nov. 30, 1849. A summary of the debate listing some of the participants appears in the Dec. 7 issue. There is more than a little evidence that the Christians and Baptists may have been trying to unite on this educational project. (The Christians always seemed to feel a compunction to "save" the Baptists, perhaps because the two groups had merged in the past and their thinking was similar on so many points.)

William Jewell, Baptist donor, was also one of the largest Columbia contributors to Bethany College, a Disciples school.

James Shannon's election to the University by Baptist curators is interesting in view of the fact that he had previously helped to establish a Baptist college in Georgia. If the two groups were trying to unite in founding a female college perhaps Shannon was considered the person who could best unite them.

12 Had Henderson, Shannon, Hatch and White succeeded in their original plans at Columbia they might not later have projected Culver-Stockton College at Canton.

13 "An Act to Incorporate a Female College," *Laws of Missouri,* 16th General Assembly (1850-51), Vol. 9, 310-312. The *Minutes* of the Board of Trustees record that "on motion of James Shannon it is unanimously ordered that the college be named *The Christian Female College."* (Bd. *Minutes,* Feb. 18, 1851.) However, in memoirs written many years later John Augustus Williams says he named the College. (Columbia, Mo. *Herald,* Dec. 21, 1900, p. 8.) The facts are not necessarily incompatible.

14 Trustee Lard's daughter Virginia married Silas Woodson who became Governor of Missouri. Daughter Elizabeth married Richard Shannon, an early superintendent of schools for Missouri.

15 Thomas Allen's own daughters were grown and had completed their schooling before Christian College was founded.

16 E. C. Davis, "Anniversary Address," delivered July 2, 1852. Columbia: Davis and Millan (publishers), 1852.

CHAPTER II

1 This account of the opening of Christian College (Columbia *Herald,* Dec. 21, 1900, p. 8, col. 1) was written by Williams himself. It is therefore to be considered authentic over those of Switzler, Carr, and others which differ from it and from Christian's early catalogs which were written in advance of each session. Other authoritative sources are Christian's newspaper ads of the period, Board *Minutes,* and particularly an allegorical account of the beginnings by one of the first students. This appears in the Columbia *Sentinel,* Aug. 25, 1853, p. 2, col. 4.

The one-room brick meeting-house of the Christian church where the first classes met from April to July, 1851, still stands across from the courthouse on the west side of 7th St. and is now a garage.

2 According to the Board *Minutes,* which possibly referred to MacMurray College, then known as Illinois Conference Female College.

3 Now Eureka College.

4 Among Christian's first textbooks were: *"Primary Class,* Butler's English Grammar, Ray's Intellectual Arithmetic, Ray's large Practical Arithmetic, Goodrich's Ancient History, Jones' Natural Philosophy, The Old Testament; *Sophomore Class,* Barnes' Notes on The Gospels, Ruschenberger's Natural History, Ray's Algebra, Goodrich's Modern History, Legendre's Geometry; *Junior Class,* The Acts of the Apostles, Boyd's Rhetoric, Jones' Chemistry, Jarvis' Practical Physiology, Mrs. Lin-

coln's Practical Botany, Hedges' Logic, Davis' Trigonometry, English Classics; *Senior Class,* Olmsted and Burrit's Astronomy, Upham and Combe's Mental Philosophy, Miss Beecher's Domestic Economy, Alexander's Evidences of Christianity, Waylands Ethics, Wayland's Political Economy."

[5] William Hitt's mansion at 100 Hitt St. (more recently known as "the Garth house") was torn down in 1933 to make way for the present Presbyterian Student Center. The two-room frame storehouse facing across the road which he rented to Christian for its first school year was later incorporated into a two-story house occupied in the 1880's by Dr. W. T. Maupin. It stood on the north side of Cherry St. and Hitt on lot number 159 of the original town of Columbia. In about 1903 the house was moved to the corner of Hitt and Elm streets. It was razed in 1923 and replaced by the Beverly Apartments.

This information comes from a study of abstracts of the two lots, from the above-mentioned memoirs of J. A. Williams confirmed by members of the Hitt family, and from the Columbia *Missourian,* March 14, 1923, and the *Tribune,* Sept. 15, 1924.

[6] Winthrop H. Hopson, M.D., was educated at Bonne Femme Academy and Columbia College and took an M.A. from the University of Missouri. He later studied at St. Louis medical college and practiced medicine in Fayette, Mo. Giving up medicine for the ministry, he became State Evangelist for the Christian Church in 1851 and in June, 1852, opened the Palmyra academy of Christian College.

Christian's educational scheme was truly ambitious in scope. It proposed to establish "subordinate, auxiliary and homogeneous academies in different sections of the State . . . to qualify young ladies for entrance into Christian College." (*Minutes,* May 1, 1852, p. 31.)

It visualized Christian as "the nucleus around which a beautiful and substantial system of Female education is being built up in the State" and promised that "auxiliary schools will soon be planted, all centering their energies to this point with the view of . . . placing female instruction at a higher standard in Missouri." (*Sentinel,* July 8, 1852.)

The Christian College academy at Columbia operated for 75 years. The Palmyra venture flourished from 1852 until 1856, when it had 110 pupils, a three-story building and a faculty of eight. (*Millennial Harbinger,* 1856, p. 534.) It was incorporated by the Legislature Feb. 5, 1855, but in 1857 was closed by a smallpox epidemic, the drouth, and subsequent financial panic. The building was used by a Baptist, then a Methodist school. Hopson's relatives, Mr. and Mrs. R. B. Fife, moved to Paris, Mo., to supervise the boarding department of the Christian academy there. (*Memoirs of Dr. W. H. Hopson,* by Ella Lord Hopson, Cincinnati: Standard Pub. Co., 1887.)

It is not known whether others than these two academies were actually undertaken as preparatory schools for Christian. It would be interesting to trace any influence the College may have had on the following schools whose founders had previously been closely associated with it in Columbia:

Northeast Academy at Canton, Mo., founded 1852 by Robert A. Grant and Sue Jones Grant.

Paris Female Seminary, headed in 1854 by Mr. and Mrs. Robert Grant.

De Soto Female Institute, Canton, started in 1855 by Mrs. Susan Grant.

St. Joseph (Mo.) Academy, founded 1855 by E. Curtis Davis (former editor, the Columbia *Sentinel*) and J. K. Rogers, former agent for Christian College.

7 Letter from Walter R. Lenoir, Boone Co., Mo., May 1, 1836, to Wm. B. Lenoir, Lenoirs, Tenn. Lenoir Mss. Collection, No. 1, Uni. of North Carolina, Photostats, State Historical Society of Missouri, Columbia.

8 Amusing accounts of the early examinations appear in The *Missouri Sentinel* for July 8, 1852, and July 14, 1853.

9 The *Missouri Sentinel,* July 15, 1852, "Communications for the *Sentinel on* FEMALE EDUCATION," by A STRANGER.

10 The "Ohio Female College" orator Davis held up as a model for Christian was undoubtedly The Wesleyan Female College of Cincinnati. It was incorporated in 1842-43 by the Methodists and in 1852 "47 resident graduates represented classes from 1847." Granted by the legislature "collegiate powers and privileges," it gave two degrees: M.E.L. (Mistress of English Literature) and M.L.A. (Mistress of Liberal Arts), the latter requiring Latin, Greek, and advanced Mathematics.

It must be regarded, says James M. Taylor (*Before Vassar Opened,* pp. 53-56) "as one of the definitely higher efforts of that era to establish a worthy collegiate course."

Davis' other model, "the Wesleyan College of Georgia," still exists, at Macon, Ga. Chartered in 1836 as the Georgia Female College, it claims to have graduated in 1840 "the first woman in . . . the world to be graduated from the first chartered college for women." While it is impossible to evaluate its early standards it was certainly one of the most prominent schools for women in the south. James Shannon, with his educational experiences in Georgia, may have pointed this college out as an example for Davis to use. (See *Before Vassar Opened,* pp. 16-23.)

11 *Circular and Catalogue of the Officers and Students of Christian College,* Columbia: Davis & Millan, 1852.

12 "Inaugural Address of Jno. Aug. Williams, A.M. . . . delivered . . . at his Installation . . . April 7th, 1851 . . . Columbia, Mo." Charles and Hammond, Book and Job Printers. St. Louis, 1851.

13 "An Address on Female Suffrage," Catharine Beecher, 1870.

14 Catalog, July, 1852.

15 "A treatise on domestic economy, for the use of young ladies at home, and at school," by Miss Catharine E. Beecher. Christian girls probably used the third "Rev. ed., with numerous additions and illustrative engravings. New York, Harper & Brothers, 1845."

16 The Patron was Dr. C. E. Williams, the President's father, who had given up a good practice in northern Kentucky to aid his ailing son. The Matron was Dr. Williams' second wife and the Assistant Matron was President Williams' wife, Louisa Hathaway Williams.

17 Mt. Holyoke's curriculum as offered in its 1838-39 catalog is reprinted in Goodsell, *Pioneers of Women's Education.* The author mentions "the close similarity between the initial curriculum of Mt. Holyoke and that of the English and scientific course offered in certain colleges for men of the same period. The extent and variety of the sciences offered seem a little surprising for that time. . . ." (p. 246.) The Sophomore, Junior, and Senior class studies outlined in Christian's first catalogs are practically the same as those of Holyoke's three classes and many of the same textbooks are mentioned. Holyoke stipulated that students must be 16 upon entering.

18 Elmira Female College was founded in New York in 1855. (Its Bulletin claims it was "the first college for women to grant a degree comparable to the degree conferred by colleges for men.") Mt. Holyoke, often cited as the cornerstone of female higher education, called itself seminary until much later. Vassar, the first endowed college for women with collegiate entrance requirements, came after the Civil War.

19 Christian's first graduates were: Mrs. Sarah A. Reeds, Lincoln Co.,

Mo.; Adeline W. Jones, Jacksonville, Ill.; Emma Jameson, Independence, Mo.; Emma Gordon, Columbia; Sallie Bedford, Boone Co., Mo.; Martha Shirley, Fayette, Mo.

Christian's first Commencement was July 1, 1853. This date, two years after the school opened, might seem inconsistent with the catalog statement that a diploma and baccalaureate degree would be granted only upon completion of the four-year course. Apparently, when the school started students were ranked according to ability and previous education. Catalogs and newspapers mention a "Junior class" that first year; hence a Senior class, Commencement and graduates the second year. Actually, three of Christian's first graduates had attended the college only one year, having transferred from other schools. Records show, on the other hand, that several of Christian's 1855 graduates had entered school in 1851, so perhaps by then the four-year pattern was established.

The age 18 as the average for Christian's early graduates is based on the fact that those students whose birth and death records survive average 18 years. The fact that some married women were enrolled, that many girls left school to marry and that occasional students entered in their twenties is some evidence of Christian's collegiate age level. A typical example might be Mary Louisa Caldwell, who was born in 1841, was graduated from Christian College in 1859 and went on to 19 years of teaching in Missouri high schools. In contrast, Margaret Jackman, a graduate of 1854, was 30 years old.

20 Based on a comparison of the catalogs of both schools for 1857 and the complete list of texts printed in Christian's catalog of that year.

21 *Reminiscences,* John Augustus Williams, F. L. Rowe: Cincinnati, Ohio, 1898.

22 The attic roof has been lowered but the original log beams are intact with hole-marks where they were chained together and floated down the river.

23 Letter from Willis Anderson, Knox County, Mo., to Nancy Anderson at Christian College, dated 11th April, 1855; property of Mr. Charles Baldwin, Novelty, Mo.

24 Jennie Robards Rogers, C. C. 1852-54, describes the life of those first college girls in the Columbia, Mo. *Herald,* Dec. 21, 1900, p. 14, col. 1.

25 Catalog for the year ending 1854. Curriculum varied slightly with different years, and course names differed from those used today.

26 Named for Mary Phelps, wife of trustee John S. Phelps, later governor of Missouri.

27 The statement that the Columbia Female Academy "closed for good" is based on a careful study of newspapers of the period and of the Laws of Missouri. Since another Columbia institution cites 1833 as its founding date claiming to be a "continuation" of this early school, the facts should be examined.

The Columbia Female Academy was organized in 1833 by citizens of Boone County and chartered by the Legislature Feb. 3, 1837. It was in no sense a church-related school, its trustees representing various denominations. It was sometimes known as "the Lucy Wales Academy" after its first preceptress who had come from neighboring Callaway county. *(Missouri Intelligencer,* Oct. 27, 1832, 3-4). Miss Wales left in 1840 to be married.

From 1848 the school had trouble keeping a principal and each semester's future was in doubt. In 1851 it was reorganized following a legislative act approved Feb. 28, 1851, amending its original charter. At this time the trustees seem to have been Presbyterians and Baptists with Wm. F. Switzler, Warren Woodson and Moss Prewitt leaders in the reorganization.

The fall of 1854 it failed to open for lack of a principal. A spring term in 1855 was held under Prof. T. J. Sloan of Pennsylvania. When Sloan did not return to Columbia after the summer it was announced the academy would close. (*Statesman*, Sept. 21, 1855.) A study of Columbia newspapers after this date gives no mention of the Columbia Female Academy ever opening again for instructional purpose under the control of its board of trustees.

Rather, on Feb. 15, 1865, an act was approved authorizing the sale of the building and grounds since "said property has not been, for several years past, used for school or any other purposes, and is rapidly going to waste." (*Missouri Laws*, 1864-65, p. 388.) The proceeds were divided among the original donors or their heirs. In this Act the academy is referred to as a high school and there is no mention of its having merged or continued in another form.

Convincing evidence that Columbia Female Academy was on a high school level as compared with Christian College is that the Academy's catalogs of 1851-55 list 20 girls who several years later show up as students or graduates of Christian College.

Christian is said to have purchased some of the defunct school's furnishings. The building was bought as a residence by Dr. S. B. Victor. Later it was sold to Turner Gordon who converted it into The Cottage Hotel, then enlarged it as The Gordon Hotel. It still stands, perhaps the oldest building in Columbia, as the Niedermeyer Apartments.

The idea that the Columbia Female Academy continued in another school seems to be based on statements of William Switzler that "the academy passed out of existence in 1853, and was succeeded by the denominational school . . . [Baptist Female College] organized in 1856 and chartered in 1857." (Switzler, *History of Boone County*, p. 807.)

Switzler was often careless. Even if his first date here were correct—which it is not—it would seem inconsistent that a school which had "passed out of existence" could merge after two years with another. The Baptist Female College charter of January 17, 1857 made no reference to Columbia Female Academy. (*Laws of Missouri*, 1856-57, Vol. 13, p. 227.) Its *First Annual Catalog* is for 1856-57. Its original advertisement of opening refers to its "first term," the fall of 1856. Its catalogs for 57 years cite 1857 as its charter date.

In contrast to Columbia Female Academy, Baptist Female College was strictly a denominational school with an all-Baptist board of trustees. In 1870 it was designated as one of the state female colleges of the Baptist church. Upon endowment by James L. Stephens of Columbia its name was changed to Stephens College. James Stephens himself recalled that "In 1851 Christian College was organized, and a few years later Baptist College. . . ." (Columbia *Herald*, 25th Anniversary Edition, 1895, p. 12.)

It is interesting that the Columbia circuit court in settling the disposal of that part of the Anthony Wayne Rollins scholarship originally granted to the Columbia Female Academy for educating "indigent youths of Boone County" divided the money equally between the two women's colleges in Columbia. Either might be called the spiritual successor of the early school just as the University of Missouri might date its origin from the Columbia College of 1833, its predecessor.

The author was aided in her conclusion by a thorough discussion of these early origins in E. A. Jensen's study "To determine the dates of beginning of Christian and Stephens Colleges . . . also to show the relation, if any, between the Columbia Female Academy . . . and the institution now known as Stephens College." (21 pp. typewritten research paper submitted to Department of Education, University of Missouri.)

28 Pres. Williams may also have built an addition to the College building proper, though this is not substantiated by Board *Minutes* or newspaper research. However, an 1855 letter-head engraving of Christian College by S. B. Victor who lived in Columbia and could have drawn it from sight, shows a two-story addition to one side of the main building. The two frame cottages, one with a three-room "L" are shown clearly in every known picture of the College. The engraving appears on the title-page of this book.

The "bill for eleven stoves" which Williams turned in to the trustees might indicate that he had added to the original 16 rooms of the mansion, for these were apparently all supplied with fireplaces.

29 Columbia, Mo. *Sentinel,* Sept. 1, 1853, p. 2, col. 1.

30 See Notes, Chapter III, No. 1.

31 Letter from W. T. Lenoir to "My dear Pa," dated "Columbia, Mo. Jan. 25, 1858" and clipped in Minute Record, Christian College, 1871-1918 volume. (Handwritten.)

32 Pres. and Mrs. Williams now had two living children: Augustus Edwin, born Dec. 29, 1854, and Katie, born Feb. 17, 1856. Dr. and Mrs. C. E. Williams had a son, C. E., Jr., born May 19, 1854.

33 The panic of 1857 followed this drought.

34 Among the names which appear in the catalogs of Christian College and are later on the rolls of Daughters' College, Ky., are: Ann E. Woods and Sarah F. Ellis of Boone County, Mo.; Eliza Basket, Mary S. Fant, and Bettie Jameson of Callaway; Elizabeth Jackson, Janeiro D. Finks, Mary J. Morris of Howard County; Josephine Bigg, St. Joseph; Mary Morrow, Jefferson City; Eliza Winston, Osceola; Mary McHatton, Lafayette County; M. Catherine Shoot, Hannibal; Roann Hockensmith, Independence; Susan Heard, Sacramento City, Cal.; Narcissa Burgin.

Daughters' College, a distinguished name in Kentucky's educational history, flourished under Pres. Williams for nearly 40 years. It functioned chiefly as a Normal school. From 1894-1914 it was known as Beaumont College (under different management) and since 1917 has existed as Beaumont Inn, a well-known Kentucky hostelry.

John Augustus Williams, after leaving Christian College, continued an outstanding lifelong career as an educator and a creator of colleges. A trustee of Bacon College, he was instrumental in its removal to Lexington, and its merger with Transylvania into "Kentucky University." He became professor of moral and mental philosophy there in 1866, and was elected first president of the agricultural and mechanical college opened that year as a part of Kentucky University. After two years he resigned to return to Daughters' College. He was an organizer of the Kentucky State Teachers' Association, prominent in Masonry, and wrote several books: *The Life of Elder John Smith, Rosa Emerson, Thornton, Reminiscences,* and *Priscilla.*

CHAPTER III

1 Christian University, incorporated Jan. 28, 1853, was the first college west of the Mississippi whose charter provided for equal education of men and women. (*Laws of Missouri,* Vol. 10, p. 293.)

2 By early March, 1856, the rumor was established that there was "uncertainty connected with the future of Christian Female College," and that the patron, Dr. C. E. Williams was planning to remove to Kentucky. (*Missouri State Journal,* March 20, 1856, p. 2.) It was predicted that unless financial aid were forthcoming the President, too, might leave.

"On the 15th of March, 1856, several earnest-hearted brethren met in Columbia, Mo., and laid plans for the organization of a Baptist female school which should be located in that city." (R. S. Duncan, *History of the Baptists in Missouri,* St. Louis: Scammell & Co., 1882.) Baptist Female College was incorporated January 17, 1857.

It is obvious from the timing and from the rivalrous tone of newspaper ads of the period that the Baptists seized the embarrassingly sudden resignation of Williams from Christian College as the opportune moment to start their own school. They doubtless felt that if Christian failed they would secure its patronage. Their advertisement of the "first term of Baptist Female College" appears side by side in the State *Journal* (July 3, 1856) with that of "the 6th session of Christian Female College." It turned out, as the newspapers had often predicted, that there were more than enough pupils for both schools.

3 See Notes for Chapter II, note 6.

4 Switzler, p. 929.

5 Allen to Gano, Dec. 27, 1860.

6 Carr, p. 152.

7 "Cynthia Ann Ream" is the name of Vinnie's older sister as recorded in Christian College catalogs for 1857-58 and in the Martha Washington Society Minute Book (November 6, 1857.) Vinnie's biographers, however, refer to her sister as "Mary."

There are many other discrepancies between the usual "facts" about Vinnie Ream and the evidence discovered at Christian College. Although she is often described as an untaught girl who had never seen a statue or painting before she went to Washington, it is obvious that in Columbia she had many opportunities for culture. While in Christian College she painted one portrait of Martha Washington for her society. (M. W. Minutes, June 30, 1858.)

O. A. Carr, writing in 1883 when she was already famous, speaks of "Vinnie Ream, who owes her celebrity to the inspiration and generosity of President Rogers." (Carr, *Memorial of J. K. Rogers,* St. Louis: John Burns Publishing Co., 1885, p. 241.) Rogers' scrapbooks offer some evidence that she was one of his St. Joseph pupils who accompanied him to Columbia. Mary Paxton Keeley, author of "Little Vinnie Ream" (unpublished 3-act play) states that Vinnie and her sister attended Rogers' academy in St. Joseph for two years. (Vinnie always referred to herself as "poor," so perhaps Rogers taught her free.) Mrs. Keeley adds (basing her claims on correspondence with the Rollins family and descendants of Vinnie Ream) that James Sidney Rollins got well acquainted with the Ream family when his travels as a land lawyer brought him in contact with Major Ream, a government surveyor of homestead lands. She believes it was Rollins' suggestion that the girls attend school in Columbia. When Rollins became a Congressman in Washington from 1861-65 Vinnie became his protégé. He introduced her to Clark Mills, the sculptor who taught her and Rollins is said to have persuaded Lincoln to allow her the daily sittings for the bust she made of the President.

Vinnie, usually described as 16 when she sculped Lincoln, was probably older. She was tiny and childlike and there is evidence that her mother falsified her age. Her birthdate is usually given as 1847 but the Danish critic, Georg Brandes, who knew her in Rome in 1870 said she was 26 then, which would have set her birthdate at 1844. This would certainly seem more plausible in the light of the poems she left at Christian. They seem precocious even for a girl of 13 or 14 and it is preposterous to think that a child of 10 could have written them. (See "My Kansas Home," reprinted in Carr, p. 295.) Minutes in Vinnie's handwriting and signed by her appear in the Martha Washington Minute Book during 1857-58.)

[8] Christian College, Record Books, Vol. 3 (1859-1875), State Historical Society of Missouri, Columbia.

[9] Bd. *Minutes,* Jan. 21, 1859.

[10] *Ibid.,* Oct. 29, 1859.

CHAPTER IV

[1] Christian College, Record Books (1859-60), State Historical Society of Missouri, Columbia.

[2] *Ibid.,* Vol. 3 (1859-1875).

[3] Allen to Gano, Sept. 19, 1861.

[4] Carr, *Memorial of J. K. Rogers,* pp. 253-255.

[5] Rogers, J. K., Journal (1858-1882), State Historical Society of Missouri. Entry for February 20, 1862.

[6] Mary Louisa Caldwell, Journal: 1858-1872, entry for July 6, 1861. (Typewritten copy, Christian College Historical Collection.)

[7] Allen to Gano.

[8] *Ibid.,* May 28, 1861.

[9] Letters from Mrs. Alice Kelly, aboard the *Belle Memphis,* to Lou Caldwell, July 12 and 15, 1863.

[10] *Statesman,* August 9, 1861, p. 3.

[11] Christian College, Record Books, Vol. 2 (1858-1865), State Historical Society of Missouri, Columbia.

[12] Christian College *Catalog,* 1859.

[13] *Ibid.,* 1860.

[14] Letter from Mrs. Henry Clay Daniel (Elizabeth Brown) of Nashville, Tenn., to Mrs. Ida Bates, Columbia. (Four typewritten pages describing school-life at Christian College, 1861-65.) C. C. Historical Collection.

[15] The bonnet verses were contributed by North Todd Gentry whose memoirs as a day student at Christian College were also helpful.

[16] Anon. letter to Robert Blackstone, December 25, 1860, State Historical Society of Missouri, Columbia, under "Christian College."

[17] Mrs. Daniel, letter cited.

[18] MS essay, C. C. Historical Collection.

[19] *Statesman,* August 9, 1861.

[20] *Ibid.*

[21] *Ibid.,* February 1, 1861.

[22] Carr, pp. 137-38.

[23] Memoirs of Minnie Winans '76, Greenwood, La., whose parents had some basis of comparison between Christian College and other schools in the country, since her sister attended Goucher College, Md. Compare with statement on Christian from Glasgow (Mo.) *Journal,* June 14, 1872: "This school . . . has the just reputation of being one of the best schools in the U. S." Also, Mrs. Daniel states in her memoirs *(supra,* 11) that in the 1860's "Christian College was considered one of the best schools in the country."

[24] C. C. *Catalog,* 1860.

[25] North Todd Gentry, miscellaneous typewritten memoirs in C. C. Historical Collection. Mr. Gentry, a nephew of R. L. Todd, vouched for the authenticity of the Lincoln letter.

CHAPTER V

[1] C. C. *Catalog,* 1871 (20th).

[2] J. K. Rogers, Journal (1858-1882) State Historical Society of Missouri, Columbia. (See entries after 1862.)

[3] Interview with Mrs. W. A. Horner ("Minnie" Winans '76) of St. Louis, who contributed much information on school life in the 1870's. (MS letters and typewritten interview.) C. C. Historical Collection.

[4] Rogers resigned April 17, 1877. (*Minutes,* June 14, 1877.)

[5] Floyd Shoemaker, *Missouri Day By Day,* Vol. 1, p. 54. Enrollment figures of Christian College were taken from the catalogs and annual reports in the Bd. Minutes. Statements about the University enrollment are taken from Jonas Viles, *The University of Missouri,* Columbia: E. W. Stephens Press, 1939.

[6] Interview with Mrs. Cynthia Wilkes McHarg, Columbia, the author's source on the Wilkes and Neville families.

[7] J. K. Rogers to the Board of Trustees of Christian College, June 14, 1877. Carr, p. 223.

[8] Letter from P. Schweitzer to O. A. Carr, April 10, 1885, Carr, p. 230.

CHAPTER VI

[1] *Missouri Statesman,* Sept. 21, 1883, p. 1. A Society of Alumnae was organized first in July, 1855, with Elmira Williams of Quincy, Ill. as president. (*Dollar Mo. Journal,* July 5, 1855.) Although local alumnae aided the College with benefits and suppers, the society held only one annual meeting at Commencement, its exercises consisting of "a Poem, an Essay and an Anniversary Address." (*Cat.* 1858-59, p. 18.) Oldham was the first president to try to use the alumnae organization in a promotional way.

[2] C. C. *Catalog,* 1888 (37th).

[3] In 1882 the Missouri State Convention of Christian Churches voted to endorse only those colleges which would allow the Convention to approve or reject any trustee. Christian College refused, citing legal difficulties. In 1884 the Convention's requirement was amended thus: "Those Colleges . . . in the state known to be conducted by men associated with our religious movement are requested to make annual reports to this body through the standing Committee on Schools and Education . . . as a matter of information to the brotherhood." (Peters, p. 118.)

[4] C. C. *Catalog,* printed 1888.

[5] W. A. Oldham, "Christian Womanhood as a Factor in the Moral Progress of the World," C. C. *Catalog,* 1889.

[6] C. C. *Catalog,* 1884.

[7] Elizabeth Forbes Soule taught at Christian College the years of 1874-5, 1884-89, 1893-5. Among portraits she painted in Columbia was one of Prof. Geo. Matthews of the University of Missouri. Several of her paintings appear in a photograph of her bedroom in the catalog of 1894-95. For her background see *Kentucky Antebellum Portraiture* by Edna Talbott Whitley, Paris, Ky.

[8] The story of "Harriet's bones" is vouched for by several alumnae. Memoirs of this colored servant—possibly a slave—are recorded from 1860 until around 1890. One former teacher refers to her as the wife of Charlie, another longtime college servant.

The legend is that Harriet had a retarded son whose greatest desire was a gold ring. She was determined to satisfy him. Braving the fearsome rumors current in those early days about the "body-snatchers" at the University of Missouri medical school, she went to the building and sold them her body after death in return for enough money to buy the gold ring. She specified, however, that her bones must be returned to Christian College. The terms of the contract were fulfilled, according to alumnae of the period. Ethel Robnett Estes recalls that her physiology class of 1902 studied a female skeleton which her mother, Laura Barton

'78, said was that of Aunt Harriet. The final disposal of Harriet's bones is unknown.

[9] Bd. *Minutes,* Feb. 1888, p. 144.

[10] *Ibid.,* June, 1890, pp. 166-170.

[11] Letter from W. A. Oldham to the trustees of Christian College, in the Bd. *Minutes,* November, 1891.

CHAPTER VII

[1] *Christian College Chronicle,* XI (1904), 31.

[2] *Ibid.,* 1 (1894), 123, quoting the *Kansas City Times.*

[3] C. C. Bd. *Minutes,* May 1, 1899.

[4] *Ibid.,* May, 1901.

[5] Luella St. Clair Moss, "The Story of Three Administrations" (Typewritten narrative, C. C. Historical Collection.

[6] *Ibid.* Also printed in the *Chronicle,* VII (Feb., 1900.) One of the four stanzas will illustrate the style of this rather touching poem written by Mrs. St. Clair on her child's death:

On a closet hook hangs a jacket brown,
And a cap of scarlet dye—
They seem to be waiting the little hands
That in quiet rest now lie.
Dear little hands, will they never come back
  To reach for the cap so gay?
Hush! did someone say in a choking voice—
  "The little girl's gone away!"

[7] *Chronicle,* VIII (1901), 133-139, quoting identical accounts from the *Christian Evangelist* and the Columbia, Mo., *Herald.* It was not generally known, when the papers made their announcement, that in order to provide the "$75,000 in improvements" Mrs. St. Clair and Mrs. Moore had incurred a $43,000 debt.

[8] *Catalog,* 1903 (51st).

[9] *Chronicle,* VII (June, 1899), quoting the Columbia *Statesman.*

[10] The beginning and growth of the Ivy Chain tradition can be traced in the *Chronicle* issues of June 1900, 1901, 1902, and 1903. Its origin is credited to Miss Lucy Laws. (The *College Widow,* 1923, p. 26.) It is possible that the "Ivy" chain was modeled after Vassar's daisy chain for Luella St. Clair at this time often cited Vassar as the sort of college she hoped Christian might become. Early *Catalog* photographs of the Ivy Chain (around 1911) show it to be made of flowers. Smilax has been used in recent years.

[11] Letter to Christian College from Mary Young McCaskill, '08 (Mrs. Clarence McCaskill), Houston, Mo., in the C. C. Historical Collection.

[12] Christian College memory book of Mayme Candler, '07 (Mrs. O. E. Hamilton), Springfield, Mo., in the C. C. Historical Collection.

[13] *Chronicle,* IX (March, 1902), quoting Hearst's *Chicago American.* The idea of teaching journalism was good for an argument in the early 1900's. Dr. Moore, in starting a journalism class at Christian College, may have been jumping into the controversy for publicity reasons. His stated reason: "A course of lectures such as I am attempting . . . by an experienced journalist on practical journalism will save [my class] from two to three years' hard work."

Christian's course pre-dated the University of Missouri's school of journalism, founded in 1908 and, according to *World Book Encyclopedia* ("M," 5146) "first . . . in the world." However, Cornell University offered journalism courses beginning in 1888 and the University of

Pennsylvania in 1893. These were perhaps the "only two schools in the United States" referred to by the Chicago newspaper article.

14 Letter from Mrs. Roy J. Curfman (Edith Petty '08), March 30, 1938, C. C. Historical Collection.

15 Actually, the annuity "granted" Mrs. Moore by the trustees amounted to rent for her share of the College property, to which she still held a lifetime deed. (Lease of June 8, 1910, Recorder of Deeds' Office, Boone County courthouse, Columbia, Mo.)

16 A. F. Lange, quoted in Walter Crosby Eells, *American Junior Colleges,* (Washington, D. C., American Council on Education, 1940), p. 10.

17 "Dorsey Hall" was in payment of an old debt of gratitude. Robert Stockton, while a poor youth in his teens, had worked in the hardware store of his cousin Jeremiah Dorsey in Columbia. It was there that Stockton met Bettie Mae Warder, the Christian College student who became his wife. It was Jerry Dorsey who found him the job in St. Louis from which he progressed to his own Majestic Range Company, wealth and prominence. He became a benefactor of Christian Church institutions and left his name in the title of Culver-Stockton College at Canton, Missouri.

18 Columbia *Tribune,* May 25, 1911.

19 Letter to Allean Hale from Mrs. G. R. Clarke (John Davis '16), Tarpon Springs, Fla., in the C. C. Historical Collection.

20 In November, 1951, Eta Upsilon Gamma commemorated the fiftieth anniversary of its founding with a gift to Christian College of a Memorial Art Library. This is a lending-library collection of fine art reproductions.

21 The "first public junior college still in existence" (Eells, p. 13) was Joliet Junior College, Ill., founded in 1902, "almost ten years before the second public junior college now existing appeared in California." Christian College became an accredited junior college one year after the California school. Following in 1915 were Hannibal, Kansas City, and St. Joseph, Mo. junior colleges, among the earliest in the country.

The validity of the early private junior colleges cited by Eells is questionable, since they originated before the term was used and "the development was so gradual . . . that it is difficult if not impossible to assign definite dates." (Eells, p. 14.) He says: "Recently published evidence indicates that Lasell Junior College, Massachusetts, organized in 1851, [named a junior college, 1932] offered two years of college work from the date of its opening and may perhaps claim to be the first privately controlled junior college now in existence." Christian College, however, could make a more valid claim. Two earlier schools for women now operating as junior colleges are Bradford Junior College, Mass. (founded 1803, junior college 1902) and Monticello College, Ill., (founded 1835, junior college 1917).

CHAPTER VIII

1 A charter chapter of Phi Theta Kappa was organized at Christian in 1918 by Dean Elizabeth Hall around the nucleus of the former honor roll society. "Christian, Stephens and Cottey Colleges bound themselves together with a chapter in each school, to form the original Phi Theta Kappa. It was, and is, an honorary scholastic society with membership limited to the upper 10 per cent of the students." (*Microphone,* Jan. 23, 1956.)

Following 1918, Dean Rose Lisenby became sponsor. "At a meeting of the North Central Association in Chicago in 1925 or '26, it was my privilege to make the opening speech and move that Phi Theta Kappa become a *national* organization for Junior Colleges. The motion was seconded by a Stephens representative and carried. I've always considered that a Christian College achievement." (Letter to Mrs. Mark Hale from Rose Lisenby, July 24, 1954, C. C. Historical Collection.) Five years later, J. C. Miller of Christian headed the committee whose recommendations made Phi Theta Kappa the only scholastic society recognized by the American Association of Junior Colleges.

2 "Christian College," the alumnae bulletin, was first issued in 1914. It replaced the defunct *Chronicle* as an alumnae organ.

3 Columbia *Tribune*, April 18, 1952, reprint of "Thirty Years Ago" (April 18, 1922).

4 The Martha Washington Society, important for three generations in the social life of Christian, survived up until about 1920 as an annual costume reception centering around Vinnie Ream's painting of Martha Washington. After 1920 it became a formal "open house" in February in the gym and by 1927 the name had disappeared from the yearbook.

5 Lee was elected president of the American Association of Junior Colleges December 1, 1926, having served as vice-president since March 17, 1926.

6 Floyd W. Reeves (Director), "Report of a Survey of Christian College, 1925-26, Prepared for the Department of Endowments, Board of Education, Disciples of Christ." (1926.) 122 typewritten pp., unbound, in C. C. Historical Collection. One bound copy, President's office.

CHAPTER IX

1 The last high school class enrolled at Christian College was for the school year 1927-28.

2 The *Microphone* had been preceded by the *Campus Coverall*, a less ambitious sheet which was published two years only, 1925-27.

3 For description, see 1934 *Catalog* (83rd).

4 Most of the articles written by Christian College faculty members between 1931 and 1942 appear in the *Junior College Journal;* others in the *American Journal of Public Health, Education,* and the *Missouri School Journal.*

5 Christian College Library.

6 A description of the guidance program, written by J. C. Miller, appears in "Christian College" (Alumnae Bulletin), April, 1931.

7 From *The Prophet,* by Kahlil Gabran; quoted as a foreword to the May, 1934, edition of "Christian College" (vocational booklet) and to the revised edition, "What Shall I Do?" (1939.)

8 Quoted in the *Minutes,* President's Report for 1933-34.

CHAPTER X

1 Mrs. Hertig is listed as Editor of the Alumnae Bulletin in catalogs from 1924-46 but seems actually to have edited the Bulletin by 1922 and probably earlier.

2 Except for the years 1936-38 when Portia Penwell Stapel was alumnae secretary.

3 The May Queen ceremony and songs seem to have been adopted from Sweetbriar College, Va. Of recent years the "May Queen" has been called "Commencement Queen."

4 The facts on Mrs. Hertig's childhood and family come from clippings and letters sent by her girlhood friend, Miss Jennie Corbin of Union City, Mich., to Mrs. Maud McConnell. (Letter dated Jan. 23, 1950.)

5 Southeastern State College, Durant, Okla.

6 Lloyd W. King (ed.), *A Statement of Philosophy, Purposes, and Design for the Secondary Schools of Missouri,* State Dep't. of Ed. Bulletin 1, Jefferson City: Midland Printing Co., 1940.

7 *Design for an Education,* 1939; *Do You Know?,* 1939.

8 *Minutes,* President's Mid-Year Report, Sept. 26, 1939.

9 *Ibid.,* President's Report, Sept. 14, 1943.

CHAPTER XII

1 Francis A. Klein, "A Century Ago a Little Group of Dixie Diehards Came to Missouri and Founded Christian College," *St Louis Globe-Democrat,* Jan 14, 1951; Mary Paxton Keeley, "Christian College at Columbia, Mo., A Daring Experiment 100 Years Ago," *Kansas City Times,* Jan. 18, 1951; Columbia *Missourian,* Jan. 17, 1951, Section B.

2 Frederick A. Middlebush, "Message of Greeting from our Institutions of Higher Learning." (Speech given at Charter Day convocation, C. C., Jan. 18, 1951.)

3 "Stephens College and Christian College, both of Columbia, Mo. . . . are the leaders among the 40 colleges which feature horsemanship as a part of their physical education program." George Coleman, "Spur of the Moment" column, in the New York *World-Telegram* & *The Sun,* Dec. 24, 1953.

4 The Christian College Historical Collection is now on loan to the Western Historical Manuscripts Collection at the University of Missouri library. It will be cataloged and housed there until a permanent place is made for it at the College.

5 *One Hundred Years of Education for Women,* 14-page illustrated historical booklet published by Christian College and containing Centennial reunion and Commencement programs, June 1-5, 1951. (Written by Allean Hale and Raymond Derr.)

6 Following the Centennial, Christian College clubs were active in Kansas City, St. Louis, Columbia, Springfield, Mo., Wichita, Memphis, Tulsa, Oklahoma City, Indianapolis, Denver, Colorado Springs, Dallas-Fort Worth, Chicago, and Cleveland. Mrs. Mark Hale (Allean Lemmon '33) served as alumnae secretary during the school year 1951-53 and edited the Bulletin in 1952-53.

7 Jane Froman received Christian's 1951 Honor Service citation at the Centennial Commencement. In 1952 she established the annual Jane Froman Award for the outstanding Junior voice student.

8 This was done in the summer of 1953 when the three-story Willett Funeral Home between the President's house and The White House on Christian College Avenue was purchased for a Conservatory of Music building. The vacated wing of Missouri Hall was converted into dormitory rooms. The basement underneath was rebuilt into recreation rooms. When enrollment for the school year 1953 topped capacity with 364 students the north cottage (original Eta Upsilon Gamma house) was remodeled for dormitory use. Conversion of old Practice Hall into a library-museum is a hope for the future.

9 "Cathy Christian" as a name for the typical Christian girl is attributed to Lois Ann Flege '47 who originated the title when she served as assistant to the dean of women in 1949.

10 Letter to J. C. Miller from Mrs. Thomas H. Chapman, Jr. (Mildred Ann Crowe, '49), San Antonio, Tex., dated 1953.

CHAPTER XIII

[1] "Master Plan of Christian College, Columbia, Missouri," prepared by Hellmuth, Obata & Kassabaum, Inc., architects, St. Louis, Mo., July, 1958. (Offset printed pamphlet, 25 pp., 10 photographs.)

[2] *Mademoiselle,* Aug. 1959; *Glamour,* Nov. 1962; *Seventeen,* Nov. 1963; *Look,* Dec. 6, 1960; *Junior College Journal,* Jan. 1963; the *New York Times,* March 7, 1965.

[3] "Christian's Future Campus," in *Christian College* (Alumnae Bulletin), Oct. 1958.

[4] Kenneth Freeman (ed.), "Trusteeship at Christian College" (Offset printed pamphlet, June 1962), p. 16.

[5] Russell Lynes, "How Good Are the Junior Colleges: a Special Report," *Harper's,* Nov. 1966, pp. 53–60.

[6] "The 2-Year College for Women," the *New York Times,* March 7, 1965, sec. 12. A *Times* supplement prepared by the Conference of Two-Year Colleges for Women with the cooperation of the American Association of Junior Colleges.

[7] See *Progressive Architecture,* January 1959; *Architectural Forum,* February 1962; *The Architect & Building News,* 2 Jan., 1963; "C F A 1964 Design Awards Program," booklet published by the federal Housing and Home Finance Agency, p. 25; *C. C.* (Alumnae Bulletin), April 1959.

[8] *Christian College Magazine* (Alumnae Bulletin), Oct. 1963, p. 10.

[9] Betty Friedan, *The Feminine Mystique* (New York: Dell Publishing Co., 1963), pp. 148–49; also chap. 7 notes 1 and 13 citing statistics from Mabel Newcomer, *A Century of Higher Education for Women* and from the *U. S. Demographic Yearbook.*

[10] F. G. Jennings, "Education Reform, 1957–1967: It Didn't Start with Sputnik," *Saturday Review,* Sept. 16, 1967.

[11] Janet Eliadis, "Bienvenu a la Maison Francaise," *C. C.* (Alumnae Magazine), Jan. 1965.

[12] Peggy Phillips, "Preparation for Life at Christian College," *Junior College Journal,* Jan. 1963; adapted from "Campus Community Program," *C. C.* (Alumnae Magazine), Jan. 1963.

[13] "Girls and Dorms," *Newsweek,* Nov. 11, 1963, p. 78.

[14] "Education," *Time,* May 18, 1962, p. 39.

[15] Alfred Kinsey and Others, *Sexual Behavior in the Human Female* (Philadelphia and London: W. B. Saunders Co., 1953); "Birth Control Pills: the Full Story." *Good Housekeeping,* Sept. 1962, p. 153.

[16] Excerpt from the report of the Trustees' Finance Committee to the Board on Feb. 17, 1960, quoted in "Trusteeship," p. 16.

[17] "Ten-Year Plan, Christian College." Statistical projections from 1962–63 to 1972–73. (Mimeographed.) The plan is also described in the April, 1963, alumnae magazine.

[18] Kenneth Freeman, "Required — A Massive Effort," the Report of the President of Christian College to the Board of Trustees, 1962–1963, p. 4. (Photocopied pamphlet.)

[19] Donald A. Eldridge, "The College Woman: 1966," reprinted in *C. C.* (Alumnae Magazine), Oct. 1966. The figures quoted on American women are U.S. Bureau of the Census and U.S. Bureau of Labor statistics; the junior college statistics are from the Lynes report.

[20] "Proposed Faculty Handbook, Christian College," submitted by the Faculty Handbook Committee, Oct. 22, 1965. (Mimeographed.)

[21] Christian occupied its original building in the fall of 1852, having held its first year's session in temporary quarters in town. (See pp. 19, 21, 22, 28.) College-level courses were taught in that first session, and the building has served some collegiate function continuously since that time.

[22] In summarizing Christian's financial progress, the author referred

to the following sources: the President's *Annual Report* (1962–1967 issues, printed), the Bd. *Minutes* (1966–67), "A Report of Development Progress" (monthly issues, 1965–67, mimeographed), the Alumnae Office annual reports (1959–66 issues, mimeographed).

23 Distinguished Alumnae awardees have been: 1963, Artie Mason Carter '00, and Jane Froman Smith '26; 1964, Allean Lemmon Hale '33; 1965, Evelyn Milligan Jones '33; 1966, Elizabeth Toomey Seabrook '42; 1967, Mayme Candler Hamilton '03; 1968, Dr. Mary Addina Crenshaw '38.

Distinguished Women of America have been: 1963, Dr. Frances Kelsey of the U. S. Food and Drug Administration, who exposed the dangers of Thalidomide; 1964, Mary Elizabeth Switzer, Commissioner of the U. S. Vocational Rehabilitation Administration; 1965, Helen Hayes, "First Lady of the American Theatre"; 1966, Dr. Blanche H. Dow, president of the American Association of University Women; 1967, Risë Stevens, opera singer and a manager of the Metropolitan Opera National Company.

24 Medallion Club donors for 1967–68 included the following: Mr. and Mrs. J. M. Allton; Boone County National Bank, R. B. Price, president; Miss Estelle Bradford; Class of 1943; Columbia Daily Tribune; Mr. and Mrs. W. Dudley Coursey; Mr. and Mrs. Allan Ferrin; Mrs. Vivian Sloan Fiske; First Bank of Commerce, Hartley G. Banks, Sr., president; General Telephone Company of Missouri; Mr. and Mrs. Herman Guttman; Mr. and Mrs. Fred V. Heinkel; Mr. and Mrs. Danal Hotaling; Mrs. Lue C. Lozier; MFA Insurance Company; Mrs. Berry McAlester; Mr. and Mrs. Warren Norton; Missouri Store Company; Mr. and Mrs. Burt F. Raynes; Mrs. Althea Whitcraft Schiffman; Mr. J. M. Silvey; B. D. Simon Construction Company; Mrs. Elbert L. Spence; Mr. and Mrs. George A. Spencer; Stover Carpet Shop; Vestal Laboratories; Mrs. Pickett L. Warren, II.

25 "The White House Conference on Education," [July 21–22, 1965], report from the President of C.C. to the trustees. (7 pp., printed.)

26 In summarizing Christian's academic progress, the author referred to the following sources: C.C. *Catalog* (1951–1967 issues); *Minutes* of the Trustees Educational Policy Committee (1965); Faculty *Minutes* (May 26 and 31, 1967); articles in the alumnae magazine: "Blueprint for the Future," (Oct.–Dec. 1958), Hoagland, "Associate in Arts with Honors," (Fall, 1961), "Teachers and Planning," (Jan. 1962), Batterson, "Faculty Summer Workshops" (Oct. 1962).

She owes much to correspondence and interviews with President W. Merle Hill, Mme. Hortense Davison, and especially, Dean Jack L. Batterson for furnishing statistical reports and his own report to the faculty fall conference, Sept. 10, 1963: "The Present Curriculum: A Revision in Need of Revising?"

27 W. Merle Hill, "Remarks to the Faculty," April 23, 1967. (Typewritten.)

28 *Time*, May 5, 1967, p. 57.

29 William Arrowsmith, "The Shame of the Graduate Schools: A Plea for a New American Scholar," *Harper's*, March, 1966.

30 Sidney Larson, "Alligators — or the Role of the Faculty at Christian College," *C. C.* (Alumnae Magazine) Jan. 1965.

31 Dan Hoagland, "A Special Place for Arts and Sciences," *ibid.*, Oct. 1965.

32 Sue M. Gerard, "Your Spare Tire Can Prevent a Drowning," *Reader's Digest*, June, 1966; also, citation, 1963 National 4-H Alumni Recognition Awards, Olin Mathieson Corporation.

33 Condensed from Pauline Tompkins, "Why a Two-Year College for Women?" the *New York Times*, March 7, 1965, sec. 12.

34 "Man of the Year: Twenty-five and Under," *Time*, January 6, 1967.

35 For sources on the life and times of the Christian College student of the sixties, the author used the C.C. *Microphone*, the *Widow* and *Ivy Chain* (annuals), the student Handbook, and interviews with Mrs. Elizabeth Kirkman, Dean of Women, Mrs. Jane Canady Crow, Director of Alumnae Affairs, and Ruth Wehmer.

36 Jack L. Batterson and Paulina Batterson, "Women and Politics: the Failure to Think and Act," *C. C.* (Alumnae Magazine), Jan. 1962.

37 Lenora S. Slaughter (ed.), "20 Years of Scholarships by the Miss America Pageant" (Mimeographed pamphlet.) Also, "All the Miss Americas, Then and Now," *Life*, Sept. 28, 1959.

38 Christina Paolozzi in *Harper's Bazaar*, 1962; *Esquire*, Sept. 1967, pp. 94–97.

39 "People," *Time*, Sept. 24, 1965.

40 John Canady, "What Miss America Is Made Of," *New York Times Magazine*, Sept. 19, 1965, p. 124. Other references on Deborah Bryant: David L. Goodrich, "The Discovery of Miss America," *Saturday Evening Post*, Nov. 6, 1966; Daniel Chapman, "Miss America, Six Months Later," *Look*, April 5, 1966; Canady, "Miss America, One Year Later," *McCall's*, Feb. 1967; *C. C.* (Alumnae Magazine), Oct. 1965, April 1966.

41 Christian's nearest rival to the "oldest in the West" claim seems to be Mary Hardin-Baylor College in Belton, Texas, which calls itself "the oldest college for women west of the Mississippi" (*World Book* encyclopedia, Vol. 12, 1962.). It originated through a charter granted Baylor University by the Republic of Texas in 1845, providing for a primary and female department. However, the female division was not organized until "prior to June 13, 1851." (Mary Hardin-Baylor catalog, Vol. XLII, No. 14, May 1951.) Christian's charter from the State of Missouri is dated Jan. 18, 1851, and the college opened in April, 1851. (See text, pp. 14, 18, 21). Moreover, efforts to organize Christian College dated from 1844, at least. (See text, pp. 3, 10, 12, 242.)

The next contender seems to be Missouri's Lindenwood College, which calls itself "the second-oldest college for women in the United States and the oldest west of the Mississippi." (*Lindenwood College Bulletin*, 1967–68, p. 129.) It claims descent from a girls' primary school that operated in the home of Mrs. George Sibley in 1827. Actually, Lindenwood College was chartered by the St. Louis Presbytery in 1853 and had no college building until 1860. (*Ibid.*, p. 128.)

The third claimant, Stephens College, also in Columbia, opened in September, 1856, and was incorporated as Baptist Female College in 1857. It was sold to the General Association of the Baptist Church of Missouri for use as their state denominational college in 1870 and that year was renamed Stephens College for an endowment gift from J. L. Stephens. The college did not operate during 1876–77. (Stephens College 15th annual catalog, 1870–71; 59th catalog, 1916–17.) Its claim to have been founded in 1833 seems to have originated with the coming of President James Madison Wood to Stephens in 1912 and is first stated in its fifty-ninth catalog (1916–17). This claim is unproven, and is based on supposed descent from the Columbia Female Academy, a town high school that legally dissolved in 1865. For evidence against the Columbia Female Academy claim see pp. 246–48. Regarding the Stephens, Lindenwood, and other "oldest in the West" claims, see pp. 241, 249. For evidence documenting Christian's own claims and its origin on the collegiate level, see pp. 10, 14, 17, 21, 22, 23, 28, 31, 32, 41, 72, 243, n. 13; 245, nn. 10, 17. Regarding Christian's origin as the "distaff side" of the University of Missouri, see pp. 10, 14, 16, 22, 23, 33, 48, 49, 51, 72, 84,

Selected Bibliography

PUBLISHED MATERIAL

Blandin, Mrs. J. M. E. *History of Higher Education of Women in the South Prior to 1860.* New York: Neale Publishing Co., 1909.

Carr, O. A. (ed.). *Memorial of J. K. Rogers and Christian College.* St. Louis: John Burns Publishing Co., 1885.

Christian College (Alumnae Bulletin). Vols. 1-100 (1914-51).

Christian College Annual *Catalogs.* 1851-1951.

Christian College Chronicle. Vols. I-XI (1893-1904). Christian College Historical Collection.

Christian College *Microphone,* 1929-50.

College Widow. Christian College Annual. (1910-50).

Collins, Lewis. *History of Kentucky.* Covington, Ky.: Collins & Co., 1882.

Columbia Daily Tribune, 1918-45.

"Columbia Female Academy Catalogs." 1850's. State Historcial Society of Missouri.

Columbia Missouri Statesman, 1848-65. State Historical Society of Missouri newspaper room.

Dollar Missouri Journal, 1852-56. State Historical Society of Missouri newspaper room.

Eells, Walter Crosby (ed.). *American Junior Colleges.* Washington: American Council on Education, 1940.

Fortune, Alonzo Willard. *The Disciples in Kentucky.* Pub. by the Convention of the Christian Churches in Kentucky, 1932.

Goodsell, Willystine (ed.). *Pioneers of Women's Education in the United States.* New York: McGraw-Hill Book Co., 1931.

History of Daughters College and its Founder John Augustus Williams. . . . Ann Shanks Bourne, Mattie Terhune Davis, Lydia Kennedy Bond, (co-authors). Privately printed.

Illustrated Historical Atlas of Boone County, Missouri. Philadelphia: Edwards Brothers, 1875.

Millennial Harbinger, 1848-52. Pub. Alexander Campbell, Bethany, Va. Bible College of Missouri, Columbia.

Peters, George L. *Disciples of Christ in Missouri.* Centennial History 1837-1937. Centennial Commission: 1937.

Phillips, Claude A. *A History of Education in Missouri.* Jefferson City: Hugh Stephens Printing Co., 1911.

Shoemaker, Floyd C. *Missouri and Missourians.* Chicago: Lewis Publishing Co., 1943.

Switzler, William. *History of Boone County.* St Louis: Western Historical Co., 1882.

University of Missouri Catalogs. 1848-57. State Historical Society of Missouri.

Viles, Jonas. *The University of Missouri.* A Centennial History. Columbia: E. W. Stephens Press, 1939.

Weekly Missouri Sentinel, 1852-56. State Historical Society of Missouri newspaper room.

Williams, John Augustus. *Reminiscences.* Cincinnati: F. D. Rowe, 1898.

UNPUBLISHED MATERIAL

Christian College, Columbia, Mo., Record Books, 1858-74. Nine volumes, MSS, records kept by J. K. Rogers. State Historical Society of Missouri, Columbia.

Christian College, Board of Trustees, "Minutes of Meetings," 1851-1951. First volume (1851-1877) in State Historical Society of Missouri; others owned by Christian College.

Hertig, Marion. Private papers. Christian College Historical Collection.

Hughes, Mary Katherine. "A History of Christian College." (1851-1900). (M.A. thesis, Dept. of History, University of Missouri, 1944).

Lemon, Amanda J. Scrapbook papers and programs of Christian College, 1870's. Christian Historical Collection.

"Letters to John Allen Gano," John Gano Family Papers. Western Historical Manuscripts Collection. (Letters from T. M. Allen.)

Martha Washington Society, "Minutes of Meetings." 1857-1897. Three record books, Christian College Historical Collection.

Royall, Regina Victoria. Scrapbook, 1850-70. Property of Mrs. Warren Branham, Columbia.

Rogers, J. K. Journal, 1858-82. State Historical Society of Missouri.

Skinner, Julia Lenoir. Papers. A large miscellany of memoirs of Christian College, 1860-1890, with a diagram of College buildings and grounds in early 1870's.

University of Missouri Board of Curators. Minutes of Meetings. Western Historical Manuscripts Collection.

*Index**

* Picture references are indexed by Roman numerals. A capital Roman numeral refers to the photography section. A small Roman numeral refers to the page within the photography section.